2X 7/01 10/02

White Hats and Silver Spurs

White Hats and Silver Spurs

*Interviews with 24 Stars of Film
and Television Westerns of the
Thirties through the Sixties*

by HERB FAGEN

with a foreword by CHRISTOPHER MITCHUM

McFarland & Company, Inc., Publishers
Jefferson, North Carolina, and London

British Library Cataloguing-in-Publication data are available

Library of Congress Cataloguing-in-Publication Data

Fagen, Herb.
    White hats and silver spurs : interviews with 24 stars of film and
television westerns of the thirties through sixties / by Herb Fagen ;
with a foreword by Christopher Mitchum.
        p.   cm.
    Includes index.
    ISBN 0-7864-0200-8 (library binding: 50# alk. paper) ∞
    1. Western films.   2. Westerns (Television programs)   3. Motion
picture actors and actresses — United States — Interviews.
4. Television actors and actresses — United States — Interviews.
I. Title.
PN1995.9.W4F28   1996
791.43'6278 — dc20   96-22997
                                                                      CIP

Manufactured in the United States of America

McFarland & Company, Inc., Publishers
  Box 611, Jefferson, North Carolina 28640

To the Memory
of
Robert Totten
Director - Actor - Writer - Friend

Contents

Contents

Foreword

by Christopher Mitchum

Since the beginnings of mankind, there has been the storyteller. From grunts and sign language, through cave paintings, to the spoken word, there have been those who must tell a story. Today, we have stand-up comedians, song writers, poets, oral historians, writers, directors, and actors, to list only a few. All of them use their given gift in their chosen art to tell stories.

Herb Fagen has compiled a collection of stories from such storytellers. The cross-section of talent gathered in these pages is a good representation of those who presented to the world the image of the old West and the American cowboy. Throughout their years of work, they told us stories, introduced us to people, and left us with lasting images and memories. Besides growing up watching many of these artists, I have, also, had the privilege to know and work with many of them.

Like most of us over ... let's say, forty ... *Rin Tin Tin*, for instance, was a part of my childhood. (My father is fond of saying, "What's so hard about being a movie star? Rin Tin Tin was the biggest star there was and he was a dog!") I have met Lee Aaker twice — well, once, but I'm not sure which time. I was a guest at the Festival of the West held each year in Phoenix, Arizona. It is a trade show gathering of Western item vendors, dinners, dances, film screenings and a question and answer session with the attendees and Western actors, which is why I was there. Another actor, to whom I was introduced, was Lee Aaker. An affable guy who, as I remember, said he now had a construction business. A few years later, I was invited to a press event in Los Angeles hosted by Michael Wayne to announce the release of *The Searchers* on video. A selection of people who had worked with the Duke were on the "invite" list. Lee Aaker was there, except, this time, it was a totally different Lee Aaker! His back was to me and I walked over and said, "Hi, Lee, good to see you again!" He turned and asked, "Have we met?"

"I guess not," I replied, stunned, and turned and walked away.

I read somewhere, recently, that Lee keeps pretty much to himself. One reason why, he said, is because he has an impostor walking around using his name! An occupational hazard. To this day, I'm not sure which one was the REAL Lee Aaker!

1

Dobe Carey I've known most of my life. His parents and mine were best of friends. His mother, Ollie, was like an aunt to me. She was that great, straight-talking, no-nonsense type woman ("Sit down, kids, and get some cookies!") who you might imagine Annie Oakley to have been. To those who knew her, she was a force who will always be missed. Early in my acting career, I had the pleasure of working with Dobe in *Big Jake*. Sorry we had to kill you, Dobe.

Hutch, Will Hutchins, was another of those people who was at the Festival of the West. Let's face it, anybody in the film business is as big a fan as anyone else is. He was one of those who held my attention for one hour a week during the Golden Age of Television Westerns, with *Sugarfoot*. We hit it off right away. Although we have not seen each other since, we send notes back and forth and know that we can call one another "friend." Before he got married, his wife Babs told him that if he wanted to marry her, he had to get a "real" job. So, he did. Now, that's love! Still, it would be nice to see him again with his other love, western movies.

I first met Ben Johnson while working on *Chisum* with the Duke. We were shooting on location in Durango, Mexico. Now, there was a tough town! Most of the men wore sidearms and you'd go to sleep hearing gunfire every night, but, that's another book. We were at dinner at Duke's house and someone's name came up who seemed to be disliked by everyone who had run into him. Ben's only comment, during the "running down" of this fellow, was, "He's the most unnecessary son-of-bitch I ever met." That was the most unkind thing I ever heard Ben say about anyone. All of which leads me to the point that Ben Johnson was about the finest gentleman I've ever met.

In recent years, I re-connected with Ben. He had a charity called Helping Hand, kind of a "Cowboys for Kids" thing. Major pro-celebrity rodeos were held in Houston, the Lazy-E in Guthrie, Oklahoma, and in Ben's stomping ground, Scottsdale, Arizona. There were two days of rodeo and two nights of live and silent auctions and dinner-dances. All the money raised went to help kids. You could see a number of western film stars competing in these events. I've won a lot of buckles rodeoing, but a Ben Johnson buckle still eludes me.

John Mitchum has known me all of my life. He's my uncle. I've had the pleasure of working with John several times, too. The first feature I ever acted in was a thing called *Bigfoot* in 1969. I was working production on it and hired John and the great John Carradine. There are some stories here, too! Two days before we started shooting, the film lost its star and the producers asked me to play the lead. So, in the credits, I'm listed as both starring and Second Assistant Director! The next time I worked with John was down in Durango on *Chisum*!

Another great from the golden days is Clint Walker. We worked together on a little film shot in Death Valley. Annie Lockhart and Eartha Kitt were also in it. It was a bizarre voodoo-snakes movie for a company in Taiwan. Clint impressed me with his kindness, goodness and gentleness. He is a man with deep spiritual beliefs which came out of facing death when he took a ski pole through his heart. He got a good look at the other side over a period of months.

Though we had worked together, once, years before, when I was working production, Marie Windsor and I became friends when I was on the Board of Directors at Screen Actors Guild for six years and then first vice president of the Guild. It was during the turbulent times of the eighties when liberals were taking over the Guild and turning it into a full labor union. We were part of the old school, spearheaded by Chuck Heston, which simply believed in helping actors, not in practicing national or world labor politics. Late at night in those Board meetings, Marie and I often felt like the Indians had us circled. As our numbers dwindled each year, Marie hung in there doing what she could to better the actor's lot.

As I write this, something is becoming glaringly apparent: the people who love doing westerns, with whom I've come into contact, are good, decent people. They embody the spirit of the American cowboy. What is that spirit? It is the ability to stand up for what's right, the readiness to take personal responsibility and the holding of positive values along with a moral code. They are people who care and who treat others with respect. They are the kind of people you want your son or daughter to marry.

Herb Fagen has pulled these people together into one book. He has acted as the catalyst and, in so doing, comes before us as a storyteller himself. This book is about the western movies, but it is, also, about the people who made them. What you hold in your hands is a collection of history, memories, and just damn good stories.

Introduction
and Acknowledgments

I am an urban cowboy pure and simple. A cowboy who never rode a range as the song says. A city kid from Chicago who fell in love with the American West at an early age. I was barely seven years old when my dad took me to the Chicago Stadium to see Roy Rogers and Trigger. It was a time when heroes and heroes ruled our days. Roy was "The King of the Cowboys," and how we loved him. I even got to pet Trigger that special day. Such was the stuff that a seven year old's dreams were made of back then.

I rode bravely through those great John Ford westerns when I was nine and ten: *The Three Godfathers, Fort Apache, She Wore a Yellow Ribbon, Rio Grande.* We all loved the Duke, even back then. Shirley Temple and Joanne Dru were better than beautiful, and handsome John Agar was the reigning heart throb of the girls in our fifth grade class.

How well I recall Gary Cooper reaching his finest hour as the courageous Will Kane in the movie *High Noon*, while I would whistle the haunting theme music for months to come. Cooper garnered a well-deserved second Oscar, but ironically it was Cooper's co-star, a relatively unknown Grace Kelly, who would shortly become Hollywood's first legitimate princess.

Soon it was *Shane*, George Stevens' western masterpiece, which enthralled me totally. Forty years later it still holds up beautifully. I was awed by an incredibly handsome Alan Ladd in the title role, and by the tears and pathos of an adoring young boy named Brandon De Wilde, particularly in the closing scene, a scene which remains one of the most haunting and memorable in the history of American cinema.

But someone else caught my untrained fourteen-year-old eye that day. He sure looked and acted a lot like a real cowboy. He played an ornery cowpoke named Chris Calloway, a barroom bully who turned into an unlikely hero before the film's final fade-out. Someone told me his name was Ben Johnson, and that he was quite a rodeo star to boot. What luck! A city boy like me had "discovered" a western screen icon in the making, and from the balcony of a gilded movie palace in downtown Chicago.

Then along came Hoppy and how he lit up our television screen. Sure he was of an earlier era, but television had reinvented him especially for us. Hoppy was everything. There were "Hoppy" hats, Hoppy lunch boxes, "Hoppy" gloves, etc. One day he was even responsible for the sibling feud of the week. I wanted to watch *Hoppy* on our ten-inch magnified screen, and my little sister was opting for *Howdy Doody*. I'm not sure who won the battle of the brats that day, but make no mistake, when it came to *Hopalong Cassidy,* I was all business.

It was a simpler world back then. There were good guys with white hats and bad guys with black hats. There was right and there was wrong. We had Gene and Roy, Duke and Matt. We cheered our heroes and we hissed our villains. But best of all we had our innocence and we had fun.

Television kept us believing in those days. It gave us Westerns aplenty: *Gunsmoke, Cheyenne, Bonanza, Wagon Train, Sugarfoot, 26 Men, The Virginian, Rin Tin Tin,* so very many. It was a time for baseball, the World Series and for Westerns. It was a good time to be growing up, and a good time to be young.

Unfortunately the old West has become a vanishing dream to some — a nostalgic retreat to a bygone era; a wasted western range covered today by slabs of concrete, billboards, and shopping malls. That's too bad. Because in truth the American West has remained in the hearts of millions of people. Westerns are a genuine art form, elevated and shaped through the medium of film.

How fortunate then to have met and interviewed many of the very people, stars of film and television, who have willingly shared their stories with me. This book is a collection of annotated interviews with twenty-four people whose contributions have left a lasting imprint on Western film and television, as performers, directors, writers, and producers. No such book can be totally inclusive, and to be sure some worthy and important names are missing. This is not due to any intentional or personal oversight, but rather to the constraints of time and space.

All those interviewed gave graciously of their time and thoughts. Each has provided us a treasure of rich anecdotes and personal histories, unique in substance and interest. All have been intimately part of the Western genre of film and television. Yet there is an added dimension and focus called versatility: these are enormously creative people with diverse and widespread talent. To each and every one, my sincere thanks and appreciation for helping write this book.

We writers are only as good as the people who read us. My deepest thanks to Bob King, editor of *Classic Images* and *Films of the Golden Age,* for first bringing my film stories to a wide public readership and to Christy Victor at *Movie Marketplace,* Craig Peters at *Remember* and Ted Okuda at *Filmfax* for expanding that readership further.

My great appreciation goes to the Tuolumne County Visitors Bureau, sponsors of the Tuolumne County Wild West Film Fest; to Dave Holland, director of the Lone Pine Film Festival; to Harold Smith at the Knoxville Western Film Caravan; to Bob Ladd at Apache Junction; and to Ray and Sharon Courts at the Beverly Garland Hotel in Los Angeles, for extending me the warm hospitality of their respective Film Shows and Festivals.

My deep thanks and lasting love go to my mom Gertrude and dad, the late Myron Fagen, who taught me early on the difference between right and wrong, and that a good day's pay always demands a good day's work.

And a sad final farewell to Ben Johnson, Bob Totten, and Virgil Vogel, who each died prior to the release of this book. Their outstanding interviews and stories now mean even more to all of us.

Herb Fagen
Spring 1996

1

Lee Aaker

*When I was about 18 or 19 years old, I just walked away
from the business. I wanted to see what else there was to do.
I became a carpenter. I never went back into show business
until I heard there was an impostor showing up at film festivals and other occasions posing as me.*

He is remembered fondly as Corporal Rusty in the popular *Rin Tin Tin*
series. But it took an appearance on Sally Jessy Raphaël's syndicated talk show
to tell the world that for the past five years someone had been pretending to
be the real Lee Aaker. Actually the former child star had gone into self-induced
seclusion nearly thirty years ago.

Born in Inglewood, California, in 1943, Lee Aaker was just a young tod-
dler when he entered show business. As a six-year-old in 1949 he appeared in
an award winning documentary called *Benji*. Subsequently, young Lee Aaker
appeared in a number of motion pictures: including *Hondo* with John Wayne,
No Room for the Groom, with Tony Curtis and Piper Laurie, *Desperate Search*,
with Howard Keel, *Jeopardy*, with Barbara Stanwyck and Barry Sullivan, and
he was one of the three kids playing hide and seek on the street in *High Noon*.
His television credits include slots on the Ford Theater with Ronald Reagan
and Teresa Wright, the *Loretta Young Show* and many more.

It was his selection as young Rusty in the long-running television series
Rin Tin Tin which really put Lee Aaker on the celebrity map. The series ran
from 1954 through 1959 and included nearly 165 episodes. Unfortunately
for Lee, as for many child stars, the later years were not as good. "Maybe it
was the hippy thing," Aaker suggests, but he too entered the world of drugs
and alcohol. In 1980 he sought treatment for his addictions at St. John's
Hospital in Santa Monica, and admittedly he has been "clean and sober
since."

An appearance with Paul Peterson, fellow child star and close friend, at
the Sonora Wild West Film Fest in 1993 was tinged with warmth and melancholy. The arena is open again and Lee Aaker, the real Lee Aaker, is making
public appearances once again.

I interviewed Lee Aaker at Ray Courts Movie Collectors Show at the Beverly Garland Hotel. Now 53 years old, he speaks candidly of his early life as a child star, the people he worked with, his early fame, his alcohol and drug abuse, his life today, and the truth behind the unraveling mystery of "the real Lee Aaker."

H.F. Lee, how did a young boy become a budding star so early in life?

L.A. In a sense it was in the family. My mother and aunt owned a song and dance studio. So when I was four years old I learned how to tap dance. We started going all over to amateur contests and winning them all. Finally my brother and I passed up our mother's ability to teach us tap dancing, so we went to a higher-rated studio, which in the forties had a show on KTLA. Then I made a feature called *Benji* which was an award-winning documentary and things began to snowball after that.

H.F. You made a number of movies!

L.A. Oh, yes! I made twenty or twenty-five features through Paramount. Fred Zinnemann, the award winning director, liked me. He was about to direct *High Noon* and said that if there was a part in the picture where I would fit, it was mine. There were three kids on the street playing hide and seek. They did a close up of me as Gary Cooper passed by. Then I made *Atomic City* for Paramount which turned out to be very successful.

H.F. Do you remember much about Cooper and working on the set of *High Noon*?

L.A. Truthfully, I was only about eight or nine then, so I don't remember much. But I do recall watching his facial expressions as he was waiting for the train to come. It was kind of a scared but confident look. Watching his face was like watching silent acting. I remember very little about Grace Kelly except meeting her. At that age I wouldn't exactly call myself an actor. I was a kid who had a gift for gab, and people never intimidated me. I could walk up to anybody and say, "Hi, I'm Lee Aaker." By the way, Lee Aaker is my real name. It's a Dutch name and it originally was spelled "Ooker." When my grandparents moved to South Dakota, they changed it to Aaker.

H.F. You did a Ford Theater Production with Ronald Reagan. How did that come about?

L.A. Well I got connected with Screen Gems which was Columbia Pictures. The Ford Theater was doing an episode with Ronald Reagan and Teresa Wright. By luck, Ronald Reagan had just seen me, and said he wanted me to be his son in this episode. Luck is ninety-nine percent of this game. So I got into the Ford Theater which got me into Screen Gems. I remember Ronald

Lee Aaker as Rusty in *Rin-Tin-Tin*

Reagan as being very confident, not bossy or pushy. I can never forget just being at Screen Gems and having him say, "I want him as my son in this show," at a time when I had only made three or four little pictures.

So in a period of a year I made three or four Ford Theater productions. This led to features for Universal such as *No Room for the Groom*. I don't think I was ever on a so-called casting call audition, because somehow someone always saw me and said, "I want him."

Then I did *Desperate Search* at MGM, and *Jeopardy* with Barbara Stanwyck, Barry Sullivan and Ralph Meeker. That was the whole cast. I remember Barbara Stanwyck as being very proud and very sure of herself. Funny, I never detected a real affected attitude about any of the stars I mentioned. Then I made *Hondo* with John Wayne.

H.F. How was it working in a picture with the Duke?

L.A. Thinking back to *Hondo*, I can only say that I wish I would have been a little older because John Wayne to me is an idol, a real idol. I wish I would have been able to have gone out with him and talked, instead of being the little kid. I would have loved doing more than just scenes with him. In one scene he picks me up and throws me in the water. I have a nice eight by ten autographed picture that says, "Lee, someday I'll give you a real swimming lesson..." *Hondo* was the first big three–D movie. We were in Mexico for three months doing it. Geraldine Page left the stage to do the picture and was nominated for Best Supporting Actress in nineteen fifty-three. But most of all I remember John Wayne as being very nice to me.

H.F. How did you land the role of Rusty in *Rin Tin Tin*?

L.A. *Rin Tin Tin* was done through Screen Gems. The producer Herbert Leonard (Herbert B. Leonard Productions) had seen me in the Ford Theater Productions and wanted me. Tommy Redding got the *Lassie* series. Three days later I heard I got the *Rin Tin Tin* series. That was nineteen fifty-four, and I think we did one hundred and sixty-four episodes. The series starred James Brown, who recently passed away, Joe Sawyer, a great character actor, Tommy Farrell, and Rand Brooks as Corporal Boone. Rand's wife was Stan Laurel's daughter. This was nice because Laurel and Hardy were my favorite comedians of all time. I always asked him when his wife was going to come on the set so I could talk to her about her father. In every episode we had a different character actor.

H.F. Who was the principal director?

L.A. Earl Bellamy directed the first show and I'll never forget him. The first day I met Earl we went up to Vasquez rocks. It was the first time I had been to Vasquez, and we went right up to that pointed rock. We had to do a scene there at the start and Earl said something like, "If you didn't know me, now you know who I am and know you can trust me. We are up here and it's windier than hell. I'm fat enough, you won't fall down." Hard to believe but that was forty years ago.

H.F. How did you handle fame at this young age? Do you feel that fame robbed you of a normal childhood?

L.A. I don't have a "quote unquote" childhood to refer to. I know I was not abused; I was not taken advantage of as many child stars are, and, I never copped an attitude. There was never a time when the parts were not there. It was not difficult for me, and it was an interesting experience.

People knew me and I was easily recognizable. This was the part I did not like. We used to go on vacation to Lake Arrowhead, go to dinner, or go on a date, and there was a line trying to get an autograph. I never minded that at the studio, but when I left the studio I needed free time.

H.F. What do you remember most about the series?

L.A. A few episodes in particular like the "White Buffalo" which was the most popular. It was like being a kid in the candy store. I could go horseback riding any time I wanted. I had a beautiful dog to work with. There was a great crew who treated me wonderfully. Looking back I have no complaints.

H.F. What did you do about your schooling?

L.A. When we were filming the series, California law said we had to have a tutor on the set. When I went to Inglewood High School, I would get my assignments and do the work. Then when we were through shooting, I'd go back to Inglewood High where I graduated from. After the *Rin Tin Tin* series, I did a lot of cameos like *The Red Skelton Show*, *The Tennessee Ernie Ford Show*, and I was still making half-hour TV shows. In nineteen sixty-two I had a small part in *Bye Bye Birdie*. It was a great cast: Bobby Rydell, Ann-Margret, Paul Lynde, Dick Van Dyke, Janet Leigh.

H.F. What started you on the drugs and alcohol?

L.A. I guess part of it was the times. The hippy thing. Then when I hit rock bottom and almost killed a couple in an accident, I said, "Hey Buddy, you better straighten up your act." So I went to St. John's Hospital in Santa Monica in nineteen eighty and have been clean and sober ever since.

I had been on the stuff for twelve years. People ask why! How did I get started? Was it the fact that I was a child star? The truth is I really don't know. Anyhow I don't think it really matters, I have been told by my doctors that it is hereditary. My father died of alcoholism. My mother suffers from depression. She is in a hospital right now. I seem to have inherited this. They call it a chemical imbalance.

H.F. Why that self-imposed seclusion for so many years?

L.A. When I was about eighteen or nineteen years old I just walked away from the business. I wanted to see what else there was to do. I became a carpenter. I wanted to try life as a "normal" person. I joined the Carpenters Union and put twenty-one years in as a carpenter. When I moved into the high desert region, I got affiliated with building schools there. Today I teach snow skiing to blind kids in the winter. I'm not rich. I have a house in Colorado with a boat. The house is in the Big Bear region. I never touched show business until I heard that this impostor was doing me for about five years, and had even gone to Jim Brown's funeral and done the eulogy. It hurt. But I was more hurt by the other cast members for acknowledging, traveling and doing shows with this impostor. They told me they didn't know, but I was upset. I had a grand relationship with these people and I choose to think they were fooled too. Remember it was twenty-five years and I had been a drug addict and an alcoholic.

H.F. Paul Peterson, also a former child star, helped you immensely on your return. Can you say something about that?

L.A. I owe Paul so much. He did help me. Paul and I go back a long time. We dated the same girls. We drag raced together. We were Hollywood brats. Paul played Jeff Stone for eight years on *The Donna Reed Show* and had several Top Forty hits. He was doing a show at the Corrigan Ranch — Corriganville where so many westerns were filmed — a couple of years ago. Just by chance I decided to give him a call after all these years. When I got to him he said, "Lee, I saw you at Corrigan's Ranch two weeks ago, and you didn't even acknowledge me." I said, "Paul, I live in Arizona now. I have not been off this mountain in years."

Paul sent me a few pictures from the Corrigan Ranch. I told Paul those pictures were not me. "Then we have an impostor," he said. "Some guy has been doing these shows for five years and saying he's you." The story I get is that because of my alcohol and drug addiction, people just thought my personality had changed. We started looking into this.

Then in September we did *The Sally Jessy Raphaël Show*, and I came out of the closet and said, "I'm Lee Aaker." The next day I got a summons from Court suing me for impersonating Lee Aaker. I looked at this and couldn't believe what I saw. Instead of going to court, I went to a lawyer. I brought all my contracts and paraphernalia with me and showed it to the lawyer. The lawyer happened to be a friend of the impostor. I told him he was backing a loser. I showed him my studio contracts, check stubs, social security cards, everything. He then said, "You are Lee Aaker and you're right. I am backing a loser."

Three days later I received an official apology from the lawyer. He asked me if I could clarify a few things with a statement or two. I said, "Sure!" I asked him if he saw the movie *Hondo*. He said he had, and that he was very good friends with both Mike and Pat Wayne. I said, "OK! On July fourth when we were filming *Hondo*, Mike Wayne and I bought these Mexican sky rockets. We lit one and it went straight down to the bottom of the swimming pool, blowing out the bottom of the whole pool. I asked him to ask Pat Wayne about the incident, then to ask the impostor if he knew about it. He did just that! He said he had made a mistake and asked if he could help me.

H.F. You were quite candid about things when I met you in Sonora. Did you find it difficult to appear in public again?

L.A. Let's first say I was a basket case. I was scared to death. Lots of people don't know that I have suffered from panic attacks for years. I was fine when I was on stage, but when I made personal appearances, meeting new people, audiences, I would suffer these attacks. When I went off by myself as a carpenter and just did my own thing I was OK. Through medication and a doctor's help, I found out that the condition is hereditary. So I'm not married and have no children.

Sonora was the first time I had been in front of an audience in thirty years. I was just moved by what happened there. All the love I received from people. When they brought out this birthday cake, I could feel love and warmth. It is such a quaint town. All those wonderful stars and western stars. I'm still a big fan, a big western fan!

H.F. Any thoughts of working again?

L.A. I committed a year of my time to teaching the disabled. I'm semi-retired. I have thought about returning to acting from time to time. I'm sure if there was a part, or something I'd like to do, I'd give it some thought.

H.F. Thank you, Lee!

L.A. Thank you!

2

John Agar

*I didn't let Ford (John) rattle me. I didn't take the old man
as seriously as the other guys. I didn't give him a chance to
really get to me. If he got mean and nasty, I'd just kid him
out of it. I'd laugh it off. He'd give it up and go after somebody else. I just didn't take all his crap that seriously.*

In 1945 Sgt. John Agar was a tall, handsome twenty-four year old physical education instructor at March Field during World War II. He was also husband to be of actress Shirley Temple. By late 1949 this dream Hollywood marriage was officially announced to be "on the rocks."

Early on film producers were quick to notice the tall 6'3" handsome
groom-to-be. They were also quite aware of the publicity coming his way
because of his marriage to Shirley Temple. When Agar went back to camp,
Shirley Temple's visits to him were always followed by scores of reporters and
photographers.

John Agar was Shirley's co-star and love interest in *Fort Apache* starring
John Wayne and Henry Fonda, the first film in John Ford's celebrated U.S.
Cavalry trilogy. The screen chemistry between Temple and Agar was appealing and convincing, and the two were a visual delight. Temple and Agar
appeared together as well in *Adventure in Baltimore*, with Robert Young in the
starring role.

John Ford soon cast the handsome actor in *She Wore a Yellow Ribbon*,
arguably the most sentimental and certainly the most beautifully photographed of all John Ford westerns. It won an Oscar for color cinematography, while Agar and Harry Carey Jr., another Ford protege, were two young
lieutenants with different styles vying for the affections of pretty Joanne Dru —
the girl with the "yellow ribbon." The evocative use of music, notably the title
song, added to the lure and luster of this splendid film. Agar gets the girl in
the movie. But more important it marked the beginning of a fifty-year friendship between John Agar and Harry Carey, Jr.

Now an acknowledged leading man and box office draw, Agar was cast
opposite John Wayne in the outstanding 1949 war film *Sands of Iwo Jima*,

John Agar

with some of the most realistic battle scenes ever filmed for the screen. This time Agar's love interest was Adele Mara. John Wayne won his only Oscar nomination before his Oscar-winning performance in *True Grit* twenty years later. Agar played Private Conway, a cocky recruit with a personal ax to grind against Wayne, his "Gung Ho" drill sergeant. With Duke's help Agar learned to soldier with the best, and after the Duke's death in the final fadeout, Agar leads his men forward in true combat style.

Soon, however, the leading man roles diminished. His failed marriage to Shirley led to bouts with alcohol, and a series of arrests for drunken driving which hampered his career. Yet he harbors no bitterness toward his former wife.

After overcoming alcohol John Agar resumed his career in a series of routine thrillers, mainly in the horror/science fiction genre. Some like *The Revenge of the Creature*, and *Tarantula* have become cult films of sorts. His other screen westerns include *Along the Great Divide* with Kirk Douglas (1951) and *Johnny Reno* with Dana Andrews and Jane Russell (1966). He was reunited with John Wayne again in *Chisum* (1970) and *Big Jake* (1971). Agar also had a small role in the 1976 remake of *King Kong*.

John Agar has become a favorite at film festivals across the country. Now seventy-three years old, his hair turned white, he has been married to his second wife Loretta for more than forty years. He is a man of strong feeling and conviction, particularly about the state of motion pictures today and the entertainment industry in general.

The scion of an old Chicago family who made their name and fortune in the meat packing business, John Agar talks freely about his film career and his short-lived leading man stardom; his marriage to Shirley Temple, an American institution; his association with John Ford and those wonderful westerns. He flavors his stories with lively anecdotes of the people he has known and worked with — from John Wayne and Clint Eastwood, to Victor McLaglen, Maureen O'Hara, Ben Johnson and others.

And make no mistake, this guy can sing too. Just ask those folks who attended the 1993 Knoxville Western Film Festival and heard him deliver, with no musical accompaniment, a perfectly phrased rendition of "I'm Glad There Is You." It was sung with warmth and sincerity.

An interviewer's delight, John Agar is clear, candid, articulate and straightforward. I interviewed him at the 1993 Knoxville Film Festival.

H.F. John, you were from a well-known family in Chicago. Any movie aspirations as a young boy growing up?

J.A. No! I really never planned for that. As you have indicated my family was in the meat packing business in Chicago; my great grandfather started it prior to the Civil War. I attended the Harvard School for Boys on the south side of Chicago. Then we moved to Lake Forest, Illinois, and I attended Lake Forest Academy. From there it was prep school in New York, where I attended the same school as Frank and Al Morgan and George Montgomery. My family moved to California, I went into the service, and my plans were to go into business once I got out.

H.F. Was it John Ford who first put you under contract?

J.A. No, it wasn't. Actually it was David Selznick who put me under contract first. I was still in the service and was home on furlough. We were at a party and got to talking about what I was going to do. Selznick offered to give me a screen test.

H.F. But Ford actually put you in films.

J.A. That's right! I got out of the service in January 1946, and on the thirty-first of the month I was tested. I did a scene from *The Farmer's Daughter*. I saw the test and thought I was terrible. But for whatever reason Selznick signed me. Then for about a year I studied.

The Ford connection happened in an odd way. My mother and kid sister went to Hawaii on a vacation. I went to the dock to pick them up and as luck would have it John Ford saw me. He happened to be on the same ship. Now Ford and Selznick were both working on the same lot, RKO in Culver City. Mr. Selznick told me that John Ford wanted to see me. He was getting ready to do this movie. It was called *War Party* originally. They changed the name to *Fort Apache*.

H.F. Ford had a tough reputation!

J.A. He sure did. I recall that meeting well. I went to see John Ford and he had me standing at attention. Then he had me doing a right face, left face, about face. He told me that he knew I had been in the service. I told him I had been a Buck Sergeant in the Army Air Corps. Then he started singing "Off We Go Into the Wild Blue Yonder," the Army Air Corps song. He ended it with a big "crash" sound.

Everyone knew Ford was a Navy Man, so I answered, "Yes Sir! I guess you're right. Were you in the service, Mr. Ford?" He looked at me and said with unmistakable pride that he was a commander in the United States Navy. So I said, "You mean 'Anchors away, sink, sink, sink!'" I pretended the boat was sinking.

I knew that he liked to tease people so he really didn't affect me like he did some others. I just gave it back to him. But lots of others would say he was cantankerous and mean. The kind of guy who would get all over your case. I thought he was kidding most all the time, but most of the guys who worked with him for years — Wayne, Fonda, George O'Brien, Dick Foran, Victor McLaglen — would say that you never knew when he was kidding and when he was serious. He really did get on my case one time about something, but I never let that bother me.

H.F. You were married to Shirley Temple when you made *Fort Apache*. How did you and Shirley meet?

J.A. People are always asking that. You see my mother was a friend of ZaSu Pitts. She lived in Brentwood and one Sunday we went over there. ZaSu lived right next door to the Temples.

While we were there Shirley came over. Heck she was only about fifteen years old at the time and I was twenty-two. I thought she was just a kid and really didn't pay much attention to her. Anyway, several months later I asked her to go to the movies with me. All of a sudden something happened. We just clicked. Eventually we got engaged, then we got married. It was 1945 and I was still in the service.

H.F. That put you in high profile!

J.A. Yes, it did. We were married on September 20, 1945. Our daughter was born on January 30, 1948. Certainly there was a high degree of profile attached to our marriage. But remember, we were both kids. I was older but just as much of a kid as she was. Shirley's mother was a very strong part of her life, and Shirley was an institution. It's very difficult to be part of an institution. We separated at the end of 1949 and our divorce became final in 1950. I never had any ill feelings toward her. I always thought she was a nice lady. I will always think that way.

H.F. Do you keep in touch at all?

J.A. We haven't really kept in touch or talked together for a long time. She lives her life as Mrs. Charles Black, and Loretta (my wife) and I have our life. We've been happily married for forty-two years.

H.F. Did Shirley show any inclinations in those days toward politics or public service? She certainly has an outstanding and interesting public career as a U.S. ambassador in different countries, in Africa and in Europe.

J.A. No. When we were young, she never showed any inclination toward politics or the kind of work she is doing today. She didn't show that to me at all. Actually, I was very surprised that she backed away from the film business. After we did *Fort Apache* she worked with Ronald Reagan in *The Hagen Girl*. Then she did *The Bachelor and the Bobby Soxer* with Cary Grant and Myrna Loy. She had something on TV in the early Fifties. Then she backed away completely.

H.F. John Ford introduced you to movies in *Fort Apache*. You played Lieutenant Michael O'Roarke, and you were Shirley's love interest. Visually you were also a very attractive couple on the screen. You also played along side John Wayne, Henry Fonda, Ward Bond, George O'Brien, and Victor McLaglen. That's quite an ensemble for a film debut.

J.A. It sure was. Of course, it was such a thrill to work with guys whom I admired as a kid. What a wonderful feeling. And they were all so helpful to me, I might add. They were behind me. Instead of looking their noses down and saying this is a beginner who doesn't know a thing, they always tried to help me out.

H.F. Were you a rider or a horseman before you were in films?

J.A. Oh, I knew how to ride pretty well. When I was a kid my mom and dad sent me to Estes Park, Colorado, and I went to a camp there. We had our own horse, and we had to groom it, feed it, and take care of it. They taught us all of that. Then for a number of years I didn't ride. But when I signed with John Ford to do *Fort Apache*, he made me meet Jack Pennick, an ex–Marine who had been associated with Ford for many years.

I would meet Pennick at his ranch in Encino. He had a horse called "Apache," a mare about "yea" wide and with a spine that stuck up like this [gesturing with his hands]. Well, I had to go out and ride him bareback every morning at eight o'clock. So after about three days of this I came home and took my clothes off. My underwear had stuck to me. I was bleeding. I went back the next day and told Pennick about it. He said not to worry about it, to go to the drug store and get a certain kind of salt then put it in the tub and soak. When I was playing basketball as a kid I used to get that stuff and put it on the soles of my feet. Anyhow, I jumped into the bath and it burned like hell. Well, Pennick proceeded to tell this to everyone on the set. I was really embarrassed.

H.F. Victor McLaglen was an interesting actor!

J.A. And an interesting guy. His son Andy became a fine director, and I worked for him in *Chisum* many years later. But, getting back to Victor. He was a big tough guy. He had been quite a prize fighter in his day. Well, a funny thing happened with George O'Brien, Victor and myself in that movie. We were on a ranch filming and the three of us were in the same cabin. They did not have any facilities in the cabin. So George and I had to get in and get to bed before Vic because he was a terrible snorer. It was just awful. ZZZ... Well, he would get up in the middle of the night, open the door and walk to the latrine. One night he opened the door and it was just so cold that after opening the door, he promptly closed it. Thinking he was still outside he went over and relieved himself in the pot bellied stove. The fire was on and that place smelled for over a week. It was terrible.

H.F. Great story. But how come you were bunking with the boys and not with Shirley during the filming?

J.A. I've been asked that before too; after all, we were married. The reason was because she didn't go on location with us. I did all my riding, but she didn't do hers. That was a stunt lady in the scenes where we were riding in Monument Valley.

H.F. How about *Yellow Ribbon*, one of the truly great westerns?

J.A. *Yellow Ribbon* was a real favorite. A beautiful film which I thoroughly enjoyed. But maybe more important, Ben Johnson, Harry Carey, Jr., and I became close friends while making the film. And we have been friends now for nearly fifty years. I actually met Ben first because he was doing stunt work in *Fort Apache*. Then I met Dobe (Harry Carey Jr.) the next year in *She Wore a Yellow Ribbon*. I was Lieutenant Cahill and he was Lieutenant Pennell. We were both going after Joanne Dru and I won. I lucked out.

H.F. You followed up with *Sands of Iwo Jima*, once again with John Wayne.

J.A. *Sands of Iwo Jima* was a real favorite of mine. I gave old Duke a bad time in that one. But it was great. Duke was with me all the way in each movie I made with him. He'd always extend that much needed pat on the back. I had nothing but the greatest admiration for him. The fighting scenes and the footage were just great and the special effects people were the best in the business. They were so very careful as to how they handled everything. There was lots of stock footage too.

Getting back to Duke. I really believe he could have lived longer. He did that movie about Genghis Khan in 1956. It was called *The Conqueror*. Well, everybody got sick because of the radiation. They were filming in New Mexico where the bomb was tested. In fact, a lot of people in the film eventually died of cancer — Susan Hayward, Agnes Moorehead, Dick Powell, who directed it, and Duke too, of course.

H.F. How does it feel looking back at those days when you were a star?

J.A. To begin with I never considered myself a star. I worked with a lot of stars, and real stars you can count on the fingers of your hand. Let me also add this. Back then you were able to imitate a lot. Remember the sincerest form of flattery is imitation. Now I'll ask another question. "Who do they imitate today?" Guys like Wayne, Fonda and Ward Bond would take their personalities and put them into the role. Guys like Brando, James Dean and others from the method school of acting try to lose themselves in the role. That is a big difference. I prefer the first way. Remember when Brando did *The Godfather*? He copied an actor named Jack Holt, Tim Holt's father. He put cotton in his cheeks to get that voice.

H.F. You also worked with Clint Eastwood very early in his career.

J.A. I know Clint quite well. When I signed with Universal in 1954 and made that second creature film called *Revenge of the Creature* with Lori Nelson and John Bromfield, Clint was under contract at the same time and played a lab assistant. We had a scene when he came in with a little mouse. The next movie I did there was *Tarantula*, and Clint played the jet pilot who dropped an atom bomb on the tarantula. Then I did another western called *Star in the Dust* with Richard Boone and Mamie Van Doren, and Clint was in that one too.

H.F. This was long before he became the big star he is now.

J.A. Yes! He left Universal about the same time as I did, and we did not hear too much about him for a while. Then all of a sudden he was in the TV series *Rawhide*. That turned out to be successful for a number of years, and when the Italian director Sergio Leone came over here, Clint caught his real break.

Yet, there was an ironic twist. The funny thing about all that was Eric Fleming who had the lead in *Rawhide* was the guy that Sergio Leone wanted for the lead in *A Fist Full of Dollars*. Fleming told him he couldn't do it because he was making a movie in South America and that he should talk with Clint perhaps. Eric Fleming drowned while making that movie, and Clint went to Italy and made *A Fist Full of Dollars, For a Few Dollars More, The Good, the Bad and the Ugly*, and came home a star. He's done great since. When he won those two Academy Awards, I called him up and congratulated him. I was so happy for him.

H.F. After making three successful movies with John Wayne early in your career, you worked westerns with him again many years later.

J.A. I sure did. It goes to show that you never know what is going to happen in a film. I worked with Duke for three years in a row, 1947 through 1949: *Fort Apache, She Wore a Yellow Ribbon*, and *Sands of Iwo Jima*. In those days, as you mentioned, I was a young leading man.

Twenty years later I worked with him again in *The Undefeated*, and you can't even find me in the movie. There was one scene where you did recognize me, because Duke and I are on horseback. I am dying from a disease, and a number of other people who followed him home from the Civil War are also on the horse trail. I know I can't go on any further and Duke knows that too. He tells me that he would send my share on to my family. It was a very moving scene but they cut it out. Lee Meriwether, who was in the film too, couldn't understand it, and neither could I. But they thought the film was too long so they cut it.

In *Chisum* I had a nice little part. I got angry when I thought that Duke sold out to Forrest Tucker. I closed out my store and rode out of town. In *Big Jake* I worked for Maureen O'Hara. I ran the ranch for her, and Richard Boone blew me away in that one.

H.F. You worked both as a leading man and as a character actor. Did you enjoy working the lead and character roles equally in your movies?

J.A. Let's say I totally enjoyed working in films. I still do. But I have particular standards that I uphold. Of course they are not going to ask an old guy like me to get involved in those huffy puffy scenes with the gals. But then I wouldn't have done it in the first place even if I was a young guy waiting to get into the business.

H.F. You have strong convictions about the movie business today!

J.A. Sure, why not! I will not use profanity on the screen. It shows a lack of intelligence, no respect for the people out there, or any respect for yourself. I think the industry today is making a big mistake. They should go back to letting the audience use their own imagination. They don't have to be as graphic as they are. People are not stupid. A guy and gal look at each other and you know very well what is going on. Do you think when Maureen O'Hara and John Wayne got together in *The Quiet Man* and in other films, that the audience didn't know what they were thinking or feeling? It was great. It was fantastic.

H.F. But aren't the studios today just giving the people what they want?

J.A. Lots of people say this. They say that the studios are doing just that, that this is what the young kids want, and they buy the tickets. I don't believe this. It is not what they *want*, it is what they are getting and are conditioned to look at. Look at the media today. Look what's on in the middle of the afternoon when the kids are out of school: Geraldo, Donahue, Oprah Winfrey. And that's just for starters. Look at the subject matter they are being fed. It's absolutely ridiculous and it's destroying us.

H.F. You feel that strongly about the issue!

J.A. Absolutely. Just look back to all the great civilizations of the past. Rome is an excellent example. These civilizations all went down the tubes from within, never from without. It resulted from lack of morals and lack of respect. It's happening fast in our society right now. People don't seem to see it. But people better start taking responsibility for what they do.

H.F. The future or the westerns, John! Do you think they can come back?

J.A. It seems like some of the westerns are coming back. Ben Johnson is filming *Bonanza*. The last picture I made was *Night Breed* in 1989. I'll say this, though, when I get a chance to work and walk on a set, it's like something that has been laying dormant. It's special, and I love it!

3

Chris Alcaide

I know very few people who enjoyed being an actor as much as I did. Here I was in my later forties still playing cowboys and Indians. And playing bad guys was fun. First, of all it's the best part usually. It's fun to do, because you can get a vicarious thrill doing these things.

"Wait a minute! All the guys you mentioned so far are good guys," said actor Cliff Alcaide when we spoke. Alcaide, the recipient of the 1993 Black Hat Award at the Sonora Western Film Fest, wore that black hat as well as anyone in the business for years. "But I was a good guy too," he's quick to point out. "At least about nine times in my more than four hundred roles."

Born in Youngstown, Ohio, in 1922, Alcaide decided to head West to see California before going into the service. He soon landed himself a job as a bouncer at the Hollywood Paladium. Strong, tall and good-looking, he was approached many times with suggestions that he try to find work in the picture business.

After being discharged from military service, he entered the prestigious Ben Bard School of Dramatics and was cast in *The Barrets of Wimpole Street*, where he traveled up and down the West Coast with the touring company. His first film part was in Warner Brothers *The Glass Menagerie*, starring Kirk Douglas, Jane Wyman and Gertrude Lawrence. Soon he was cast with western star Charles Starret in the *Durango Kid* series. Some other film credits include *Miami Story*, *Chicago Syndicate*, *Monkey on My Back*, *The Big Heat*, *Flight of the Phoenix*, and *Kid Galahad*.

But, Chris Alcaide was becoming one of the most recognizable bad guys around town. He wore that black hat in films like *Smoky Canyon*, *Massacre Canyon*, *Gunslinger*, *Cripple Creek*, *Day of the Bad Man*. Yet it was as a television bad man that Chris Alcaide carved his true mark, appearing in over 400 television westerns and working in such hit series as *Rawhide*, *Kit Carson*, *Annie Oakley*, *Bonanza*, *Broken Arrow*, *Cheyenne*, *Sugarfoot*, *Daniel Boone*, *Rin Tin Tin*, etc.

Ironically, after making more than 400 westerns, he injured himself in the pilot for a new television series to be called *The Black Saddle*, which was to be his first lead as a hero. The injury ultimately ended his days in the westerns, although he continued to work regularly for another ten years in less strenuous bad guy roles.

For many years Chris and his wife Peri, once a top Hollywood foreign correspondent, owned and operated an art gallery in West Hollywood, catering to stars and collectors. He continued to act in occasional television movies and feature films through the mid 1980s. Today, Chris and Peri Alcaide are both semi-retired and spend much of their time in Palm Springs, California. And just forget that "menacing bad guy" image for a moment, because in real life Chris Alcaide is simply a genuinely nice man.

H.F. Chris, you were born in Youngstown, Ohio, light years away from the Hollywood sound stage. Did you ever have any acting ambitions as a young guy growing up?

C.A. No, not at all. When I was first approached for this business it was all very foreign to me. My early background was in the Youngstown steel mills. I left when I was sixteen and went to New York. I lied about my age and got a job on the *New York Mirror* covering the World's Fair. That was 1939-40. In 1933 my parents had taken me to the Chicago World's Fair and I got very upset because my dad and my older brother went in to see Sally Rand, and they wouldn't let me go in. I guess I was all of eleven years old at the time.

H.F. What brought you out to Hollywood?

C.A. Once I got to New York, I knew I wanted out of Youngstown. In 1942 I was almost twenty years old and thought I'd like to see California before going into military service. After a couple of odd jobs, I ended up with a job at the Hollywood Paladium as a bouncer. I had to lie about my age again. I was nineteen but jacked my age up to twenty-two so I could kick the minors out of the cocktail lounge. I am 6'3" which in those days made me pretty big. While working at the Paladium I was approached many times for pictures. Remember too with the war on there was a shortage of people available.

H.F. But you admit to having no acting background at all.

C.A. No, I didn't. As a kid I was the greatest movie fan in the world. Still I never considered myself material for that kind of thing. Yet, as I mentioned, when I walked around the Paladium I was approached about four times by agents and twice by producers. So while I was in the service I gave it quite a bit of thought. Even when I came out of service in 1946 and went back to the Paladium, I did not consider it something I'd end up doing. Then I met an agent. He was a very smart man. He suggested that I see if I liked this kind of work first before really deciding to get into it. So with his help and influence, I ended up at Ben Bard's School of Dramatics.

Chris Alcaide

H.F. Lots of big name stars went to that school!

C.A. Sure! Alan Ladd, Jack Carson, Marilyn Monroe, Ben Gazzara, and a number of other names you would recognize. After doing a number of plays and going up and down the coast and on the road with these plays, my first touch was at MGM where they held me in option for a while. But I never quite fit into their stock of leading men.

H.F. Did they sign you on as a contract player?

C.A. No, I was not ever signed. I was held on option for a while to do a test. Then the same thing happened to me at 20th Century–Fox. One day I was having lunch with a friend of mine who worked at Columbia. Through him I met a director named Fred Sears. Sears was famous at Columbia for taking a small budget and making it look like a million-dollar picture for those days. My first one was *Smoky Canyon*, the Durango Kid thing with Charlie Starrett. I met Jock Mahoney. He was a stunt man turned actor. So all of a sudden, here were the westerns.

H.F. So you started your career making westerns.

C.A. No, actually my first picture was *The Glass Menagerie* at Warner Brothers. There were only about three or four speaking parts other than the principals. I'm in the factory with Arthur Kennedy when the foreman criticizes him about the rush. I had one line; this was my great debut. I also did some amateur stuff in the true sense. I did a video with a guy called Steve Gibson and his Redcaps. Then I did something else with a fly-by-night producer that was called *The Curse of the Ubangis*. I was one of the white hunters. It was ridiculous stuff. But then the westerns came up, and my god, I was at home!

H.F. Did you have any experience riding a horse?

C.A. No, growing up in Youngstown I had never been on a horse. But I was lucky. I said how I met Jock Mahoney. I also met the guys who had all the cast horses. I mean the good horses they used in the westerns. The first thing they did was have Red Morgan and LeRoy Johnson lean on me every time we went around a curve to keep me in the saddle. Then for about three months they wouldn't let me have a saddle. I had to go bareback. Fortunately there were a lot of stunt people who come out there. Jock Mahoney was a great help. There were three men whom I watched carefully. Tim Holt was one. Joel McCrea was another. Those men sat on a horse so beautifully that I tried to copy everything they did.

H.F. You mention Tim Holt. He was also a very fine actor.

C.A. Absolutely! He did *The Magnificent Ambersons* with Orson Wells and the Mercury Players and, of course, *The Treasure of Sierra Madre*. He could do westerns and non-westerns alike. He was marvelous on a horse; watch some of his old pictures and see how that fanny remains on the horse. He was a far underrated actor.

H.F. You mentioned three men. Who was the other?

C.A. The third, of course, was Ben Johnson. I watched him and he was poetry. I remember picking up on him early in his career when he had three lines in a John Wayne picture. But when he got on a horse, "Oh boy!" But then Ben became one hell of a performer, a hell of an actor, too. How about *One-Eyed Jacks*, when he played the heavy. So aping these men and, of course, getting a lot of help from so many wranglers, things began working out.

H.F. The wranglers, too, helped you a lot.

C.A. They sure did. If you go to a wrangler in the morning and say, "Hi, my name is so and so and I'm playing so and so in this, could you please tell me what horse I'm going to ride and let me find out a little about him." Heck, those guys would bend over backwards for you. The first thing I'd do would be to get up on the horse and take the reign to get the horse to do what I wanted him to do. If he responded just by the shifting your weight, then at times you could make it work without even using the reigns. So, I may not have become a good horseman, but I sure as hell knew how to look like one.

H.F. Were you ever a good guy in a western?

C.A. Yeah! At least about nine times out of about four hundred TV westerns. Then I did a pilot for my own series for Four Star. It was released under *A Thread of Violence* with Cesar Romero. The series was sold, then five days before we went into production, we heard that a new ad agency man was a little worried about me because of all the vicious heavies he had seen me do. He asked whether I would consider doing the second lead instead. Well, I was hot at the time and had three other series offers, so I told him "No chance!" Then suddenly in the mid-sixties all the westerns started to fade out. In fact, the motion picture industry as a whole had some bad times right about then.

H.F. While you found a home with westerns, you also did a lot of non-westerns.

C.A. Oh, yes! At Columbia I did a whole bunch of things, some with Fred Sears. I played practically the same part every time. The head of the syndicate had a personal assassin whom he would send off to knock off witnesses, even our own lieutenants. I was that guy. We started out in Miami with *The Miami Story* with Barry Sullivan and Beverly Garland. Then we went to Chicago and called it *The Chicago Syndicate* with Dennis Morgan, Abbe Lane, Xavier Cugat and Paul Stewart.

H.F. What do you recall about *Chicago Syndicate*? I was born and raised there.

C.A. That we got thrown out of there. They didn't like us shooting about the syndicate. We shot about half of it in Chicago; then we had to wrap it up and finish it in Hollywood. I remember one place on State Street where Paul Stewart was supposed to run down with his snub-nosed .38. One of the cops who was helping us out said that Paul could start out there, but he might not come out the other end. There were dead rats all over. The cooperation was not good because of the syndicate theme. We couldn't get the cooperation, so we went back.

I also recall there was a little late night place called the Corner House. I went in there wearing the hat I was wearing in the picture, since I had to get used to it. I also had my trench coat. I sat down at the other end of the counter and had some bacon and eggs and coffee. The waitress said to me, "We don't have to give you a check, do we?" I just looked at her. She thought I was a cop, to her I either had to be a cop or a hood.

H.F. What about *The Houston Story*?

C.A. More of the same thing. After Chicago we went to Houston to do that film. At the beginning Lee J. Cobb was the head of the mob and once more I am the killer. About three days into the shooting Lee gets a heart attack. Barbara Hale, who was in the film too, goes to the second-in-command and says,

"How about Chris doing the lead?" We sat around for two more hours to see if we could get anybody to play my part. We couldn't find anybody in Houston, so we wrapped it up and went back to Hollywood and brought in Gene Barry for the lead.

H.F. You have a reputation for just being a real nice guy. How were you able to get all that venom to play such sinister parts?

C.A. Let me put it this way. First of all, it's the best part usually. It's fun to do because you can get a vicarious thrill doing these things. But getting back to all these films. We ran out of cities and Lee J. Cobb still owed them one more picture. We went back to Miami and did *Miami Expose*, with Lee and Patricia Medina, who had been married to Richard Greene. After that the westerns really began coming along on TV, and I found myself doing more and more westerns. Maybe once in a while a Perry Mason or something.

H.F. How many westerns?

C.A. Let's say this. At one time there were forty western series on the air. Going back, my wife, Peri, and I tried to figure out the ones that I did not work on. The ones I did not work on were *Wyatt Earp*, *Wagon Train*, and one other. My god, I did just about them all.

H.F. Many westerns feature films?

C.A. Only a few. Nothing important. Things like *Crippled Creek* with George Montgomery, and *Whiplash* with Richard Widmark and Donna Reed. In TV I could come in and be the main protagonist. But in the feature films I would be up against the big names, but I did do a picture with Elvis Presley.

H.F. Which one was that?

C.A. It was *Kid Galahad*. I was one of the syndicate men who came down to try to get everyone straightened out.

H.F. What did you think of Elvis?

C.A. Big surprise! I must have gone on the set a little biased because I didn't care for his music. It wasn't my type. You are stuck with the music you went to high school with. Remember I worked at the Paladium in 1947, and the next year I worked at Dave's Blue Room as *maître d'*, a famous after dinner spot. Then, I went back to the Paladium and through a series of promotions, ended up managing it. So the Bid Band Era was really my kind of music, that was the music I loved.

So, when I went on the *Kid Galahad* thing, Presley's music was not for me. Well, I'm watching him as he makes an entrance into the boxing ring. He's listening to the director attentively. He takes very good direction. He's a very polite young man. He looks down at ringside and sees me with Edward Lewis, the other syndicate man, and makes like a fast draw. He remembers me from the westerns. I was blown over. So now I was captured. He's got me. Now I like him.

H.F. What TV westerns stand out in your mind?

C.A. I think my favorite was the Zane Grey Theater. I had a lot of fun with *The Rifleman* too. And in the early days I liked the *Gunsmoke*s, the way it used to be done. I did a lot of the half-hour episodes, not many of the hour ones. When it became an hour show, a new outfit of producers and directors came in and I didn't know any of them. I couldn't quite break the ice.

H.F. What do you recall of James Arness?

C.A. He was just a nice big guy. I also liked Milburn Stone. He was a very nice man. In fact, I did a story where I came into town with two hench-men. I'm a bad guy, there's no doubt about that, and it turns out that years before Doc Adams and I were after the same woman. I had taken her off, so naturally he hates me from the beginning. Then I get shot in the back and Doc has to operate on me. They are not sure they want him to operate because they think he might be the one who shot me since he hates me so much. Well, it turns out that my own brother, one of the henchmen, shot me in the back. Of course, I had to play someone Milburn's (Doc's) age, so they died my hair gray. I have a still shot from that show in 1953, where my hair was as gray as it is now, and today, it's natural.

H.F. What about Chuck Connors on *The Rifleman*? He played first base for the Chicago Cubs for a while.

C.A. He also was a big guy and lots of fun to work with. I did a lot of *Rifleman* episodes. It was a good income for me too. I got co-star or guest star billing later on. My god, today someone who has three lines on TV is a guest star. That ridiculous!

H.F. As primarily a character actor then, you had pretty steady work.

C.A. Yes, I worked a lot. As I said Peri and I added all my work up and it was quite steady. An actor's superstition is that as soon as you are out of work you go and register for unemployment. For two reasons: one is the super-stition that if you register you get a job right away; the other is that it is tax-free money which helps you through the lean days. But really, I know very few people who enjoyed being an actor as much as I did. Here I was in my late forties, still playing cowboys and Indians. But eventually it took its toll when I got seriously injured.

H.F. Was the injury work-related?

C.A. You bet! I was doing a pilot for my own series when the stirrup broke and I went off the horse. I had enough left in the right stirrup to start a roll before I went off the horse. I hit the ground and got a ridge in the small of my back.

Now they didn't know it, but I spent all three nights in traction when we finished the film. I got it fixed but it would go out again. Then in 1969 I couldn't walk anymore. I went into the hospital for forty-five days; they found that two disks had disintegrated. My left leg was completely paralyzed and my right one was going. They patched me up with fusions and I was in a brace for almost a year. After that I was stronger than ever. But, you go tell that to somebody who is going to hire you for a western. So, in a sense, that was my swan song in the business, and the business was in bad shape itself.

H.F. What happened then?

C.A. For a long time I worked for a friend of mine who did live shows. I did staging, promotion, and publicity for him. Meanwhile my wife, Peri, had a hobby of collecting almost all sorts of things. One of the things she was collecting was old calendar art out of the Decco period. She was a foreign correspondent from Turkey covering the movie industry for three papers and a couple of magazines. Little by little she turned her hobby into a business. She'd buy photographs for a reasonable price, and put them in frames which she would buy at a reasonable price. She was able to put the two together and make a remarkable profit from it. She had a marvelous ability to know what people were going to want next year. Now I had never worked with my hands, as my father and brother did, but I became adept at making trains. Little by little we built this into a good business. We bought a building on Santa Monica Boulevard in West Hollywood, and every year it improved and improved. The moment we'd hit an area that was selling our type of thing, we'd purchase it. We continued to build up our business and called it "Peri's Pictures." We had the business on Santa Monica Boulevard from 1972 till 1985.

Then I found that my insurance eligibility had dropped because my residuals were getting too low. I mentioned this to an agent who asked me if I would like to do some work. I told him "Sure!" So, I worked in *The Assassination* with Charles Bronson in 1987. I played the chief justice swearing in a new president. Heck, I'd take anything: an elevator operator, a waiter, a minister, just to keep the eligibility for the insurance. When you turn sixty-five, of course, you don't have to worry about all that. But it was enough of an experience for me to realize what a different business it is now, from the days when I was in there having lots of fun.

H.F. What's the difference between then and now as you see it?

C.A. Today it's in the hands of the "bean cutters," the accountants. Those old moguls who ran the studios could be nasty men, but their interest was in making movies. When they made them close down all their theaters, they could no longer grind out those B movies which was like the training ground, the minor league for actors. They had everything going on an even keel. It was great. Moreover, they also knew how to build stars.

H.F. To retreat a bit Chris, you never had any formal acting training as a kid. Did you go to a lot of movies as a youngster?

C.A. Are you kidding? As a kid, if they couldn't find me, they'd go to the Uptown Theater. Fredric March was one of my movie heroes. I liked Clark Gable. In the western genre my favorite was Buck Jones.

H.F. Any favorite screen westerns?

C.A. Of course everybody has to have *Shane* right up there. Then you've got to put *Red River* in there. Then *My Darling Clementine*. One of the greatest lines ever came from that film. Fonda is standing at the bar, and he is very despondent because he is in love with Clementine, and she is crazy for Victor Mature (Doc Holiday). The bartender is a marvelous character actor named J. Ferrell McDonald. Fonda looks down at his drink and says, "Mack, have you ever been in love?" Ferrell thinks for a minute and says, "No Sir! I've been a bartender all my life." I loved that line.

H.F. Which directors most impressed you?

C.A. John Sturges who did *Bad Day at Black Rock*. I liked John Ford a lot. I liked a lot of things George Stevens did. Richard Whorf, an old-time character actor, was a fine, fine director. Of course, Fred Sears who died rather young was a fine director. So was Virgil Vogel.

H.F. And what about today's westerns?

C.A. Remember, we created something when two guys walked down the street and one said, "I don't think you are such a fast draw!" Now, if you believe that, then you are about as bright as the man who is about to go out and do that. We did all that fast draw stuff, and we had forty westerns on the TV at one time.

It's just like the old saying that every time something is a success, there's twelve imitators out there. We overdid it so much with the westerns and created a lot of fallacies, like the wardrobe, the way women looked, and men reacted. A lot of it was just farce, like the so-called situation comedies. People won't believe that stuff any more. It's still nice to watch though. It's nostalgia and everything, and in that way, it is great. But we overdid it to the point that people say, "Oh come on," or something like that.

H.F. Did you see *Unforgiven*?

C.A. Yeh, it was very well done. But when you think about it, a lot of it was really simplicity. It was good, but not as good as a lot of people wanted to think it was. Clint simplified a lot of things. Remember this, when Clint was in *Rawhide*, he rarely had anything to say. When he went to Italy, he rarely said much either. He was "The Man with No Name." So, they were smart, they tailored it for him.

H.F. Do you know him personally?

C.A. Only from working with him on *Rawhide*. Incidentally, he's one hell of a nice guy. I did one *Rawhide* episode which was quite good. It was with Cloris Leachman and Russell Arms.

H.F. Are there many good things coming out of the picture business today in your estimation?

C.A. Well, I'll tell you this. Without the training ground we used to have, some of the performers I see today are so good. In the old days we had all these little theaters where performers got an excellent apprenticeship. Actors could get experience and training, along with drama schools. Then there were all those "B" pictures going on constantly. I guess TV in some way takes the place of that, but there isn't the amount of work today that there was for actors then. With the lack of places to go where actors can get away with being bad, I'm amazed at the quality of some of the performers I see coming on. Today I think a lot of people are getting their training in college.

H.F. But the films were better in the old days!

C.A. That's what they say, and I certainly love to watch the American Movie Channel, though we made our share of clunkers then too. However, there is one thing I'd like to point out because it just amazes me. Look at the credits after an HBO movie. They list everything: "the man who got the coffee for the wrangler," or "the man who helped sweep on Saturday afternoon." There are five minutes of credits. They rush through the credits so fast that if you want to know the actor who did a certain role you liked, I defy you to find him. When I look at the amount of people listed on the crews I can't believe it. It's so ridiculous what the studio costs are today to put a movie on.

H.F. How did John Wayne strike you as an actor?

C.A. Nothing as an actor. But let me explain. As a screen image he was magnificent. I always tell people who might criticize him by saying, "Who else would you get to play the part?" Talking about actors, how could I forget my all-time hero; the greatest actor for me was Cary Grant. Once in a while he could be miscast. But he learned his framework and that was what he worked in. Movie acting is much more personality than it is acting. Do I have time to tell you a little story?

H.F. Sure! Please do!

C.A. I'm at Metro in 1954 working on a picture with Esther Williams called *Jupiter's Darling*. I started in Catalina in May and finished the thing in Silver Springs, Florida, at the end of August. It was a nothing part, but they needed a guy who could ride a horse well and swim underwater a great deal, and look muscular next to Esther because she is a big gal.

In the morning I would come in the commissary and there was a guy with a big heavy coat, sort of a bulky guy. He said, "Hi." I said "Hi" back! One morning I'm having my coffee and he asks if he could join me. I told him to please sit down. He said, "You are making a picture with Esther Williams, aren't you?" I told him I was. Then I asked him what he was doing. He replied he was doing the musical *Oklahoma* and was playing Judd.

Of course, the guy I was talking to was Rod Steiger. He told me he had just got a break back east to do a picture with Marlon Brando called *On the Waterfront*. Anyway, there was a little bar across the street from Schwabs called the Lorelei. Rod would come in, drink some scotch, and I'd have my scotch and some beer. It was just a nice hangout, and Rod and I would talk quite a bit. He was the first major star who would try something different every time out of the box. To me Brando was always Brando. Steiger was the only major star around at the time who would always try something different. He's my other hero. He's had a lot of trouble since then, but I still consider him one of the finest actors around. He was marvelous.

H.F. Any big regrets career-wise?

C.A. Yes, there is! I should have turned more things down. I would have been able to get better parts and more money. If I wanted to be more successful at the time, I should have definitely turned more things down and have been a little more discerning. But major regrets? No!

H.F. You mention your wife was a foreign movie critic.

C.A. Peri came to this country from Turkey to visit. She was in New York for a while, and in San Francisco for a while. Being from the middle east, she loved to gamble. She went to Las Vegas where a couple of people connected with a film called *Ataturk* contacted her. It was the story of the man who modernized Turkey. Lots of money was invested in the script, but the Turkish government would not approve it because it delved into the man's life. He was a real swinger.

They canceled the picture because the Turkish government would not approve, but since Peri was here, they asked her to do a picture with Errol Flynn called *Istanbul*. They cast her as the guide to the city in the film. Peri had worked in some films in Italy but didn't like working in American films because she didn't like standing around all day to work on the right set. So she decided to go to Hawaii, and bought her ticket since she is leaving out of San Francisco. Then she got a bad break; she met me. We met on a Wednesday night and got married on Saturday. She returned her ticket, and we bought a refrigerator instead. That was 1956. There's another interesting story I think your readers will like.

  H.F. Sure! Go ahead.

  C.A. Two years ago Peri got a phone call. I am in the garage where I am making frames and I hear Peri say, "Hello Georgia! How are you?" Georgia is my ex-wife, and she just loves Peri. It seems that Georgia just bought a house here in Palm Desert. Actually, her daughter bought it for her. You see, when Georgia and I were married in 1947, she had a little girl two years old from a previous marriage. He name was Cherilyn and she was the most beautiful baby. She was sort of dark-skinned, as I am dark-skinned, too, so a lot of people thought she was my daughter from a previous marriage. And although Georgia and I were completely wrong for each other, what kept us together was the way that baby took over me. Anyway, Georgia went on to be married quite a few times. And when Cherilyn grew up a little, she decided to shorten her name to Cher. I guess you heard of her. The rest I guess is history.

  H.F. So Cher was the captivating little baby that kept you and Georgia together.

  C.A. That's right. She is my stepdaughter. But I'm not alone. I think there are five or six other guys who are stepfathers.

  H.F. That sure is a great story! How about these film festivals? And, how do you feel attending them?

  C.A. I enjoy the hell out of them. I imagine it will get old after a while. But I find them just great. What I particularly enjoy here in Sonora are the panel discussions. You really learn a lot and are able to share your experiences in the industry with so many people.

  H.F. Congratulations on the "Black Hat" Award, Chris. It's well-deserved.

  C.A. Thank you!

4

Randy Boone

It's just amazing how many people remember me from The
Virginian *show. After all, Lee J. Cobb and James Drury
were the real stars. I was surprised how loyal the public was.*

Born in Fayetteville, North Carolina, Randy Boone's southern roots are
clearly recognized in his singing and acting. While country music has been a
part of his life from the start, his good looks and slow-moving manner put
him on the receiving end of many cameras over the past years. He was Vern
Hodges, a series regular in *It's a Man's World*, and Francis Wilde in the western series *Cimarron Strip*. But, it was as Randy Denton in *The Virginian* for
which he is best remembered. Randy Boone was a popular guest star as well,
with roles in popular westerns like *Gunsmoke, Bonanza, Wagon Train*, and
non-westerns like *The Twilight Zone, Alfred Hitchcock Presents, Combat, Lassie*,
and *The Dinah Shore Show*.

A fine singer, Randy Boone recorded from California to Nashville on several labels including "Decca." He is a master of troubadour singing, needing
neither special effects nor a crafty chorus to make him sound good; his "old
guitar" is all he needs to delight audiences. And, he has done that from cafes
and coffee houses across the land.

I interviewed Randy Boone in North Hollywood at Ray Courts Movie Collectors' Show. In the following interview he tells of his youthful cross-country
odyssey with that "old guitar," his years as a folk and country/western singer,
and his lively experiences in show business. Most of all he talks about his role
as Randy Denton in *The Virginian*, highlighted with wonderful stories about
the late great Lee J. Cobb with whom he worked with and greatly respected.

H.F.   Randy, what inspired you to grab your guitar and hitchhike cross-
country?

R.B.   Well, my last year in high school I just began playing the guitar
and got the romantic idea of hitchhiking. Of course, things were much safer
back then, so that's what I did. I thought I'd like to see the country before I

got drafted, so I took my guitar and thought I'd have some fun, which I did. It was June 1960, and folk music was becoming real popular in the country.

H.F.   How many years did you travel around with your thumb to the road?

R.B.   Oh, I'd say a couple of years. I went to New York and Cape Cod, and to Florida the year they had the big riots after the filming of *Where the Boys Are*. I came out to California in 1962. The folk song/coffee house scene was very big then, and I used my guitar as a way to meet people.

H.F.   And this led to television!

R.B.   Yes, but in an indirect way. I was doing the clubs when I ran into a guitar player who had an agent. The agent sent him to try out for a part in a series called *It's a Man's World*. He saw that there was a part for a kid with a guitar who could look realistic. He took me to see the producer. They brought me a script and had me read. I never had any real experience, just one high school play. But, they had me come back and do another scene which was put on film.

H.F.   Did they sign you right away?

R.B.   Not really! I already had gone to San Jose and was playing in a folk club when they called and said I was the guy they wanted. This was 1962-63. Wow! I was on my way, or so I thought. That show took me through the year and was very successful. Yet, it was canceled to make room for TV movies which were becoming quite big. The cast of *It's a Man's World* included Glenn Corbett, Ted Bessell, Michael Burns and myself. It was based on a houseboat in some little college town. We all felt we were doing really well, but the show somehow just got bounced by the movies.

H.F.   Did you go right into *The Virginian* from there?

R.B.   Not quite! I did some work with *Wagon Train* first. Then I landed the part in *The Virginian* series, and what a great cast: James Drury, Doug McClure and Lee J. Cobb, who was just a wonderful, wonderful man.

H.F.   Did Lee J. Cobb have that same powerful presence off the screen as he did on the screen?

R.B.   Yes, he really did. It was a personal thing with him. But there is a story which I like to tell. I was working downstairs with the music guy and we were working together on some songs I was going to do. I'm down there one day rehearsing and the guy from the music department has this little gadget he blows on. He also has a little keyboard like a piano, and we are busy at work.

Well, Lee J. it seems was down there too, and he and the music guy remember each other from the old vaudeville days. There was a piano on the set, and one of the others, a third guy, could play a little piano. So Lee J. picks up some prop canes and three hats which were laying there. The three start

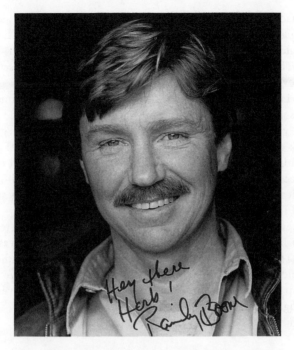

Randy Boone as Randy Denton in *The Virginian*

doing some soft shoe dancing side-by-side. The whole set just stopped cold and watched the show which went on for about half an hour. It was great. Talk about talent. Here's this guy who is such a powerful actor, the guy who played Willie Lohman on Broadway singing and dancing. This was a side of Lee J. that few people ever got to see. I feel very fortunate.

H.F.   What was it like doing scenes with him?

R.B.   It was great. You'd forget all the action and all the stuff going on around you. You would just get taken into the scene. You'd really get taken in. It was different, very different. Sometimes he would even play tricks on the set.

H.F.   Anything in particular that you recall?

R.B.   Sure! We had this one scene when all the guys in black ties were down from the front office — all the brass, as you say. They were wondering why it was taking so long to get this one particular scene done. It was a scene where Betsy was lost and we were all looking for her. James Drury said something like, "You go down the bend and up the ridge, around the draw, and I'll come over the ridge, and through the pass and down the slope. And Randy, you come over the mountain and through the woods, down the creek."

We had all these cliché things. But every time we tried it, somehow we just kept giggling. We couldn't get our lines in rhythm; we just had a bad case of the giggles. Everyone was angry. The businessmen were mad. The director was mad. The professionals on the set were mad. They were all scowling at us. Finally they lost patience.

Now Lee J. had this clause in his contract saying if it is time for him to leave the set, they would have to wait until the next day to shoot the whole scene. They would have to hold everything for him. So Lee J. is giving us this awful look on the set. A look like "you unprofessional group of punk actors. Get this thing together." The director said that we'd better get ourselves together "because we have a real professional, Lee J. Cobb, waiting to do the scene." Meanwhile, Lee J. is looking "real disappointed." He's smacking his lips — that little characteristic of his.

Well, we finally get everything together and he is supposed to say his line, "All right! Is everything in order," right after James Drury gives us his long directive. This time Lee J. looks at each one of us and says something just hysterical which had absolutely nothing to do with the script. We all instantly cracked up and that was it. We were through for the day. Everybody now started laughing. The black tie guys and all, they cracked up too. They laughed for half an hour. They wrapped up the set and that was it!

H.F. Who played the young lady in the series? She was very good.

R.B. You bet she was. That was Roberta Shore. You bet she was good. She was also a delight to be around, real personable! She was a sweetheart of a person, genuine, bright, fresh. She was a Mormon and was going with a guy who came to Los Angeles to study at their church. She said that when he got through with his studies she was going to get married and quit show business. And that's what she did. They got married and went to Utah to live. I had breakfast with Doug McClure the other day and he said he had talked to her recently. They are still living in Utah and doing fine.

H.F. What do you recall about James Drury?

R.B. A great guy to work with. We hit it off right from the start. We didn't have as many close and intimate scenes in the show as I did with Lee J. What I mean is that there weren't as many long, drawn-out scenes. I had many more scenes with Doug McClure who played Trampas. In one episode, however, I got to hit James because in that episode the Virginian fired a guy that I liked. But James was often out doing appearances. He was extremely popular at the time, so he would come and go a lot. I got to know him better later in the show. He was always great to work with. Doug McClure and I were pretty close. We did lots of rodeos and fairs together.

H.F.   How many years were you in the series?

R.B.   Four years, from 1963 to 1967.

H.F.   Did you have a lot of western skills when you began doing *The Virginian?*

R.B.   Oh yes! When I first got into *It's a Man's World*, I started going with a girl, she knew a few things and thought I would be good for westerns. She talked me into buying a horse, so by the time they put me in *The Virginian*, I was a pretty good rider.

H.F.   How about handling guns?

R.B.   Oh, I learned enough. I never really got into it though because I banged my hands around a few times. I played the guitar and I had to be careful. But I did well enough.

H.F.   Any movies?

R.B.   Just a few. I did something called *Terminal Island*. Tom Selleck was in it, and I was billed ahead of him. Try to believe that! Then I went to Nashville and did a movie called *Country Boy*. And I did a movie out here. I can't remember the name, but I was a kid who gets enticed by an older woman who is a doctor and wants me to murder her husband.

H.F.   After *The Virginian?*

R.B.   I did a series called *Cimarron Strip*, with Stuart Whitman. Stuart Whitman once got an Academy Award nomination for a film called *The Mark*. He was a super talented guy. The kind of guy who could do anything. He was also a super talented businessman. He owned a lot of the production company in the making of *Cimarron Strip*. I played a guy named Francis Wilde and was a regular on the series.

H.F.   Your work then was mainly western!

R.B.   A western TV actor, that's me! And during that time I switched the kind of music I did. When I first hitchhiked across the land, I did a smattering of country music, but mainly I did folk songs. I began going more and more into western and country/western music. I was booked in lots of country music clubs, and I started playing country music like mad. After *Cimarron Strip*, I spent years playing the country/western clubs.

H.F.   It's thirty years now since *The Virginian* and the heyday of TV westerns, do people still remember you well?

R.B.   It's amazing, they do! I was surprised how loyal the public was. They would come to see me in the clubs. Right now I'm really hopeful about getting back and doing some more work.

H.F.   Best of luck, Randy — and thanks!

5

Harry Carey Jr.

Red River *was the last film my father ever did. It was the only time we were in a film together. Even though we didn't have any scenes together, I was very proud to be in it.* Red River *was one of the great all-time westerns. I never really felt the impact of what I was doing. My first three directors were Raoul Walsh, Howard Hawks and John Ford. What a way for a guy to start out.*

Those who know him well call him Dobe. Harry Carey Jr. has been among the industry's most durable actors for almost fifty years. It's a safe bet that Dobe Carey has appeared in as many top flight films as anyone around today, appearing in over one hundred feature films and scores of television shows. Moreover, no living actor can boast a more impressive list of western credits.

Although he was the son of a screen icon and an actress mother — his mother, Ollie, appeared with him in *The Searchers*— Harry Carey Jr.'s earliest dream was to be a Big Band singer. Instead he achieved western protege status when John Ford cast him in the role of "The Kid" in *The Three Godfathers*, the film which Ford dedicated to the memory of Harry Carey following his death in 1947. Many years earlier his dad and Ford had filmed a different version of the same touching story.

Ford would cast Harry Carey Jr. in six more western films in the years ahead: *She Wore a Yellow Ribbon*, *Rio Grande*, *Wagonmaster*, *The Searchers*, *Two Rode Together*, and *Cheyenne Autumn*. All told, Harry Carey, Jr., appeared in nine John Ford films, including *Mister Roberts* and *The Long Gray Line*, where he played a young West Point cadet named Dwight Eisenhower.

But the John Ford films are only a part of Dobe Carey's resume. He has also appeared in *Pursued*, *Red River*, *The Comancheros*, *Shenandoah*, *Alvarez Kelly*, *Big Jake*, *Something Big*, *Gentlemen Prefer Blondes*, and *The Great Imposter*. More recently his films have included *Crossroads*, *Tombstone*, and *The Whales of August* with Bette Davis and Lillian Gish. This confirms what the film industry and movie buffs alike have known for many years, the fact that Harry Carey Jr. is a first-rate talent in his own right.

Born on his father's ranch in Saugas, California, in 1921, Dobe Carey was weaned in the western genre. His dad was John Wayne's idol, while John Ford was his godfather. When Harry Carey Sr. died in 1947, John Wayne, John Ford and Harry Carey Jr. were each at his bedside. Today, Harry and Marilyn Carey live in Durango, Colorado. Westerns still remained very much a family affair. After all, his wife Marilyn is the daughter of the late Paul Fix, one of the best character actors of his day. Harry Carey Jr. is also the author of *Company of Heros: My Life as an Actor in the John Ford Stock Company*, an intimate look at John Ford at work.

I met Harry Carey Jr. at the Knoxville Film Festival in 1993 and have spoken with him many times since. In the following interview he discusses his life in and out of the western arena. He highlights his early years on his dad's ranch, explains how his failed singing dreams eventually turned into a successful movie career. He talks about that special friendship between his father and John Ford, and about his own, the ups and downs of working with Ford. "As Renoir said, he knighted those who worked for him." He tells about some of the great westerns he has made, his work in television, and of course, the people he has known throughout these many years — John Wayne, Henry Fonda, Maureen O'Hara, Ward Bond, Richard Widmark, Ben Johnson, Howard Hawks, Bette Davis, and Lillian Gish.

H.F. Harry, could you tell us about your dad's ranch in Saugas, California, and your early years there?

H.C. Saugas, California, where I was born was about forty miles north of Los Angeles. It's pretty built up now, but in those days it was really open country. It was pretty wild up there too. My dad didn't even have electricity on the ranch. He didn't want it. We didn't get it until about 1935 because he wanted our place to be like a real ranch. We also had a wood stove rather than gas. He only put electricity in when my mother finally put her foot down.

H.F. Your dad was a great film star. Did you want to follow in his footsteps and get into movies?

H.C. Actually I had a big dream that I wanted to be a singer. It wasn't realistic, but when you are eighteen years old you think you can do anything. My hero at the time was a wonderful baritone named Lawrence Tibbett. I was also a big fan of Paul Robeson. So that was my big dream. I got out of the Navy in 1945, and by 1946 I had aspirations of being a big band singer like Dick Haymes. But nothing materialized from this dream. I seemed to freeze up at auditions, so I gave up the idea of being a crooner and really didn't know what I was going to do.

Harry Carey Jr.

H.F. Yet, you have sung in films. *The Three Godfathers* comes to mind. Your voice sounded very good.

H.C. I do have a deep resonant voice. It didn't really fit the way I looked but it was my voice. Anyway it's nice to hear you say that.

H.F. How did your foray into film start? Was it the Ford connection from the start?

H.C. Well, as so often happens in life, fate intervened. Marilyn and I were living in Studio City, California. I was standing on Ventura Boulevard waiting for the Roy Rogers Parade to come down. I'm not sure what the celebration was; it might have been the Fourth of July. There was a fellow standing next to me named Bill Berke. He produced lots of those quickie westerns, the kind you make in eight to ten days, and had produced a number of westerns with my dad. I was twenty-five years old and I guess he recognized me. "Aren't you Dobe Carey?" he said. Then he asked me what I was doing with myself and I told him nothing right now. He said he had a little part in a picture he was making with Russell Hayden and Jean Parker and asked if I wanted to do it. I told him I didn't belong to the Guild, but he said not to worry about it. I went out and did the part. It was a small part, but I did it very well.

Then, I got a test at Warner Brothers for a picture called *Pursued*. It was a wonderful western directed by Raoul Walsh. Robert Mitchum played a cowboy who searches for the murderer of his father. The whole cast was great: Bob Mitchum, Teresa Wright, Dean Jagger and Alan Hale. They tested about twenty-seven guys for the part, but it was made to order for me and I got it. Soon after that I went into *Red River*. "Wow," I thought, "nothing can stop me now!"

H.F.   Was *Red River* the only time you worked with your father in a movie?

H.C.   Well, we had been on stage together once in Maine in Summer Stock, but *Red River* was the only film. Yet, we didn't work together. He had finished his scenes when I started working on mine. It was the last film he ever did; he died a short time later. So, even though we didn't have any scenes together, I was very proud to be in it. *Red River* was one of the great all-time westerns though I never really felt the impact of what I was doing then. My first three directors were Raoul Walsh, Howard Hawks and John Ford. What a way for a guy to start out!

After *Red River*, I did a thing called *Moonrise*. Then, I did a musical short with Tex Williams and his band over at Universal. I followed that with a shot in a Bob Mitchum/Robert Preston movie. These were just small roles. After my father passed away, John Ford put me in *Three Godfathers*. I was supposed to go into a Gene Autry western in Palm Springs when I heard that Ford wanted me. I had to call the producer of Gene's movies and tell him that I had a shot with John Ford. He said I should take it immediately.

H.F.   Then, you didn't start out with Ford?

H.C.   No! But I was very lucky to get with Ford. What happened was the day my father died, John Ford, Duke Wayne and I were at his bedside. After he passed away and after the shock which was reverberating around the house, Ford came up to my mom and said he wanted to make *The Three Godfathers* with Duke Wayne, Pedro Armendariz, and me playing the kid. He dedicated *The Three Godfathers* to my dad.

H.F.   Can you say something about the friendship between your dad and John Ford?

H.C.   There was a very special relationship. My dad, more or less, started John Ford out as director at Universal in 1916. They were a great team. They made twenty-five westerns together. A lot were two-reelers. *Straight Shooting* was their first five- or six-reeler. My dad and Jack Ford made a great team. They wrote their own scripts. In fact, they wrote a lot of them in the kitchen of this little farm my father had at the time. It was way before I was born.

After about twenty-five films, they had sort of a breaking up. Not that they weren't speaking any more, but there was political jabbing going on between some of the actors who were in the stock company who were jealous of my father's friendship with Ford. The gossip became very nasty and Ford started to believe what people were telling him. Then my father started believing the same. You see, my father was very much a liberal and Ford was the other way. Yet, I do remember that when we were making *Yellow Ribbon*, it was during the Truman/Dewey election in 1948, and Ford voted for Truman. Jack wasn't always a hard-line, right-winger. He switched when Barry Goldwater came around. He really believed in Goldwater. John Ford was a very strong patriot.

H.F.   Was he as tough a task master as he was reputed to be?

H.C.   Oh yes! Yes, he was! The other night my wife Marilyn and I went down to where the DeMille Barn is. It's on a parking lot across from the Hollywood Bowl. It's where DeMille first shot *The Squaw Man*. They ran three of my father's silent films that night. Two one-reelers — one made in 1912, the other in 1914. The next was *Straight Shooting*, which my dad and Jack Ford made in 1917. It was Ford's first feature.

The audience wanted to know something about Ford. I told them that with Ford, if there was a hill to come down, you came down as fast as you could on horseback. If there was water, you had to go through it. If there was a river, you had to go across it. He loved that wild west stuff; he really loved it. Ben Johnson and I always made it a point to give him exactly what he wanted. In fact, I wrote a book about him. It's called *Company of Heroes*. It's a good book because I took it picture by picture. There's no baloney about it. I have total recall of all these movies and what went on during shooting all those pictures.

H.F.   Many of your early films were with John Wayne!

H.C.   Well, Duke got me the part in *Red River*. That's a fact! What happened was there was a kid who was supposed to play that part originally. The actor Howard Hawks had under contract was told to practice his riding. Finally, when the day came when he was to work on the scene, he said he was sick and couldn't work. Hawks said it was okay, no problem, he would just shoot something else. That night Hawks went to Tucson and found the kid drinking and having a good time. Hawks fired him, and supposedly said that he didn't know whom he could get to play Dan Lattimore. Then Duke, I'm told, said, "I don't know if he can act or not, but the guy who looks just right is Dobe Carey." So, that's how I got it.

H.F.   Harry, would you comment on some of these early films separately? How about *The Three Godfathers*?

H.C. That was a rough one. Ford made it real tough on me. He rode me something awful and I wanted to quit a few times. Duke was a great help. He told me that I'd just have to take it, that Ford did the same thing to him in *Stagecoach*. He said to listen very carefully to him, because sometimes you couldn't understand what Ford was saying. He'd have that handkerchief in his mouth.

H.F. You did the last two films in his Cavalry trilogy, *She Wore a Yellow Ribbon* and *Rio Grande*. Did he ease up on you at all?

H.C. Yes, he did. He was just fine in those films. Yet, he did get me in a big mess with that buggy scene in *Yellow Ribbon*. I was to take Joanne Dru to a picnic, and he rigged it up so I couldn't get the buggy through the gate. Then, he called me a lousy driver. He fixed it first so I would have to back the buggy up, then turn it around and go through the gate, which took a lot of time. He just wanted to give me a hard time.

But, *Yellow Ribbon* was a wonderful experience, a beautiful film. It was in color and won Winnie Hoch an Oscar for Best Color Cinematography. I was Lt. Pennell and Johnny Agar was Lt. Cahill. We were both after Joanne Dru and Johnny won out. John is a nice guy. We've remained friends now for nearly fifty years. Ben was in that one too, and did a great job. Then, Ben and I were in *Rio Grande*. That's where we did that Roman riding that people still talk about.

H.F. What about *Wagonmaster*? It's been said that it was Ford's personal favorite.

H.C. We made it 1949 and it came out in 1950. It was just a fabulous film. *Wagonmaster* was a great experience! It was like a vacation. It was just marvelous. We were the first picture company ever in Moab, Utah. Some people associate Monument Valley with *Wagonmaster*, but it wasn't. Moab is sort of a miniature Monument Valley. There was just one motel. There are dozens now. A lot of the guys stayed at rented houses. There was a big catering outfit called Anderson. They came up here and built these marvelous tin cities with wooden floors. It was called an Anderson Camp. That was where the crew stayed and where the Navajo stayed.

H.F. *Wagonmaster* was Ben Johnson's only leading role, except perhaps for *Mighty Joe Young*. The two of you worked great together in the film.

H.C. In *Wagonmaster* Ben was very convincing. I played kind of a hot-headed kid who wanted to get in a gunfight all the time. Ben was the hero and I was the sidekick. It was small scale, but something that Ford always wanted to do. That's what they tell me. Very low budget. It was $500,000, and Ward Bond was so powerful as the Mormon elder. He was wonderful. We had a good time. I think Jack (John Ford) enjoyed making that more than any other film.

H.F.   Jim Thorpe's name is in the credits. Was that the great athlete?

H.C.   Yes, it was! He was on the sound stage back at the RKO lot in Culver City. There's the greatest athlete who ever lived, and he was around the campfire when they were dancing. Jim Thorpe played the Chief.

H.F.   Was he down on his luck at the time?

H.C.   Oh, he was for a long time. He became an alcoholic. He had a hard time. One of the things which caused it, I feel, was because they took his Olympic medals away. They said he was a professional. I think he once got paid five dollars to play a baseball game.

H.F.   Could you touch on your friendship with Ben Johnson.

H.C.   Oh, we've had a lot of fun together. As I said, we have been friends since 1948. First, let me say that no one ever looked better on a horse than Ben Johnson. And, Ben is a hell of an actor. He has a real presence, not to the degree of John Wayne, nobody did. But, Ben fills a room by just walking in. Yet, he is one of the best natured men I have ever known. I've only seen him mad once. I asked him if he ever had any fist fights. He said, "Ol' Dobe, I never have. I always figured if you are mad enough to punch a guy in the face, you're mad enough to kill him." Yet, Ben is tough. He is the only World Rodeo Champion to ever win an Academy Award.

I'll tell you something else, too. Ben always drove a new car, and he always dressed as if he was worth a million bucks, but he had some tough years along with me. There were years in the fifties when Ben took wrangling jobs. A talented guy like that worked as one of the wranglers in the musical *Oklahoma*.

H.F.   You may know that Gordon MacRae has publicly credited Ben with teaching him to ride a horse. He commented once in an interview that when he got the role of Curly in *Oklahoma*, he went to the best horseman in the business and that was Ben Johnson.

H.C.   That's just great. I didn't realize that. I really believe that Ben was one of the best cowboys I ever saw in my life. He could do anything around livestock.

H.F.   So rough times were something you had to expect in the movie business!

H.C.   Well, that's the movie business, unless you are a big star like Jack Nicholson. When I was a kid and things were going good, there were quite a few parts. I was in my twenties then. When you get over forty — which was thirty years ago — they don't know how to cast you. Hindsight is often twenty-twenty, but I have often thought that if I had grown this bright red beard, it would have worked in every western that came out. Nobody was growing beards then. I have had a beard now for twenty-five years.

H.F. You had mentioned much about John Ford as a movie-maker. You knew him from the time you were born. Did you ever have real problems with him, other than on the set?

H.C. There was a time when Jack Ford got mad at me. I'd see him socially and I'd call him, "Uncle Jack!" I always called him "Uncle Jack." He was at the ranch when I was born. I was never baptized, but he was my unofficial god-father.

What happened is that we were doing *The Searchers* in 1955. I remember it very well. I had to be back in Hollywood to start with Walt Disney on July 12. It was the latter part of June. Every night at dinner Ford would ask me when I had to be back at Disney. I would say July 12. He would ask the next night and the next night. I'd say July 12. What he wanted to hear was "whenever you are through with me." I never came up with that answer and that made him very angry. I didn't work for him for five years after that.

H.F. He could carry a grudge!

H.C. Yes, he was very vindictive!

H.F. How did your career go after that?

H.C. Oh, I did a lot of small roles. *Gentlemen Prefer Blondes*. That was starvation time. I took it to eat. All we did was stand there and wave at Marilyn Monroe. I don't think I had any lines. Howard Hawks gave three of us some work. One was Joseph Cotton's son-in-law; the other was a guy who still makes commercials, and myself. We were the Olympic athletes. I guess it was barely a credit, but it made me five or six hundred dollars so that was all right. I also did *Mister Roberts*, and *The Great Imposter*. There was lots of television going on too. Television really kept me working.

H.F. What about *Mister Roberts*? It was a fine film. Jack Lemmon won an Oscar as Ensign Pulver. Was his extraordinary talent easy to recognize?

H.C. *Mister Roberts* was lots of fun, and Jack and I were pretty friendly on the set. As far as his talent: everybody knew he was going to steal the picture.

H.F. What about James Cagney?

H.C. Oh, he was scary. I was frightened of him. I was thirty-two years old at the time and I looked in my mid-twenties. I just idolized him, as I did William Powell and Henry Fonda.

We had a young actor named Nick Adams who later killed himself over a girl. He played Johnny Yuma on television. He didn't drink or use drugs.

He got a broken heart and did himself in. Nick was a delightful guy, and he loved to do imitations of Richard Widmark, Jimmy Cagney and Clark Gable.

So Jimmy Cagney, this overpowering movie star, was sitting next to the hatch on a ship over in Midway trying to get tanned. He had one of those reflectors and was sunning himself. Everyone kept their distance, no one is bothering him. He had his shirt off and suddenly Nick Adams runs up in front of him and yells, "You dirty rat!" He does a Cagney imitation right in front of Cagney. It was the funniest damn thing. Cagney looked at him like he was crazy. Then in a very soft voice he said, "Is that the way I sound?"

H.F.   It's said that Jimmy Cagney was the ultimate professional!

H.C.   Was he ever a professional! You bet! He was very nice to me. Right after *Mister Roberts*, he played the "gimp" in *Love Me or Leave Me* with Doris Day. He told me to come on the set and visit. It would be educational. I don't think he was that excited by his role in *Mister Roberts*, but he was just dying to do the part of the "gimp." I went over to the set and we had lunch together.

H.F.   Going back to the westerns, you certainly played in some of the best.

H.C.   Because of being raised where I was, and because my father knew some great cowboys, many of whom lived in the town where I grew up, I had a definite bent for the west. When I got to be about eighteen, I started hanging out with these guys and learned to rope. I had always been a good horseman and a good rider. I had been riding since I was about three. Some people are like that on skis. I was that way on a horse. It was very natural for me.

H.F.   How about *The Searchers*? You mentioned the film earlier in discussing your rift with Ford.

H.C.   Oh yeah, I played a kid named Brad Jorgenson. When Duke comes to tell me he found the girl I loved dead, I run off and get killed. His line was "What do ya want me to do, draw ya a picture? I wrapped her up in my coat and buried her with my own hands." It was a great line which Duke did particularly well.

H.F.   What do you recall of Natalie Wood in the film?

H.C.   Well, she was sixteen, absolutely gorgeous. She was so pretty and a real nice kid. At the end of the film when Duke picks her up in his arms and says, "Let's go home, Debbie." It always makes me cry.

H.F.   You did so much work with John Wayne. What are your memories of him?

H.C.   I loved him and he loved me. The thing is I don't think he ever forgave me for being the son of Harry Carey. Harry Carey was his absolute hero. When I watched those films of my dad the other night, and now that I'm a much older man and can watch my dad and see him totally objectively, I don't wonder why he was Duke's hero. He had a really unique screen personality, and he was a strong actor who could carry a picture. But, what Duke loved about my dad was his mannerisms, and the way he always added something to his roles.

H.F. So your dad was a great influence on Duke in developing his technique!

H.C. No doubt about it! I'll tell you something else. Duke could have been quite a director. When Ford was directing him, Duke was like a pussycat around the set. But later in such films as *Big Jake* and *The Undefeated*, and all those things we did in Durango, Mexico, late in his career, he was a hard guy to talk to on the set. That was because he always knew more than the director. Duke would have been a wonderful director if he held his temper. But he really knew what he was talking about. He knew the film game. He knew the film business. But he had no tact. So he really wasn't full of camaraderie on the set in those later years.

Yet with Ford in those earlier films, *The Three Godfathers*, *She Wore a Yellow Ribbon*, *Rio Grande*, and *The Searchers*, he was a warm, wonderful guy. That was as long as you didn't get in a political discussion with him.

H.F. What was the full extent of his politics? We hear different accounts.

H.C. First, he wasn't an extremist. He was a Republican. He was a conservative, and he was very, very patriotic. His love for his country was real. He didn't go into the service because he had four kids and he was thirty-eight years old. But, he was right on the line there. His love for his country was immense. The only man I think who loved his country more was John Ford, and Ford was military; he was an admiral in the Navy Reserve.

H.F. Ward Bond was another whose politics have been questioned in many sources.

H.C. Oddly enough, Ward always wanted to be John Wayne. He wanted to be a big star like John Wayne. He was the backbone of a lot of those films. He was just marvelous. Ward, too, was a warm, friendly person. He was the kind of man if one of those "unfriendly ten" came around, Ward would sit down and talk with them. But Ward got some notoriety by being on the Motion Picture Alliance thing. He thought he was doing the right thing. I don't think it was ingrained in the marrow of his bones. I actually think Duke Wayne was more set in his belief in his conservative politics. I think Ward could have been swayed later on. He was friendly with Humphrey Bogart and a lot of guys who were Democrats. Although I often didn't agree with them — guys like Duke,

Ward and George O'Brien — I have always found the political conservatives to be much warmer and friendlier on the whole that the super-serious political left of the movie business. I'm not sure why this seems to be, but that's the way it is.

H.F.   John Wayne had a reputation as being a pretty good drinker in his own right. Those all night poker games with the boys are pretty well documented.

H.C.   Duke was a good guy and fun to be with. But I'll tell you this, thirty-one years ago I quit drinking. That almost broke his heart. I was getting in trouble with booze, waking up in strange places and things like that. Finally, to keep my family together and to try to get more organization and productivity, I knew I had to stop. I got a lot of help and did. But from that point on, he just couldn't accept it.

If I had told him some of the things I was doing, maybe he would have changed his mind. But, Duke could get in trouble with booze too. Yet, he was a warm, wonderful guy. Another thing about him is that you never saw him turn down an autograph. The public loved him and he always said they were his bread and butter and he loved them back.

H.F.   And he's remained as large in death as he was in life!

H.C.   Yeah! They are going to have him right up there with George Washington, which is really kind of silly [laughing]. But I'll tell you another thing about him. If you ever saw him work, the first time he came on set you would say, "Here comes a movie star!" A whole quiet came on the set, because he was the most impressive looking man I have ever known. He was handsome, and rugged and a huge guy. He had an aura that was just movie star. I think he was the biggest movie star that there ever was. I loved him very much.

And a good actor! My god, yes! In *The Shootist*, *The Searchers*, and *The Three Godfathers*, he was a superb actor. A lot of people don't want to give him the credit he deserves. The critics seem to like message pictures. They like the guys like the British actors, and things and stories nobody can understand. They can't either, but they think they do.

H.F.   During the sixties and seventies, was there still a lot of work for you?

H.C.   Well, I kind of grew up in the business with Andy McLaglen who directed every big star in the business. He's a great big guy like his father, Vic. He was a damn good director. Andy wouldn't do a picture without me and he wouldn't do a television episode without me. The last time I saw him, we figured we did more than forty shows together. Richard Boone like me too, so if Andy wasn't directing a *Have Gun, Will Travel* episode, Dick Boone would give me some wonderful roles. I worked for *Gunsmoke* a lot, particularly when Bob Totten was directing. This kept me pretty busy.

H.F.   Looking back over your career, what really stands out?

H.C.   Well, there has been a couple. *The Three Godfathers* was special. For a kid with very little experience, I think I did a good job. I've always had a soft spot in my heart for the part of Brad Jorgenson in *The Searchers*. He was an intense sort of kid, and he was so in love, that when he loses his girl it drives him crazy. Then later in life in 1986, I made *Whales of August* with Bette Davis and Lillian Gish. I was the handyman, a guy called Joshua.

H.F.   What was Bette Davis like to work with that late in the game?

H.C.   Oh, I got on great with her. She chain smoked. She loved to drink too. She jumped on people who appeared weak. The first day I was on the set, she was sitting on a rocking chair. I went over to her and said, "Miss Davis, I'm Harry Carey Jr., and I've admired you so much." I got down on my knee like Essex and kissed her hand. Well, my god, I was "In like Flynn." She kept saying, "No use talking to Lillian, she can't hear a god damned thing you're saying." Lillian paid no attention to her. She tried to boss Lillian Gish around, but Lillian paid no attention to her.

H.F.   Any main regrets in your career?

H.C.   Oh, hell yes! A lot! I really never talked about this too much. But all that celebrating and the alcoholic camaraderie after a day's work affected my work the next day. Much of the time as a supporting actor, I was just trying to make a living. Also, I regret not going to New York and being on the stage.

H.F.   But all told, it has been fulfilling work!

H.C.   Oh yeah! It had two advantages. One are all the memories, and I met some legendary people. A director recently told his group, that I had been in more great films than practically anyone. That I really treasure. Another thing is the marvelous pension and residuals. I get great health insurance.

H.F.   You mentioned four kids earlier?

H.C.   My oldest son passed away from a heart attack about five years ago. Now there are three. My son had been in a rock and roll band and became involved in drugs. Then about twelve years ago he got involved with the Episcopal Church. He's a brother in the church today and travels all over the world, and has a marvelous program going in Brooklyn with these troubled kids. My daughter Melinda is married to a cameraman. They live in Santa Barbara. She works for the Episcopal Church. She is secretary to the priest. My daughter, Patricia, has her own restaurant business and is also in Santa Barbara.

H.F.   Your wife's father was Paul Fix, the actor!

H.C.   Yes, he was a fine actor and a nice guy too. He was in *The Rifleman* series, and before that he played lots of gangsters. He was also a strong influence on Duke Wayne. He helped Duke develop that unique walk of his.

H.F.   How did you and your wife Marilyn meet?

H.C.   Well, I knew her as a kid. I was four years older than her. I was sixteen and she was twelve. Paul would come over to the ranch and visit my mother and dad. But I never paid any attention to Marilyn. We both went our ways. I was dating a couple of girls, and she was dating lots of guys including Eric Fleming. When I was in the Navy, I came to visit my folks who were staying at Paul and Taddy's house. This blond comes up the stairs, pretty as can be. I said, "Marilyn!" She said, "Oh, hi!" That was it! I was stuck! We only went together six weeks, then we got married. We've been married for more than fifty years now.

H.F.   The film industry today, what do you think?

H.C.   Well, Ben and I sometimes disagree. Ben won't watch a movie. He says they are all filthy. But Marilyn and I enjoy the modern films. Maybe they are not the Bogarts, the Waynes, the Gary Coopers and Jimmy Cagneys, but as far as sheer ability, I think there are some incredible actors around today: Gene Hackman, Robert Duvall, Jack Nicholson are just some. Tommy Lee Jones is another. But one thing you don't see is the magic those older actors had on the screen. Brando had it. So did Montgomery Clift until he destroyed himself. Ben Johnson has it.

H.F.   Are you satisfied with the work you did?

H.C.   Definitely! I'm not upset that I don't have that special presence of Duke or Ben. Because of that, I was able to do all different kinds of roles and characters. Today's leading men are small in stature. Some of them look much taller on the screen.

H.F.   Any personal favorites on the screen today?

H.C.   I like Anthony Hopkins. But I think my personal favorite is Nicholson. I love his manner.

H.F.   What do you feel are some of the major drawbacks in the films of today?

H.C.   For one thing, all this sex. All this simulated intercourse on the screen today makes me angry. It's totally unnecessary. It's awful and makes me very embarrassed. I watched a little old picture the other night with Gene Raymond and Loretta Young. It was called *Zoo in Budapest*. It was a terrible movie. But the two of them were something. They were hiding in the bushes and they turned toward each other and simply looked at each other. The sex in that scene was unbelievable. You wanted them to kiss and they didn't. They turned their faces at the same time and it was just marvelous.

H.F.   Do you think the films coming out today are of the same level as what they were?

H.C.   No! No, not of the same caliber. Not like *The Grapes of Wrath*, *Citizen Kane* and so many others. They were great films. The demise of the studio system has a lot to do with the quality of movies today. The people making films today are bankers and brokers. They are wheeler-dealers not interested in making good entertainment. They are interested only in making money.

The old studio bosses, for all their reputed meanness, really cared about motion pictures. They had a code of ethics and they knew how to build movie stars. They knew how to make movies, and there were lots of good directors. What's wrong with the films today is that too many dodos are trying to direct pictures. I just did a picture called *Tombstone*. They started out with this young man who wrote a very good script. It was a thirty-five million dollar movie. They gave him the director's job and in ten days he was ten days behind. That cost them about six million dollars. The next day they had to hire another director.

H.F.   You also did a TV special called *A Return to Tombstone*, with clips from Hugh O'Brien's old TV series. Would you say something about the film?

H.C.   Sure! It was a two-hour TV special. A friend of mine produced a series in Europe called *William Tell*. He asked me to do one of the parts. They wanted to bring back the old Wyatt Earp, Hugh O'Brien, who did the series on television. Earp comes to Tombstone looking for somebody. The first thing he does is meet me in the grave yard. Then he meets Bruce Boxleitner, Bo Hopkins, Alex Hyde-White, and all these different people. They then flash back to the old Wyatt Earp episodes.

H.F.   Do you keep pretty busy these days, Harry?

H.C.   Oh, I've had some pretty good roles. I have also done some interesting documentaries which have paid well. One was called *John Ford's America*. Another was *Legends of the American West*. Then there was my book. There are also film festivals which I attend. It's good to keep the American West alive.

H.F.   This is what we all hope to do. Thanks, Harry!

6

Carolina Cotton

Looking back over my years in show business, what I enjoyed doing most was entertaining the troops. I went to The Hollywood Canteen and they said, "Carolina, would you like to yodel for the boys?" I did and those boys were so appreciative and so nice to me. They wouldn't let me do anything for myself.

Today Carolina Cotton teaches special education in Bakersfield, California. Her students love her as much as audiences did in the 1940s and early fifties, when she appeared in a number of western films. During those years she appeared opposite Gene Autry, Charlie Starrett, Jimmy Wakely, Eddie Arnold, and Jock Mahoney to name a few, and when it came to the business of yodeling, she had few, if any, peers in the industry.

Although she did a few films at Republic and Universal Studies, most of her work was at Columbia as a contract player. Already a show business veteran when she was eleven years old, Carolina Cotton has touched almost every avenue in the western scene. She had her own show during the Korean War for Armed Forces Radio called, "Carolina Cotton Calls." She made eighteen movies starting with *Sing, Neighbor Sing* at Republic where she did her first "little yodel." Her last three films were in 1952 when she did two features with Gene Autry and one Durango Kid movie.

In the following interview Carolina Cotton tells the story of a young girl smitten by show business at an early age, her preteen and teenage years trying to cope with school and show business at the same time, and her warm experiences entertaining the GIs before and during the Korean War.

At the 1993 Knoxville Western Film Caravan, she delighted one and all with her singing and yodeling.

H.F. Carolina, how did you get started in this business?

C.C. My family was from Arkansas and they traveled a lot. We were living in San Francisco, and it seemed that all the kids were taking dancing

56

Carolina Cotton

lessons. For a dollar you could get one lesson a week. My teachers were a group called the O'Neil sisters, and they also had a contract with the Golden Gate Theater. If you took dancing lessons at their studio, twice a year we'd go to the Golden Gate Theater for the Christmas show and the Easter show. It was a kiddie show, but it was good for us. We got to sit there and watch all the different shows. This happened right before the war. One thing I recall well is that cars were lined up for miles and miles because Bing Crosby was playing close by.

H.F. How did you learn to yodel so well?

C.C. When the war started I was taking dancing lessons. My big sister was babysitting for me because everybody else was working. She'd drop me off at a studio to watch the show while she would go to the library to do her homework. I'd sit there and watch the show every night, and I got to know the group pretty well. San Francisco was very Union and in order to play a musical instrument at the Golden Gate Theater you had to belong to the musician's union — even if you were a kid. If you just picked up an instrument, you had to have a card.

So in order to join the union I took guitar lessons. There was also another rule. To stay on the stage you had to have seven musicians with a union card. Well, one day the girl singer on the show ran off and married a sailor. So they needed somebody on the show with a union card who could sing.

You think you can do anything when you are a kid, so I started singing with them. I'd jump up on the stage. Then every time a new musician would go in the service they'd put me on that instrument. I could play "Steel Guitar Rag," and "Song of the Islands." I never learned to play any instrument too well, but I could play a few instruments, and I had enough nerve to try to stand up there and sing and yodel. So that's how I got started. I was only a kid.

H.F. How did this eventually lead to films?

C.C. Well, I needed a western costume. Now San Francisco had a lot of great shops, even some for cowboys. But, there weren't any western shops for women with the type of western outfit I needed. So my mother let me go to Hollywood one day to get measured for my costume at Turks, rent a cab for the day, stay overnight at the Roosevelt Hotel, then get up the next day, get on the plane and come back.

Well, I was walking around looking at all the big buildings when I ran into someone named Johnny Marvin. Johnny was pretty well known in the record industry. He told me to come back to his house, meet his wife and son, and I could call my mother to tell her that they were putting me up. There was going to be a big party at the Knickerbocker Hotel for the cast of *The National Barn Dance*. They had just finished a movie and I sure wanted to meet some movie stars.

I was still in school in San Francisco, but during summer vacation, I got a call from Johnny. "Would you like to come down and do a movie?" he said. Well, who is going to say no to that. I flew down to Hollywood and did a film called *Sing, Neighbor Sing* where I had an eight-bar yodel. I was dressed up like a college person. But, when I went to breakfast one morning I ate some sausage which wasn't good and got sick. So they had to take me back to San Francisco. All I got to do in the picture was three scenes and a yodel. But my name was up there in the credits.

H.F. Was that for RKO?

C.C. No! It was Republic. I got to know the Sons of the Pioneers. They were just great. In fact, I met them the day I ate in the commissary and got sick.

H.F. Did you start making pictures regularly now?

C.C. Oh, no! I went back home and did radio with Dude Martin. My day would go something like this. I'd get up in the morning. At 5:30 I'd be at the radio station to rehearse. From 6:30 to 7:30 we'd broadcast, and rehearse a little bit on the next day's show. Then I'd take the streetcar to school. After school, I'd go downtown to the radio station and the musicians would pick me up and we'd go to a place called Eastshore Park in Richmond. We'd rehearse and do a TV show there on Wednesday from 5:30 to 6:30 at night. Then we'd eat dinner and do a broadcast for a dance. I'd sleep all the way back. They would take me home, and I would start the next day all over.

H.F. And you were in high school then?

C.C. No! I was still in elementary school. I'd do my homework between numbers. So when kids complain today that they don't have time to do their homework, I really get upset. By the time I was in high school, I'd go down to Hollywood and do the Hollywood Barn Dance and fly back again. So I was commuting between San Francisco and Hollywood when I was still in high school.

Finally Dude Martin asked me if I was going to stay in San Francisco or go to Hollywood. Shirley Temple's brother and Hal March both worked for the radio station and they were the ones who encouraged me to go to Hollywood. So I went.

H.F. What happened in Hollywood?

C.C. I sang in Spade Cooley's Band. Spade was doing the Hollywood Barn Dance, and his manager was a great lady named Bobbie Bennett who said she would manage me. So I lived with different musicians' families with Spade's band. I was going to Hollywood High now, and Spade was doing a lot of movies, so I got to sing in the movies with him. There was something called *I'm from Arkansas*. Most of the films were made at Columbia. I did one at Universal, *Say and Share* with Bob Crosby. I did some voice-over cartoons at Warners. I did one with Ken Curtis called *Stallion Kings*. There's another terrific person.

I had an excellent publicity man named Charlie Pomeranz. You know how it worked in Hollywood. They'd lend me out to another studio, if your studio would help them. So I got in a lot of things I normally wouldn't have been able to do.

H.F. Anything you enjoyed particularly during your career?

C.C. I made eighteen movies including two with Gene Autry, but entertaining the troops is what I enjoyed most. I went to the Hollywood Canteen and they said "Carolina, would you like to yodel for the boys?" Well, I did and I'll tell you those boys were so appreciative and so nice to me. I couldn't go out and do anything without their helping. We'd do shows around the Bay Area. There was more talent out there in the audience than there was on the stage.

When I got to Hollywood I was older so I could go overseas. The first show overseas was in Christmas in 1950. We went to Germany, North Africa, Naples — all in about three weeks. By now I had made recordings with MGM so I went out with the MGM Troupe. I did several with Keenan Wynn and Walter Pidgeon. I went to Korea with them along with Debbie Reynolds and Carlton Carpenter. During the Korean War, I had an Armed Forces Show out of Hollywood called "Carolina Cotton Calls."

Walter Pidgeon had a great singing voice, so he and I got together and sang a duet. He didn't want to do anything too serious, so he yodeled with me. That was the funniest thing you have ever seen. Here is this great actor, distinguished person doing a hillbilly yodel. We did this act on several tours. Keenan Wynn was another wonderful actor. He played the type of roles that didn't give people the chance to know the true depth of the man. I met his dad, Ed Wynn, at a party once. What a thrill that was.

H.F. You also did a lot of western things other than films?

C.C. Oh sure. In those days you did everything. I did rodeos, car openings, everything. There was a wrestler in those days named Baron Michele Leone who was quite popular. I worked with him. He said, "Carolina, when you go to Italy, look up my family." Everyone there knew him. He decided that I should really be strong. He told me that to be strong, I should eat raw liver at least once a day. Well, he put me on a diet. Raw liver, exercise, everything. It really built me up, because I was doing so much that I needed additional strength.

H.F. You stopped making westerns in 1952. How come?

C.C. Well, they stopped making the type of pictures I was in. They began making the psychological western. The studios started cutting loose all their contract players, and I was a contract player for Columbia. A real nice guy was Bobby Cohn, I recall. He was the son of Harry Cohn who owned Columbia. Bobby would try to make things easier. He'd be on the lot and offer to bring me coffee, and was always available to talk to.

H.F. You don't hear many nice things about Harry Cohn.

C.C. Well, I guess that's why I don't do too well on interviews, because I never knew the dirt about people.

H.F. You were in a film called *Hoedown*.

C.C. Yes, I was. Eddie Arnold was in it. He is a sweetheart. Jock Mahoney was in that, too. I kissed him in a lot of the scenes. Here I was kissing a married guy on the screen. I was really embarrassed. I also got to meet Tyrone Power. Boy, was he handsome.

Jimmy Wakely and I were on an Armed Forces show with all of these big stars. It was one of those shows with all the big producers running around. There was some time left over so they grabbed Jimmy and asked him to do a number with me. This was a network show and they came to us for help. We did "You Are My Sunshine." The catch of all of this was neither one of us had enough money to get us back home. We didn't know the show was going to run over.

H.F. And you have been teaching school since you left show business?

C.C. I went back to college, took all the necessary courses, and received my degree in special education. I love teaching. I find it so very rewarding. Sometimes my kids hear about my career in show business. They'll ask lots of questions. It's really very pleasing to me. And yes, I think my years in show business and in film helped make me a better teacher.

H.F. The two businesses aren't that far apart. Thanks, Carolina!

C.C. Thank you, Herb.

7

Warren Douglas

So many of the people who helped me start out as an actor also became part of my later career in writing. I can't over-emphasize the importance of friendship and loyalty in the picture business. The circle became complete with these dear friends, and how grateful I am.

From Warner's to topnotch westerns, actor/writer Warren Douglas has done it all. At Warner Brothers in the 1940's, Douglas appeared in such feature films as *Destination Tokyo* with Cary Grant and John Garfield, *Pride of the Marines* with John Garfield and Eleanor Parker, *Task Force* with Gary Cooper and Walter Brennan, and *The Man I Love*, where he was Ida Lupino's bad-boy kid brother. He was also featured in the Oscar winning Warner Brothers short, *I Won't Play* with Dane Clark.

The long road to film and TV stardom began in Minneapolis, Minnesota, where Warren Douglas was born and raised. Here he began his fledgling acting career at South High School performing in school plays, where baseball and show business were mutual passions. Choosing show business, he followed the usual route of local theater, summer stock, a stint with the Federal Theater, a part of FDR's Depression Era WPA project, Robert Breen's Oxford Players, and eventually to Broadway. So impressed was actor Lyle Talbot when he saw Douglas doing summer stock in Pennsylvania, he wanted Warren Douglas in his production of *Separate Rooms*. Bob Longenecker, who was with the Selznick Studios at the time, saw him and brought Warren Douglas out to Hollywood. He later signed with Warner Brothers where he stayed for five years as a contract player.

Douglas would also work for Republic and Monogram/Allied Artists Studios in such movies as *The Babe Ruth Story*, *Charlie Chan and the Chinese Ring*, *Cry Vengeance*, *Torpedo Alley*, and many more. He also narrated Monogram's 1947 Oscar-winning two reel short subject, *Climbing the Matterhorn*.

Yet beneath all this, quite unbeknownst to himself, was an innate talent for writing. With the coming of television as an important medium, and with considerable writing talent now a given, he began to focus more and more on

Warren Douglas

writing and production. He quickly became one of the industry's most prolific film and television writers.

Included in his fourscore of film and TV writing credits are such movies as *Jack Slade, Dragoon Wells Massacre, The Return of Jack Slade, Torpedo Alley, Cry Vengeance, Sierra Passage, The Night of the Grizzly,* and *The Cruel Tower.* His TV credits are equally impressive: *Bonanza, Cheyenne, Sugarfoot, Bat Masterson, The High Chaparral, 77 Sunset Strip, Lassie,* and Ralph Edward's *This Is Your Life.*

"Warren Douglas was a sleeping giant among the industry's top writers," says veteran actor Clint Walker, "The man has enormous talent." In a similar vein actor Will Hutchins credits Douglas with writing the best *Sugarfoot* episode he was ever in.

Douglas can also be seen in some of his own movies, occasionally writing in small parts for himself. He joins the impressive array of actors and actresses who have appeared in movies he has written: Sebastian Cabot, Jack Elam, Mona Freeman, Don Haggerty, Skip Homeier, Martha Hyer, Katy Jurado, Barton MacLane, Dorothy Malone, Wayne Morris, Barry Sullivan, Clint Walker, Ida Lupino, Frank Lovejoy, Sterling Hayden and Anne Baxter.

Douglas also wrote the books and lyrics for two musicals successfully produced in England starring Betty Grable, and two novels: *One Rode Alone* and *The Man from Wells Fargo.* His considerable talents are still clearly recognized.

During his acting days, the Warren Douglas International Fan Club had members in more than thirty states, Canada, England, and Scotland, the Philippines, and Australia.

In the following interview, Warren Douglas discusses the many facets in his world of acting and writing. He credits the people who helped him along the way with an unwavering appreciation. He recalls the industry he knew in his day with precision and detail, and deplores the sad state which he finds it in today, especially the recent films which degrade "our wonderful West." He gives a rare and compelling account of what a writer feels from the moment he places his first word on a blank sheet of paper until he sees the finished product, the movie itself in its completed form — tracing and commenting on each and every step along the way. Warren Douglas and his wife, Bonnie, have been married for more than thirty-five years, and reside in the Mother Lode area of Northern California.

H.F.   Warren, it's a long ride from the Minnesota of the Depression Era to Broadway and Hollywood.

W.D.   There is an interesting twist also. I consider my acting career to have started in high school. I was in two class plays. The year I graduated I did a play called "Captain Applejack." Around the same time a young man in Dixon, Illinois, named Ronald Reagan also did "Captain Applejack." Ronald Reagan landed at Warner Brothers, and I landed at Warner Brothers.

H.F.   Did you always have an interest in movies?

W.D.   I started out loving movies. I was about three or four years old when my mother started taking me to the old movies on Lake Street in Minneapolis about as often as she could. I loved all the old westerns. Tom Mix, Buck Jones, Art Acord, all those guys. Also I loved the serial heroines like Pearl White and Ruth Roland. When I was about four years old my dad sent for a little Charlie Chaplin thing with a gold tooth and a little mustache and cane. So for years I was doing Chaplin around the house.

H.F.   So acting was your first love?

W.D.   I had two loves actually, baseball and show business. The Northern League was just being formed in Fargo, I wanted to play ball, but I got a job in the theater just a short time before. My high school play coach, Helen Fish, was a wonderful woman and a fine, fine coach. She had a little theater she was directing. After I graduated she wanted me to come down and do some work for her. I did a couple of things: "Enemy of the People," and "The Torchbearers," which was a funny light comedy. In "Enemy of the People" I was Dr. Stockman. I was actually half of the play. An interesting thing happened. The director of the university theater, Tim Ramsland, saw me do

"Enemy of the People," and asked me if I wanted to go to the University of Minnesota to do the same play. I told him I didn't even want to hear that Stockman name again. Dr. Stockman is the worst and longest part I ever did in my life. He said it wasn't what he had in mind for me. He wanted me to play his brother Peter, which meant learning the entire script. Well, he talked me into it. So now I had done both parts in "Enemy of the People," thereby memorizing the whole play.

H.F. You worked for the Federal Theater which was part of FDR's WPA project.

W.D. Yes, I did. But before that I had met a chap named Robert Breen, a wonderfully creative person who got a deal with Halle Flanagan about the time FDR was starting the WPA. After I did "The Drunkard" at the Old West Hotel in Minnesota, I went on the road with Breen's Oxford Players. It was the forerunner of the Federal Theater, A WPA project. We did "Hamlet," "Romeo and Juliet," "The Ivory Door," and "Faust." This was 1938-39, and we toured the south. It was wonderful. I really learned a lot about theater. Actually Robert Breen was the finest director and actor I ever worked with.

After the tour we went to Chicago to open the shows. But the opening was delayed and delayed, so I waited and waited as you do with a government project. Finally, I went back to Minnesota and got myself into radio. One day "Tobacco Road" came through and one of the chaps left to do another part. I went on the road with that show for a season. Then I went to New York to try to get into theater, but I didn't have much luck. So I went to Hollywood and started getting little bits in pictures.

H.F. How did you get established in Hollywood?

W.D. A director named Frank McDonald gave me my first part in films. I worked in a picture called *Freshman Year* with Johnny Downs and Frank was the director. Frank later became a great friend of mine and directed pictures that I wrote. In fact, all the people I have worked with somehow played a full circle in my life in my second career as a writer.

H.F. How did you land with Warner Brothers?

W.D. Well, I did three seasons of summer stock in Pennsylvania. Lyle Talbot came through and was doing *Separate Rooms* and wanted me in it. I played it on Broadway and later on the road. Bob Longenecker, who was with the Selznick Agency at the time, saw me and brought me out to Hollywood where I got a contract with Warner Brothers. So I became a contract player with Warner Brothers for about five years.

H.F. You mentioned how some of the people who helped you along as a young actor later became a part of your second career as a writer.

W.D. It's really interesting how the circle became complete with these dear friends. I want to emphasize the importance of friendship and loyalty in the picture business, and how grateful I am for their friendship. Frank McDonald, who I have mentioned, directed the first picture I ever wrote, *Sierra Passage*. Harold Schuster who put me in a film called *Swing That Cheer* also directed many of my pictures including *Jack Slade*, *The Return of Jack Slade*, and *Dragoon Wells Massacre*. Lou Landers who directed me at RKO in *Anabel Takes a Tour*, directed many of my *Files of Jeffrey Jones* segments on television.

Lou Appleton the producer of *First Offenders* for Columbia wound up living about ten miles from me. We have a standing lunch date every Thursday. Originally there were three of us. John Dehner, Lou and I, but John passed on a couple of years ago. Burt Dunne ferreted me out of the Mother Lode to work on *Sugarfoot*, *Cheyenne*, and *Bronco*. I owe that man a lot. He and Clint Walker got me *The Night of the Grizzly* screenplay to do at Paramount.

H.F. You worked in some great war films for Warner in the forties. Films like *Pride of the Marines* with John Garfield. It was one of the first films I ever remember seeing.

W.D. I was one of the guys in the hospital when John went blind in the picture. I liked Johnnie Garfield. He was a kind-of-by-himself guy. He was a nice guy and I never heard of anybody having a beef with him. He was pleasant and had an enormous charisma. His performance in the boxing picture, *Body and Soul* with Lili Palmer, was one of the best I've ever seen. It was beautiful. Great picture!

H.F. How about *Destination Tokyo*? You worked with Cary Grant.

W.D. I spent the whole picture manning the periscope in that one. Six weeks and I didn't get out. Johnnie Garfield and Dane Clark were also in that one. Cary Grant was the ultimate gentleman, warm, friendly, courteous, a bit reserved. A real professional.

H.F. You were also in a lot of training shorts and short subject films at Warner during those years.

W.D. And some very good ones. Some won the New York Critics Award and Academy Awards. I appeared in Warner Brothers Oscar-winning short, *I Won't Play* in 1944. *It Happened in Springfield*, *Devil Boats*, and *Mountain Fighters* each won the New York Critics Award. I narrated the Academy Award winning *Climbing the Matterhorn* for Monogram Pictures in 1947. That was a great thrill.

H.F. Any favorite role?

W.D. There was one I did with Monogram Pictures called *Below the*

Deadline. It was a gangster film. The kind of thing Alan Ladd might have done. In fact, I almost got into an Alan Ladd western. The film was called *Branded.* I tested extensively for it and it was a good part. But after what seemed like a number of deliberations an actor named Pete Hanson got the part.

H.F.   Alan Ladd did good work!

W.D.   Yes he did. The two best things Alan ever did were *Shane* and *This Gun for Hire.* He was far more capable than many of the pictures they gave him to do.

H.F.   You also did *The Red Pony.* Was this the one with Robert Mitchum?

W.D.   No, I worked with Henry Fonda and Ben Johnson in that one. It was a TV movie directed by Bob Totten. Maureen O'Hara and Jack Elam were also in it.

H.F.   What do you recall about Henry Fonda?

W.D.   I liked him very much. I thought he was a fair man, a fair-thinking man. He was a gentle and loving man. Henry could be gentle and tough at the same time. That's a quality I admire in a man.

H.F.   A couple of other films you were in were *The Babe Ruth Story* and a Charlie Chan movie.

W.D.   I was in the original *Babe Ruth Story* with William Bendix and Claire Trevor. I didn't have a very big part in it, but I loved the part I had. I was the guy who didn't like the Babe, kept calling him a "bum." There were a couple of sequences, but it was a good little part. I took his place when Babe was sold to the Boston Braves. After they let the Babe go, I was entirely in his corner.

H.F.   The picture has been panned a lot!

W.D.   Well, they should pan the new one. It was awful. Goodman was grotesque. Babe never looked like that. When he first came up he didn't even weigh two hundred pounds. Later on he had a little paunch, but never looked like Goodman in the film. I was under contract with Allied Artists. I got to know Bill Bendix casually on the set. He was a little standoffish, but a nice guy.

H.F.   How about the Charlie Chan film? Did you work with Sidney Toler?

W.D.   The film was called *Charlie Chan and the Chinese Ring.* Roland Winters was Charlie, and I played a newspaper man. It was a featured role and I enjoyed it. There is a cute story here. When Roland tested for Charlie, I assisted him. We both had terrible hangovers and we had to get our trembling hands in sync before I could pass a cup of tea to him. But in the long run I probably did more writing than acting. It was this second career where the westerns really became a forte. Out of more than a hundred writing credits, forty-eight were westerns.

H.F. What were some of your favorite screen westerns?

W.D. *Shane* was the best. It had everything going for it. I liked the John Ford westerns for their scope and integrity. I liked them for their realism. All those Ford pictures were marvelous. And that stock company of his was well-versed in everything, all distinct types and good actors. John Wayne was great. I've always admired Ben Johnson, too. There is a definite strength in him. But for sheer western poetry in action, I still go back to *Shane*. As I said, it was sheer beauty.

H.F. How about *High Noon?*

W.D. They didn't quite know what to do with that one. Then Dimitri Tiompkin wrote the score. And wham, the song saved the picture. The music pulled it together and got it off the ground. Gary Cooper did a great job.

H.F. Any western stars who were particularly special?

W.D. John Wayne was great. He was the best — unless you go back to Richard Dix in *Cimarron.*

H.F. And the westerns today?

W.D. These guys who are writing the westerns today are making everybody a masochist, a sadist, dirty, rotten heavies, wearing long trench coats they trip over. They have made our wonderful west look like a land of terror, a land of psychos, masochists and sadists, and I resent it deeply.

H.F. How did you get in the writing end of the business, Warren?

W.D. I was working at Monogram when I got an idea for a western. I met a psychologist at a party. She talked a lot about certain tests. I said that I would like to take one and she told me that I should. So I took it. The psychologist said that while acting was awfully high on the list, I should think about writing. I had never even thought about writing. I said that I couldn't write a good letter. She told me to try. Well, Dalton Trumbo's sister lived next door to me. She let me use Dalton's typewriter and also said I should give it a try. I wrote something and the first thing I wrote I sold. When I told the psychologist I'd written and sold a screenplay, her comment was something like, "Well, I'll be damned."

H.F. So you really wrote your first story with Dalton Trumbo's typewriter?

W.D. Yes! The story just came to me, from beginning to climax, to the ending. It never stopped. I took it to Lindsley Parsons to read. Lindsley in turn said that he would give me less than anybody in town for it. So we did it. It was a picture called *Sierra Passage* with Wayne Morris and Lola Albright. It was a good little picture. I stayed with him when he did a TV series called *The Files of Jeffrey Jones* for CBS. I became associate producer, story editor, location scout, second unit director, anything. What a picnic it was! What total fun!

H.F. So you owe quite a bit to Lindsley Parsons.

W.D. I sure do. Lindsley Parsons took one of the biggest chances in his life when he gave me full responsibility for his first series for CBS, *The Files of Jeffrey Jones*, both in writing and in production. Actually, Lindsley was responsible for much of my success, both in acting and in writing. Lin knew more about production and good film making than anybody I ever knew or worked with. He knew how to get every production value possible out of an available budget. I always said that Lin could spit on the sidewalk and shoot the Johnstown flood. He also had a story mind that was uncanny. I wrote fifteen screen plays for him plus twenty-six segments of *The Files of Jeffrey Jones*, and supervised the entire thirty-nine segments. Just a couple of years ago, we were talking about another project. I got him interested in it. Then sadly he passed away. Lindsley Parsons was one of the wonderful pioneers of the picture business. We'll miss him.

H.F. Did all your stories just flow freely from your mind to keys of your typewriter?

W.D. Here's what I do, and it works very well. I find characters, and I find situations. Then I put the characters in the situation. If your characters are honest and your situation is a good one, they'll follow it. It's amazing!

H.F. When you write a screenplay or a TV script, do you go from beginning to end, or do you write in segments?

W.D. I write from beginning to end. But what we do is start a small treatment like three or four pages and hand it in to the producer. He says to either enlarge the treatment or turn it into a screenplay. But you got your whole plot and the action into that treatment. You must follow that. So I was able to follow a screenplay from a blank page one, to the final cut, to the dubbed and scored product one would see in the preview. And I'm telling you right here, it is one of the most satisfying, exhilarating, fascinating, thankful experiences a man could have in so many ways.

H.F. Can you explain it in some more detail?

W.D. Sure! The story which started on a blank page begins to come alive with the people you created. They are dependent on you for their very lives and well-being, for their happiness and joy, and sometimes for their sorrow and despair. You created them and you are responsible for their behavior, good or bad. It is exciting and scary.

Then, in a quiet way, you marvel and are terribly grateful that your characters and your talent are in a sense responsible for putting hundreds, maybe thousands, of people to work: the actors, the director, a film crew, camera crew, sound crew, assistant directors, make-up people, office people, casting people, scenic artists, set construction, set dressers, laborers, publicity people and ad artist, printers, newspaper people, theater owners and workers. It's overpowering!

During the shooting you experience periods of elation and despair. You see the dailies each night, and they can be pretty deadly static pieces of film. But as the picture progresses, you begin to see some sense of improvement. Then one day they let you see a rough cut and you note some fluidity and grace to the movement. You begin to see some hope. The final cut makes a person have a grateful feeling and to take a tentative step back into the real world for the first time in many weeks. The picture, your baby, is finally dubbed and now it begins to move, feel and sound like a motion picture.

Then the fateful day arrives. You sit in the furthest back seat in the farthest corner of the room. The musicians quietly troop and quietly unpack their instruments as the conductor frowns thoughtfully at the score. He lays the music sheet on the podium and taps it with his baton lightly. The musicians come to attention, straighten their sheets and ready themselves. After a few tunings, scrapings, piping and blowing, the conductor raises his arms and waits for the film to begin on the big screen in front of him and the orchestra. A moment of silence and the main title flashes across the big screen. The baton swings up and sweeps down and you are treated to a volume of spine tingling music that sends the goose bumps racing down your arms in shivering, quivering battalions. Wham! God bless the musicians. It takes hundreds of artists to make an excellent film. But it takes ASCAP to breathe a soul into it.

H.F.　Do you always know the ending of your story or script?

W.D.　Not always! Sometimes I think I know it, but my people don't always go the way I send them.

H.F.　You not only write and act. You know almost every avenue of production and casting.

W.D.　Again I go back to Lindsley Parsons. Lin was a very wise man. I had worked for him as an actor before the both of us discovered I could write. He knew I liked actors, actors liked me. So he kept me on the set to troubleshoot whenever and wherever I could. When any trouble developed about a line or a speech, I was there to fix it without fuss or long expensive delays. I worked as a dialogue director and the cast usually had faith in my judgment. If a director had a technical problem, I could change it on the spot. I knew what change Lin would make and I did it. It was a wonderful arrangement for everyone. I would not suggest, however, that a producer should send a writer with no production or acting experience down on the set. He might get the poor man killed.

But no matter how good the script, the setting, the director, the producer, the make-up, the costume, without an excellent cast your film hasn't got a chance. With the right cast, your people come alive. A good actor likes to be challenged by a good actor. It sometimes makes him play "over his head." Freddie Messenger was Lin's casting director and he did an excellent job.

H.F. Any specific actors who gave a particularly good treatment of the characters you wrote?

W.D. Most all of them. But I did *Jack Slade* with Mark Stevens and Dorothy Malone. Mark was excellent in that, so was Dorothy. Mark was a taut little guy. Tense. He had a series shot in New York. Later he became a producer. Dorothy, of course, won a Best Supporting Actress Oscar for *Written in the Wind*. Lovely person. A real sweet person. Pretty both inside and outside. She was also a darn fine actress, cooperative — wonderful.

H.F. Then you gravitated to TV westerns?

W.D. I spent a lot of time with the westerns. I had become pretty well known for my feature pictures. My agent started following along the western line. I came up here to Mother Lode country and let the guns cool for a while. Barry Dunne who had been producing *Sugarfoot* started asking, "Where the hell is Warren Douglas? I have a script and I have to have him." He heard I was here in Mother Lode and wanted to get me. He dragged me back down to Hollywood and my career went boom again. Barry was a dear friend and I owe that Irishman a great deal. I did *Cheyenne*, *Sugarfoot*, and *Bronco* for Warner Brothers. David Dortort caught me and took me to Paramount for *Bonanza* and *High Chaparral*. So for a while I was doing five of them.

H.F. What do you recall about Will Hutchins?

W.D. There was a guy who was perfect for *Sugarfoot*. You'd hand him a script and he'd frown and say, "I don't know about this!" But he'd say every word and not change a thing. The character and Will molded into a beautiful performance. I'm not sure how they found Will for the series. But I'll tell you this. Will was *Sugarfoot*. He was a by-himself type of guy back then, but a gentle, nice guy. You know he hasn't changed much. He looks about the same as he did years ago.

H.F. You and Clint Walker are rather close.

W.D. Clint is another real nice man. He's a deep-thinking guy. He's a simple guy. He won't stand for any dishonesty, any moral lack. Clint's a real straight-shooter. He did westerns for a livelihood, but I don't think the West itself meant that much to Clint. Rather, it's the caliber of the thing he is doing which means an awful lot to him.

H.F. What about *Bonanza*?

W.D. Oh, I loved that one too. They all fit beautifully. But I didn't meet the guys too much. I wasn't on the set. At Warner Brothers I was out there all the time because I was a personal friend of Barry Dunne, the producer. A lot of producers would let you go on the set; others would tell you to mind your own business.

H.F. How many episodes did you do at Paramount?

W.D. *Bonanza* and *High Chaparral,* I guess about ten.

H.F. And the work was pretty constant!

W.D. It was! Remember this was the heyday of the western. At the time *Bonanza, Sugarfoot, High Chaparral, Cheyenne* and the rest of them are going like wild fire. That was a little nucleus for me.

H.F. And *Gunsmoke!*

W.D. I did only one at the end of the series. They were quite impersonal. They had their own niche and their own way of doing things, so they didn't let you get too close. There again, I didn't get to meet the people who acted in the show.

H.F. Did you continue acting after you started writing?

W.D. Oh sure! In a lot of my feature films I wrote myself a part. I had a little part in *Cry Vengeance.* We shot that up in Alaska. Mark Stevens and Martha Hyer were in that. She married Hal Wallis and is living in Palm Springs. She was and is a good little actress and another real nice person.

H.F. Then you feel that most of the people you worked with were pretty decent.

W.D. Yes I do. In westerns and non-westerns alike, the people I worked for or with in that era were nice people. I loved the business. I loved the people in it, and I still do. I would love to get back in it.

H.F. The industry in general today?

W.D. So much seems to revolve around ego. There are a lot of people out there who don't really have talent. They are getting by with stuff that twenty years ago would never work. Everyone thinks they are so marvelous.

I think the demise of the studio system was a tragedy. They developed their own talent. Not by going to school, but by using them in little parts. They even developed some people who didn't have talent in the first place.

H.F.   Your feelings on method schools?

W.D.   I feel that no one can teach you how to act. Acting is inside of you. If you haven't got it, nobody is going to put it inside of you. You can read a line the way someone tells you, but it will still be phony. You've got to love what you do. You have got to love people and situations. You've got to love life. To be a good actor you've got to be able to dream with your heart, your mind, and your feet. You must be rooted in reality, does that make sense?

H.F.   The Warren Douglas Fan Club. How did it start?

W.D.   In 1947 Toni Paterson wrote me and wanted to start a fan club. She was just a young girl back then. And she is still working at it. She is a wonderful person and I consider her a very good friend. So is her daughter, Beverly. It's a good feeling. When you get somebody as nice as Toni who appreciates you, it is very special. When you get someone like Toni, it is a miracle.

H.F.   You also worked with Ralph Edwards on the *This Is Your Life* show?

W.D.   Yes I did. The writers researched all the people connected with the subject. Then you would interview them and write what they said in script so Ralph could keep track. So he asks questions, and they can answer the questions from the script we have made.

H.F.   Are you fully retired now?

W.D.   Not really. There is a lot of stuff I have been working on and hope I can get someone interested in. I still miss the active working participation in the industry. I sure do. But I have enjoyed what I have done. It's been great. All the wonderful people I met along the way. It's a joy. It's been a real joy. And I am very grateful to have been part of a wonderful era of film-making. I thank God for giving me the tools, the opportunity, and the friends to help me along the way.

8

Lois Hall

*I think the westerns are coming back. I think people are a
little tired of all this sex and craziness. I just hope they don't
fill them with unnecessary sex. I think people are ready for
something better. Working with western people is special.
They are just plain nice.*

Born in Grand Rapids, Minnesota, in 1926, Lois Hall was just a girl when
her parents moved to Long Beach, California. It was in high school that Lois
Hall had her first experience with theater as a set designer, stage manager, and
head electrician. This led to a set design scholarship at the famed Pasadena
Playhouse.

Acting eventually became part of her life, and her first film role was a gag
walk-on in an MGM feature. She made three more films for Republic Studios,
including her first lead in *Daughter of the Jungle*. Then she started doing the
Monogram westerns. During the next five years she was featured in twenty-
five other films including many B westerns. She also appeared in some two
hundred television episodes, including a year's stint in the hit television series,
One Man's Family.

Since 1953 Lois Hall has been happily married to Maurice Willows. They
have three daughters and two grandchildren. Today Lois and Maurice Willows live in Beverly Hills. She was the recipient of the Lady of Western Fame
Award at the Fifth Annual Tuolumne County Wild West Film Fest in 1992.
Although her stock and trade has been the screen and television western, her
career high point, she insists, was working with the great Laurence Olivier in
the film *Carrie*.

I interviewed Lois Hall in Sonora, California. The years have not diminished her beauty and charm. She was a good interview, glib, candid and direct,
and she offers an interesting account of what the B western was all about.

H.F. Lois, you began your career with Republic Pictures. How did it all
start?

Lois Hall

L.H. I started doing bits, like so many other actresses. I did *Love Happy* with the Marx Brothers in 1949. A young Marilyn Monroe was also in the film. I was walking across the stage in a slightly skimpy costume carrying a tray. That was the second thing I did. Earlier I had done a bit part in *Every Girl Should Be Married*. It was a gag walk on with Don Hartman and Dore Schary, director and producer of the film. Then somehow I got the lead in *Daughter of the Jungle* out at Republic.

That was wonderful, crazy fun. I was scared to death of course. I fell out of trees and did all those silly things. Terrible film! In fact, it was named in one of those books as one of the hundred worst films ever made. I might add, accurately, that the people who were playing the natives were wearing shoes. Sheldon Leonard was the leading heavy in it. The director would look at the script, tear out about five or six pages, and say, "This is a bunch of junk!" I did a couple of more pictures at Republic, although I wasn't under contract. Then I started doing Monogram westerns.

H.F. Then your formal training was not in westerns? You became a woman of the west through your work in film and TV.

L.H. Yes! Unless you call riding the workhorses on the farm back in Minnesota, "West!" In the late 1940's though, the B westerns were still absolutely in vogue. There was a theater in Hollywood called "The Hitching Post" where they only played the B westerns. Kids would have to check their toy guns at the box office. And they were good. The B westerns were wonderful. They were hard work. You would get on a stretch-out or a bus to go on location. The moon would not have set yet, but we'd get out a bacon and egg sandwich.

H.F. Where were most of these westerns shot?

L.H. Most were not shot on location. Perhaps close location would be more appropriate. Places like Chadsworth, Corriganville, and Lake Sherwood.

H.F. Was it steady work making those B westerns?

L.H. Well, looking back at the number I did, it was pretty steady. They paid almost nothing. Maybe $150 or $200 a week. Sixty dollars a day. Whenever I was going a little broke, I'd go to my agent and say, "Hey, Gus! Can I borrow a little money for my rent," and suddenly there would be another job.

H.F. You were living in Los Angeles at the time?

L.H. Oh yes! That's where the people who wanted to be in movies were living. I did a couple of serials, *Pirates of the High Seas* with Buster Crabbe. Tommy Ferrell was also in that. I also did *Sir Galahad* with George Reeves.

H.F. He was Superman on TV!

L.H. Oh, George did a lot of work. He was in *Gone with the Wind*, *So Proudly We Hail* with Claudette Colbert and many others. George was a good friend, I'd known him at the Playhouse.

H.F. How much television work did you do?

L.H. Oh, I did a lot. Maybe about two hundred segments. Actually, I did a pilot for what should have been the first TV sit-com, if it had sold, called *Sadie and Sally*. I was Sadie. Then I did three *Unexpecteds* at the Hal Roach Studio which were fifteen minutes of heavy drama. We tried to do classics in fifteen minutes. Imagine trying to do Pushkin in fifteen minutes.

H.F. Did people recognize you from your television work?

L.H. I'd say yes, considering I wasn't a big star. I was on *One Man's Family* for a year on television.

H.F. Did you work with Eva Marie Saint?

L.H. Eva Marie Saint played Claudia on the TV show which was done in New York. I was in the second series which was done in Hollywood. I played Beth Holly! It was fun to do. We had a good cast and we did it every day. And it was live which was a little different. It's a bit funny, but when I started playing it, I recognized many of the scripts because I heard them on radio when I was a kid.

H.F. All told, how many films did you make?

L.H. I think about forty films if you count the bits, and about two hundred TV segments. And I worked with some of the best: Jimmy Wakely, Johnny Mack Brown, Charlie Starrett. Funny, sometimes they would cast me as the ingenue. Other times they would cast me as the heavy. That's what made it nice. I had different roles for different studios. I started with Republic, then I worked for both Monogram and Columbia.

H.F. You worked during the heyday of the westerns. Do you see an indication that they might be coming back?

L.H. I think they are. I think people are a little tired of all this sex and craziness. I just hope they don't fill them with unnecessary sex. I think people are ready for something better.

H.F. *Unforgiven* captured an Oscar for Clint Eastwood. How did you feel about the film?

L.H. I loved it. I loved it because it was an anti-violence film. A lot of people disagree and don't realize that. But, its very essence was anti-violence.

H.F. Any people particularly stand out in your mind in the western genre?

L.H. Fred Sears over at Columbia who directed the Charlie Starrett films was delightful. He was such a gentleman. But there were so many that were very nice.

H.F. In a television special made when he was alive, John Ford commented that the people who made the westerns were the very best people he ever worked with.

L.H. That's so true. From the crews to the stars. Never underestimate the crews. Whenever you worked a B western or a TV western, you could not walk on the set where you didn't know these guys. And then there were the stunt men. You can't find a better bunch.

H.F. Congratulations on your selection as the Lady of Western Fame last year at Sonora. How do you enjoy these film festivals?

L.H. It is an astonishment. But the great fun of it is to see all the people whom you have worked with before, whom you would not see otherwise. About half of those here today I have worked with. I think I did about eight things with Tommy Ferrell. But it really doesn't matter if you worked with them, because you have so many things in common. It's like a stock company. Working with western people is special. They are just plain nice.

H.F. Any favorite movie stars when you were a kid?

L.H. Well I loved Spencer Tracy from the time I was a kid. I'm proud of my taste. I also liked Olivia DeHavilland, Katharine Hepburn and Errol Flynn.

H.F.   The highlight of your career, Lois?

L.H.   I think working with Laurence Olivier, if only for two weeks. I was in *Carrie* with Olivier and Jennifer Jones. Most of it landed on the cutting room floor, but I played Jennifer Jones' roommate. It was a thrill. The movie was based on *Sister Carrie* by Theodore Dreiser.

H.F.   What do you recall about Olivier?

L.H.   Oh, he was sweet and wonderful to me. He made sure I had my own dressing room when he heard I had to share a dressing room with lots of others. I remember having been handed half a page of script changes one day. It was supposed to be shot that afternoon. "You can't do that! You can't do that," he said. "You have to have time to study." I answered, "Oh I guess you haven't worked in the kind of pictures I have" [laughing].

H.F.   Major disappointments along the way?

L.H.   I'm not the kind of person who regrets. I think it is a big waste of time.

H.F.   How come you stopped working when you did? Your career was going well.

L.H.   I had been on the soaps for so long and at the end, I became pregnant with my first child. At the same time my agent died. So I guess I thought someone was telling me something. It was time to spend more time with my family. I had been married in 1953 and have been with my husband, Maurice Willows, for more than forty years. All you hear is how movie people never stick together and get divorced. Just look around at the room here. Most of us have been married to the same person all our adult lives, or at least to the same person for many years. This is a side to the industry a lot of people don't realize.

H.F.   The movie industry today, what do you think?

L.H.   To me the sex scenes were so much more wonderful when they left something to the imagination, and much more sexy, I might add. Sex isn't really a spectator sport as far as I am concerned.

H.F.   Do you feel people have reached a saturation point with all this?

L.H.   Well let's say I think things are starting to turn around at least. And I see underlying and very positive things beginning to come out. I was so excited when *Driving Miss Daisy* won the Oscar for Best Picture. It is a very telling story. Some very nice things are starting to do well at the box office.

H.F. Do you think there is a definite correlation between the excessive violence on the screen and TV, and the violence in society in general?

L.H. Oh, I can't see how it doesn't have an effect. I heard a statistic the other day that by the time kids are six, they have already seen eight thousand acts of violence. It's like we have been endorsing it as an expected part of life.

H.F. Do you feel that film makers and the networks have a moral obligation to clean-up their act?

L.H. Oh, absolutely! This whole thing of "let it all hang out, and let's not repress anything," just hasn't worked out. You don't have to tell everything or say everything. You can walk along the street and see the garbage cans, but you don't have to stick your head in them.

H.F. Do you miss performing, Lois?

L.H. Actually I have returned to film and television and have appeared in seven films and ten television shows. I love to work, but thank God I don't have to earn a living that way. But it's wonderful when I do work!

H.F. Thanks, Lois!

L.H. Thank you, Herb!

9

John Hart

I worked on The Lone Ranger *show when Clayton Moore
was the Lone Ranger. I had played the bad guy in some of
the episodes. I had done the lead heavy in a number of
things. I guess they looked at a lot of guys but I got the part.
I think I made fifty-two episodes as the Lone Ranger 1952.
Sometimes it's me and sometimes it's Clayton Moore.*

He has been called "the other Lone Ranger" by fans who recall his stint
as the famed "masked man," when Clayton Moore took a year's hiatus from
the show. But John Hart's long and distinguished career in show business has
included so much more. A native of southern California, his career has
included almost every facet of film: acting, stunt work, production, lighting,
soundtrack, dialogue.

In addition to the *Lone Ranger*, Hart was the star of the successful TV
series *Hawkeye and the Last of the Mohicans* with Lon Chaney Jr. Hart has
appeared in more than two hundred pictures and TV episodes, including such
films as *The Buccaneer, Union Pacific, The Ten Commandments, Longhorn* with
Wild Bill Elliott, *The Cincinnati Kid* with Steve McQueen, *The Sandpiper* with
Elizabeth Taylor and Richard Burton, and *Jumbo* with Doris Day. He also
appeared in more than twenty episodes of *Rawhide*.

An avid camera buff, Hart has also made travel films in Europe and
Hawaii, and a successful film for school kids called *Animals Can Bite*. He
played *Jack Armstrong, The All American Boy* in the 1947 movie serial, and in
later years was one of the producers for the successful TV show *Quincy* with
Jack Klugman.

But Hart still likes to go back to the westerns. He was a skillful rider and
a crack shot even as a youngster. He talks about his days as "The Lone Ranger,"
and his close friendship with Jay Silverheels whom he greatly respected; and
the *Hawkeye and the Last of the Mohicans* series for which he is best remembered. His stories are alive and plentiful, and he weaves some interesting yarns
concerning the history of the highly successful saga of *The Lone Ranger*. John
Hart is a trained and disciplined actor. His credits are many and varied. He

was a natural for westerns from the start. "To tell the truth," he adds, "I don't know why I didn't get into them sooner."

H.F.   John, you have had an extraordinary career both on and off the screen. Let's just start from the beginning.

J.H.   Sure. I was raised in the LA area, and my mother was a fairly well-known drama critic in Southern California. She covered the Pasadena Play-house extensively. So when I was a teenager I was exposed to a lot of theater. I started out acting in high school. Before high school though I had played "Scrooge" in *A Christmas Carol*. Interestingly, Bill Holden was a classmate of mine. His name was Billy Beedle back then, and we both took drama courses.

So I got the acting bug pretty early. I used to drive a truck all day, then rehearse and do shows at night. I did a lot of little theater, The Pasadena Play-house, etc. There were lots of productions. Through a friend of mine I was introduced to the Myron Selznick Agency, one of the industry's big agencies. They got me into a DeMille picture out at Paramount. It was *The Buccaneer* with Fredric March made in 1937. Boy was I thrilled. Here I was driving a truck for peanuts, and all of a sudden I'm making all this money and getting to know a lot of people in the movie business — I loved it.

H.F.   Did Paramount put you under contract?

J.H.   Yes they did! But I really didn't do too much afterwards. I worked in some gangster pictures, but that's how I got started. Then my contract ended in a year-and-a-half, and that was when I really started working more. The casting guys knew me and used me in many more pictures.

H.F.   The Army really influenced your career a lot, didn't it?

J.H.   Yes it did. I learned a lot in the service. I was drafted way before Pearl Harbor, an out-of-work actor — let's get that guy. I went into the Coast Artillery. It was the Army Coast Artillery, a famous old branch of the service, now long gone. After a couple of years in the artillery, someone pulled a few strings and I got into the Air Service Command to do a recruiting show. I went to Special Services school in Lexington, Virginia, and when I had finished there, I went to Texas to set up a whole big special services program there. I wrote, produced, and directed a new show every week for almost a year. From there I was sent to the Philippines and wound up in a signal service battalion attached to the Fifth Air Force. From there it was on to Okinawa and that is where I was when we dropped the bomb on Japan. Soon after I was in Japan. I was one of the first GIs most of the Japanese civilians ever saw. I drove around to a lot of places in Japan. In those first days it was pretty spooky.

Then I produced a big show for the Fifth Air Force and toured all over Japan and Korea with it. I had also done some training films at Fort Roach —

The Lone Ranger (John Hart) and Silver

Hal Roach studios. I thought I had a contract going for me at MGM. But by
the time I got out of the Army and came home, I couldn't find anybody that
I had worked for and my career was a disaster.

H.F.   But you never had given up the notion to pursue a film career?

J.H.   Oh, I never thought of doing anything else. I had a lot of fun, and
a good taste of it before going into service. It is a heady thing for a young person. During the War, I had known Jon Hall who was married to Frances Langford. Tony Romano was one of my best buddies and he played guitar for her.
I bummed around with a lot of those people. So I finally managed to get hold
of Jon, and he got me on a western at Universal. I played a bad guy, but I was
on salary for about six weeks. The picture was called *The Return of the Vigi-
lantes*. Things started slowing up and Jon Hall went to do a picture at Columbia. I got a job as his stunt double on the picture.

H.F.   Did you have a lot of training to do that type of work?

J.H.   Oh yes! I had worked as a cowboy as a young man. I worked on cattle ranches and was handy with horses. I also boxed so I could fight pretty well. So I doubled Jon Hall and got into doing stunts.

Then I got back into acting because I could do pages of dialogue easily in one or two takes. This was a great advantage for low budget pictures. So I worked in a lot of little pictures, including *Red Ryder* and serials at Columbia, and other movies playing the bad guy or the second bad guy. At the end of it you usually got beat up or shot. I'd get extra money for doing stunts. The westerns were kind of a staple in those days. Lots of action. You didn't pay too much attention to the story if you kept the action going, riding and shooting and all that stuff.

H.F.   How did you become involved in *The Lone Ranger?*

J.H.   I worked on the show with Clayton Moore as the Lone Ranger. I played the bad guy in a couple of those episodes. I had also done the lead heavy in a number of things. I guess they looked at a lot of guys, but I got the part. I made fifty-two episodes in 1952. If you see them now, sometimes it is me and sometimes it is Clayton Moore.

H.F.   What about Jay Silverheels?

J.H.   Jay played Tonto for both of us. Jay Silverheels was a very good friend of mine. He was a pure-blooded Mohawk Indian from Brampton, Canada. And he was a good actor and just a wonderful person. He was also an athlete. He played lacrosse and I think he was a boxer too. It was a delight to work with him.

H.F.   When you did *The Lone Ranger* series, did a lot of people actually know you were The Lone Ranger?

J.H.   Clayton made a life and a career out of being the Lone Ranger. When you have the mask on during the show, you are not easily recognizable. In other words, if I went to the store or out in public, people wouldn't point at me and say, "That's the Lone Ranger." Later when I did a very nice series called *Hawkeye and The Last of the Mohicans* with Lon Chaney Jr., everybody knew me from that show. However, it's kind of faded away today. The story has been made a few times. I especially enjoyed the Randolph Scott, Binnie Barnes movie in the thirties.

But getting back to *The Lone Ranger.* When I did the series, every episode I made was done in about two days. The scripts were about thirty pages which is unheard of now. So we were doing about fifteen or sixteen pages a day on *The Lone Ranger.* There is a lot more dialogue there than you think. God, I talked and talked and talked. Jay used to laugh at me working so hard, with a lot of bad things going on, and bad guys riding off in a flurry. Tonto would say, "Ah — what do we do now, Kemosabe!" Then I'd talk for two more pages, and he'd jump on his horse Scout and say, "Me go. Get 'um up, Scout!" That would be his dialogue for the day. Then he'd go back to his dressing room and watch me do pages and pages of dialogue.

H.F. What did "Kemosabe" mean?

J.H. Well nobody really knows. With all this mystique about *The Lone Ranger*, it was made up by a bunch of radio writers in Detroit. And one of the kids went to a Camp Tonto or something. They didn't seem to know a lot about the Indians, the cowboys and the west, so they dreamed up this whole big thing and it was good. It worked. Anyway, Jay and I used to go talk about this and we figured that the masked man was always a mystery. "Who is that masked man?" they'd always say. So in Spanish "who knows" is "quien sabe." So we figured it might be a derivative of that.

H.F. You mentioned earlier that you worked well with horses! Did you have any training with guns?

J.H. I used to shoot a lot when I was a kid. And of course the Coast Artillery had infantry training as well as the artillery. I ran a rifle range for a while and had high scores as an expert rifleman. Oh, I was a crack shot.

H.F. So you were really a natural for westerns?

J.H. Yes! I don't know why I didn't get into them sooner to tell the truth.

H.F. You did a film with Bill Elliott in 1951 called *Longhorn*. The film has received a lot of nice credits.

J.H. Yeah! It sure turned into a good picture. It ran at Grauman's Chinese Theater on Hollywood Boulevard. It was probably a five- to seven-day screen shooting schedule and everything worked well, so they had a good picture.

H.F. Did you work often with Bill Elliott?

J.H. I did several pictures with him. He was a very pleasant, nice, unassuming and quiet guy. He worked at Republic Pictures. All these guys worked at Republic Pictures mostly, but I hardly ever worked there. I worked at Columbia, Paramount, and later I did a lot of work at MGM.

H.F. Did you make *Longhorn* for MGM?

J.H. No, there were a lot of other independent producers. A guy could get some money, get a writer, get a script, and put together these low budget quickies. But when you had a decent script, the actors had a chance to do something, so they could turn out to be pretty good little pictures. I worked in many of those, some better than others.

H.F. Can you say something about those early days of television?

J.H. I did *The Lone Ranger* in 1952. Since there were fifty-two weeks in a year, I guess they thought they had to have fifty-two episodes. Today, of course, twenty-four is the accepted number of episodes for a season. So things were very different. Another thing was that they thought if you did the lead in one series, you were identified and nobody wanted you to work in another series. I had a hell of a time getting a job for a year or two after *The Lone Ranger*, which was absolutely ridiculous, especially as I wore a mask in the series. Finally, I got to working again and did some nice pictures. I did a real nice episode of *Fury* with Peter Graves. I had a very strong part as a crippled rodeo rider who comes out to the ranch to recover. It was because of that role that I was picked to do the lead in *Hawkeye*. I went up to Canada later in the year and made thirty-nine episodes of *Hawkeye* with Lon Chaney Jr. That was a good show. It was a top twenty show for a short while.

H.F. Lon Chaney Jr. was a much better actor than a lot of people gave him credit for being!

J.H. He certainly was. I think he was a consummate actor. His father died in 1929 or 1930, I think. We'd go to a party or something and some young guy would say, "Oh, I remember your father!" It would get him so damn mad. They were not a happy family, the Chaneys. For me, working with Lon Chaney Jr. was an education. He was a strange guy, but a great actor. After working with him for a year, I never got to know him very well, only a little more than when I started. He was the best man at my wedding. I met a beautiful lady in Canada when I was working on *Hawkeye* and we're still married.

H.F. Your wife was an actress in Canada?

J.H. Well, she had a big radio show there for eight years. She is a graduate of the Royal Academy in London. We were married only two or three weeks after we met. It's more than thirty-five years now that we've been married.

H.F. What was it like making the series?

J.H. Well I was in Canada for about a year, then I toured the United States with my new wife to promote *Hawkeye*. We drove all over the country and I made many appearances. So when I got back to Hollywood after a year and a half or more, nobody knew where I had been. *Hawkeye* ran on television about 5:00 or 5:30 in the afternoon in California. In the picture business most people work until about 7:00 every night, so no one in Hollywood really heard about *Hawkeye* or saw it except the kids. I'd run into people and they would say something like, "Hey, John. Where have you been?" And here I thought I was a star by now.

So I wound up working on *Rawhide*. I had a running part as one of the cowboys. I was in about twenty or thirty *Rawhides*. Then producer, Andre Bohem, developed a part for me as a cowboy who wore glasses and could read.

I would read all the other guys mail for them and answer their letters. Just about when the thing started to go, some deal occurred and the company moved out of MGM and to Republic. They got another producer and directors and changed everything. I never worked on the show again.

H.F.   Then you worked with Eric Fleming!

J.H.   He was a nice enough guy. I think he and Clint Eastwood were actors in New York and they came out here. It was kind of funny watching them play cowboys. But they soon assumed the cowboy role real fast and were very good at it. Eric died tragically in South America making a film. He went into the river to go swimming and no one ever saw him again. There was a funny thing about him. He wouldn't wear shoes. He'd go to a black tie party for a premier, he'd have on a beautiful tuxedo and he'd be barefooted. He was quite a likable guy and so was Clint.

H.F.   In those early years could you detect the potential which would make Clint Eastwood a "super star" in the industry?

J.H.   Yeah, sure I did! He had a very convincing powerful way about him. This dry strong character. It was quite an event then. It was just a matter of when it would happen and it did.

H.F.   Those Spaghetti westerns really did it for him!

J.H.   They sure did. you know a few people suggested that I should go to Italy after I had done *The Lone Ranger*. They said I would get lots of work there. I'm sorry I didn't go. I've gotten to know Steve Reeves. He made many films in Italy and had a successful career.

H.F.   What happened after *Rawhide*?

J.H.   Oh, I got back into acting and chugged along looking for jobs. I did a scene with Elizabeth Taylor in *Sandpiper*. I worked with Doris Day in a couple of pictures. One was the musical *Jumbo*. I did *The Cincinnati Kid* and sat in on a card game for about five days. That was Steve McQueen, Karl Malden and Edward G. Robinson. I had fun yakking with those guys.

H.F.   You mentioned how you got into pictures. At what time did you decide to get out?

J.H.   Let's just say I got tired of the same fighting for a living as an actor. It was either feast or famine all the time. I was always interested in camera work, so I made some travel films in Europe and Hawaii. I made a school film that cost about $18,000 that grossed $200,000. It is called *Animals Can Bite*, and it is distributed by Pyramid. I still get small residuals. It was about how little kids can keep from being bitten by dogs or other animals. Nobody wanted to touch the subject, so I figured a way to do it.

H.F. You mentioned a scene with Liz Taylor in *The Sandpiper*. Which scene was that?

J.H. I was the highway patrol guy, and it was in the very early part of the picture. She had a youngster and the kid was trying to run away. I am trying to find him and I was standing on the beach with Elizabeth. I had about a page of dialogue. I might also add that she was just a total delight. She had found out that I did *Hawkeye* and the show was very popular in England. It ran for years on English TV. They must have run it for ten years over and over again. I was on salary for days but just worked about one. She and Richard Burton invited me into their dressing room. I had lunch with them and we talked all day long. It was one of the most fascinating afternoons I ever spent in my life.

H.F. What was Richard Burton like?

J.H. Oh, talking with him was just like music. The guy had a beautiful speaking voice and was lots of fun, and Elizabeth Taylor would look at me with those lovely violet eyes and smile. What a great day that was!

H.F. How many films did you make, John?

J.H. Well we are making a list now for somebody. I figured I worked in two hundred pictures, movies, TV, everything. You figure fifty-two *Lone Rangers*, thirty-nine *Hawkeyes*, *Jack Armstrong*, *The All American Boy*, and a great many shows as the heavy.

H.F. Were you Jack Armstrong on radio?

J.H. No, I was Jack Armstrong in a Columbia serial made in 1947. They were doing all the famous radio shows. The serial was made in forty-seven and it ran forever I guess. But it was in nitrate film and I've never found anybody who has a copy of it.

H.F. You also switched gears and became involved in the production end of things.

J.H. That's true. I was one of the producers of *Quincy* for three years at Universal. I was very good at dubbing sound tracks. *Quincy* was a very quality series with a big budget, and we did everything first class: doorbell, dialogue, dialogue over the phone, it just goes on and on. I would have maybe twenty-five or more soundtracks working at once. You have to bring all this together in one track. You have mixers which are responsible for different amounts of the track, the level and the music, etc.

H.F. How did you develop these varied skills?

J.H. Well I had done it all myself. When I got to a big studio, I just had to figure out how the system worked. When *Quincy* shut down I got a job working at Marvel Productions for about a year, doing all these Saturday morning cartoons. Boy, don't you think they are not complicated sound tracks. My God, I would have thirty reels going at once.

H.F. So you have touched almost every aspect of film making!

J.H. Yes I have, and it was a very important change in my life. I've actually made more money the past five or six years of my life than I did as an actor. With *The Lone Ranger* and *Hawkeye* we got paid nothing compared to what they are being paid now. When *Hawkeye* first came out we were twenty-second or twenty-third rating, and Chaney and I were working for under a thousand dollars a week. Nowadays, it's different. I remember Jack Klugman on *Quincy* making around $120,000 or $130,000 an episode. He was making twenty-four episodes a year and then the residuals. My God, you are talking in the millions. When I got in production at Universal I had a nice little office, a secretary, and a nice check every week. That was great.

H.F. Would you have done anything differently if you had it to do over today?

J.H. I would have done the same thing. I loved acting and it was a great satisfaction to me, especially when I completed a good day's work as an actor.

H.F. Any favorite movie stars when you were growing up?

J.H. I always liked Gary Cooper. I loved Bogart too. I grew up in San Marino which was a little town that didn't even have a high school. But there was the Rialto Theater and boy, we didn't miss anything. We loved the movies.

H.F. And some of your favorite westerns?

J.H. *Red River* is up there. I think *The Treasure of Sierra Madre*, but I'm not sure it can be considered a western. I guess in a sense it can. I'm sure you heard that originally they considered *High Noon* to be a total disaster. Then they got the music and Tex Ritter to sing it. They edited the film to the music, picked it up and turned it into a terrific picture. But then Gary Cooper never did a bad thing in pictures.

H.F. Tell me something about your stunt work. You did quite a bit of stunt work and doubling.

J.H. There was a picture called *Warpath* with Forrest Tucker and Edmond O'Brien. I doubled for both of them in that picture. I did a long fight scene that is considered one of the classics at Paramount.

I also did some work for DeMille. I did some early things like *The Buccaneer* and *Union Pacific*. If DeMille liked you, you could always get some work with him. Once I remember I was sitting at a little bar right across from the studio gate at Paramount nursing a beer and wondering what the hell I was going to do next. A guy said, "Hey, DeMille is starting a new picture."

Well, I knew DeMille personally. I had been to his house and knew his secretary quite well, and she knew the people he liked. I went down to see her and she told me to wait a few minutes, that he would be out shortly. So I waited until he came out with all these guys. "Hello, John," he says. He knew my name. He was a real gentleman you know. He said that he and his associates were putting out a new picture. It was *The Ten Commandments*. Remember when Moses throws down his spear and staff and it turns into a snake. The princes from the far country were standing around yelling. I was one of those. I made one hundred fifty bucks a day for ten days. Not bad in those days.

H.F.   The high point of your professional career?

J.H.   I really think looking back, that wonderful afternoon I spent with Elizabeth Taylor and Richard Burton. And *Hawkeye* when the stories were good.

H.F.   How does it feel seeing yourself on the screen today, looking back at your earlier work?

J.H.   Well, it's kind of interesting. You'd rather not get old and fall apart. But I had a tremendous experience in Knoxville last week. Someone brought out all the old stills from Paramount, and he had about five or six pictures of me when I was about nineteen or twenty and a contract player at Paramount. My God, I was a good-looking kid. No wonder the girls liked me [laughing]. I showed them to my wife and she liked them.

H.F.   How are these western film shows? Do you enjoy attending them?

J.H.   Oh, I get a kick meeting people who remember Jack Armstrong. I'm old enough and have been through enough and have spent a lot of time on the other side of the camera also to really have an appreciation for everything. Of my career I can really say, looking back, that I really enjoyed it.

H.F.   The industry today, John?

J.H.   I think it's gotten all out of hand and it's crazy. It's a free-for-all. What are you going to make that will make people buy tickets? That's your basic premise. When they broke up the theater chains, it changed things. When I worked at Paramount, for example, they wouldn't let a really bad picture out of the studio gate. They had their own music department, their own stock company, their own actors and potential starlets. When that broke up, it became a free-for-all.

The movies have gotten so expensive it is ridiculous. People like David Selznick who had such immaculate taste about his pictures and had such class, were replaced by people who could raise the money. You could make a hell of a good picture for a million dollars twenty or twenty-five years ago. Now you start at twenty million. All these people have moved into the industry today, especially in TV — wives, girlfriends, relatives. They waste so much money. They really don't know what they are doing. These guys are in it to make money, nothing else. And if you are going to buy tickets to see sex and violence, well that's exactly what you are going to get.

H.F.   Do you see a lot of good stuff coming out today?

J.H.   In spite of what I just said, sure there is. There is good stuff and there is bad stuff. We just saw *Four Weddings and a Funeral* the other day and thought it was wonderful. I haven't seen *Philadelphia*, but that's supposed to be quite good. I haven't seen *Unforgiven* yet either, and everyone says I should.

H.F.   Do you feel there will be a revival of the western as we know it?

J.H.   I don't think it will ever be the same. People are so much more sophisticated today, especially the kids. They don't go to the movies every Saturday for a quarter and have their idols. Now they have TV thrown at them twenty-four hours a day. Their excitement level is dulled, until you get all kinds of things for stimulation. I get so sick of seeing cars blown up each second. It was fun for a while, for a few years. Now, everybody blows up cars. Sex, if it is put into the context as something natural, is fine. But that's it. But I do like the new series *NYPD Blue*. It's the best new show on television. It's quite realistic. But I don't think they are going to go back to the handsome little westerns that I used to work in. That's never going to happen again.

H.F.   What about the actresses you worked with over the years?

J.H.   I usually worked with horses [laughing]. I didn't do too much with romantic leading ladies, but I got to know a few. They were beautiful and wonderful.

H.F.   Thanks loads, John!

10

Kelo Henderson

I'm an old timer whose mind goes back to a better and slower pace and different scripts. It's the nostalgia that we are trapped in and we can't break out of it. This is new, and we don't accept the new too well, especially when it comes to westerns.

Like Ben Johnson, Kelo Henderson is one of a handful of real cowboys who made that transition from the business of ranching to the movie sound stage. Best remembered for playing Arizona Ranger Clint Travis in all seventy-eight episodes of the popular *Twenty-six Men* television series in the fifties and sixties, Paul "Kelo" Henderson was born on a ranch in Colorado in 1923 and ranched with his father in Blyth, California.

Twenty-six Men told the story of the Arizona Rangers, the group formed by the Arizona Territorial Legislature in 1901 to stamp out outlawry and violence which plagued the Territory at the turn of the century. Produced by western actor Russell Hayden, perhaps best known as "Lucky" in the Hopalong Cassidy films, *Twenty-six Men* became the world's largest syndicated show at the time. At the height of its popularity, the show had a 90.2 audience and rated over such shows as *Gunsmoke*, and *Have Gun Will Travel*. It also brought instant fame to Henderson, who in 1962 was made an honorary citizen of the State of Arizona by Governor Paul J. Fannin.

Kelo Henderson's prowess with the lariat and six gun brought many big name actors to him for training. In his heyday, his proficiency at six gun martial arts won him first place at the first international fast draw contest held in the United States. A quick look at a recently released video verifies clearly that in his time and era, Kelo Henderson was the Michael Jordan of the fast draw.

In the 1960s Henderson accompanied actor Lex Barker to Europe where he made films in Germany, and in Yugoslavia. Paul "Kelo" Henderson has been married to his wife, Gail, for more than ten years and they live in Ridgecrest, California. He has two sons from his first marriage, both of whom did some film work when they were young. He loves the American West, and today his hobbies reflect that wonderful part of the country which he knows and

Kelo Henderson in *26 Men*

loves. He is a true cowboy and the following interview reflects beautifully on the American West as he has lived it.

H.F.   Kelo, you went from ranching to show business, how did this happen?

K.H.   Well, just before I went into show business, I was a ranch foreman on a cattle ranch and horse ranch for three years. While I was doing this in Malibu, I met a fellow who raised ponies and worked at the contract department at Republic Studios. Each time we met he would urge me to drop by the studio and have a cup of coffee with him. I kept saying "Yes, yes!" Then a couple of years went by, and one day I had a truck with me. On my way to see him, I made my way to the bottom of the hill where there was another ranch called "Yearling Row," owned by an actor named Ronald Reagan. That was the one and only time I talked with Ronald Reagan. I was driving by, and he was out by himself. I introduced myself and we spoke briefly, and I drove on.

H.F.   How did you learn the tools of the ranching trade?

K.H.   My father, Paul Sr., taught me to ride, rope calves, and handle a six gun. We had horses and cattle there. I even had buffalo on one of my ranches. I always had my foot in ranching in one way or another. It certainly helped me in show business.

H.F. So you decided to visit your friend at Republic Studio. What year was that?

K.H. It was the end of 1956, and little did I know that my life would never quite be the same again. He insisted I meet a friend of his. I'll never forget. We went through a maze of office buildings and came upon this office ... a gentleman came to the door. He invited me in and we talked for about twenty minutes. He asked me if I had done any picture work and I immediately said, "No!"

That was it. The man I was talking to was Harold Rossmore, casting director of Republic Studios. He asked me if I would be interested in meeting an agent and starting an acting career. In a matter of minutes we were off to Sunset Boulevard to meet the agent. He talked me into quitting my job and moving to the San Fernando Valley where I would be closer to interviews.

H.F. You had an interesting drama coach.

K.H. Oh, I sure did! Not only interesting but extraordinary. My drama coach was Josephine Dillon, Clark Gable's first wife. Her home was in the Valley. Apparently the home was hers for life and then it reverted back to the Gable estate. She was a very nice lady and Gary Cooper was one of her students. Paul Fix of *The Rifleman* was another. Lots of people don't know that it was Josephine Dillon who helped Cooper get rid of his Oxford accent and gave him his "Yep" and that stuff.

H.F. Did you learn a great deal too?

K.H. To tell the truth, the most interesting thing about working with her was that she would lapse back into reminiscing about Gable, and I found that more interesting than the drama lesson.

H.F. With no screen experience, did you find it hard working in front of the camera?

K.H. Strange as it seems, the answer is no. I had no trouble because I totally ignored it. When you have the wardrobe and you have the armament and wardrobe under you, you fall into the part. Nothing else exists.

H.F. Did you work much before the *Twenty-six Men* series?

K.H. Yes, the parts had already started coming in. I did *Saddle the Wind* with Robert Taylor and Julie London. My son played the son of Royal Dano in the film. Then I did *Gun Glory* with Stewart Granger, Rhonda Flemming and Chill Wills on location in El Centro. I helped Stewart Granger quite a bit with his gun work. I also helped John Cassavetes a lot in *Saddle the Wind*. Robert Taylor didn't need much help, he was pretty good with guns...

H.F. There is a story that you helped Will Hutchins prepare for the *Sugarfoot* series.

K.H. Yes, that's true. When I was with Josephine Dillon, Warner Brothers called to ask me if I could train the young fellow who was going to do the series. The actor in mind was Will Hutchins. About twice a week, Will would come over to my house in the Valley and I would train him with a six gun and a rope. That was before he was *Sugarfoot* and I went to Arizona to do the *Twenty-six Men* series. I hadn't seen Will Hutchins all these years until we met in Scottsdale at a film festival a couple of years ago.

H.F. How did you get cast as Clint Travis in *Twenty-six Men*?

K.H. Well, my agent called to tell me that I should be at a producer's office and at a certain time. The producer turned out to be Russell Hayden, the ex-cowboy actor best remembered as "Lucky" in the Hopalong Cassidy films. I brought a little eight millimeter film clip shot on the ranch, which displayed my horseback riding, gun work and related cowboy skills. He signed me on the spot. I signed a five-year contract with ABC for syndication for *Twenty-six Men*.

H.F. But you had been trained in these skills long before you signed the contract?

K.H. Oh yes! I was thoroughly trained before I went into the series. I was trained to use a pistol, to ride and to rope. Some shows had doubles to ride and such, but Russell Hayden didn't like that. He wanted someone who could ride and do everything. As I indicated I learned a lot of gun tricks from my father and picked up some from the Arizona Rangers when we filmed there. Four of the gentlemen (the original rangers) were still alive. I have a picture with them taken in 1957 which I really treasure.

H.F. Russell Hayden was a real matinee favorite in the days of the B western. Can you say a few words about him?

K.H. I'd love to. Had Russell not become a movie cowboy, he had the skills to become a real one. He was born on a ranch near Chico, California, and spent the first seventeen years of his life breaking horses and raising cattle. Before becoming a star, Russ held dozens of odd jobs in the movie industry—from fetching water for actors to working in the printing labs at Paramount. Of course the role that catapulted Russell to fame and the one for which he is best known and remembered is that of "Lucky," Bill Boyd's womanizing sidekick in the Hopalong Cassidy series. I think he did something like twenty-seven films with Bill Boyd in a short four-year period. He decided he was getting too old for the part.

Russell was very handsome and starred in nearly one hundred films with almost every Hollywood cowboy from Hoot Gibson to Roy Rogers. Before the *Twenty-six Men* show, he co-starred with Jackie Coogan in *Cowboy G Men*, which was the first television serial filmed in color. But make no mistake,

Russell Hayden could ride, shoot and hunt with the best of them. He did such a wonderful job with *Twenty-six Men*. He was a good man and a good friend. I was very saddened by his death in 1981.

H.F.   Can you say something about the Rangers?

K.H.   Sure! They were a group of twenty-six men formed by the Arizona Territorial Legislature in 1901. Remember Arizona was still a territory and not yet a state. A lot of violence and lawlessness plagued the territory at the turn of the century, and the Rangers were formed to help stamp this out. Incidentally, each of the seventy-eight episodes produced by Russell Hayden is historically accurate. Tris Coffin played the Captain of the Rangers and I played Ranger Clint Travis.

H.F.   And you always wore a white hat!

K.H.   That's right. I was easy to recognize. A white hat and handkerchief, and we didn't have stand-ins or stunt men. We did our own jumping from cliffs, swimming and fighting.

H.F.   Was each episode shot on location?

K.H.   They certainly were. *Twenty-six Men* was shot entirely on location in Arizona. Filming began in 1957 and ended in 1959. It included seventy-six half-hour shows and became the world's largest syndicated show at the time. At the time we filmed entirely in Phoenix and there was lots of coverage. It was a big thing because it was the only show shot in its entirety in Arizona and about the Arizona Rangers, which is the history of Arizona. So we had full cooperation from the Governor's Office all the way down. Of course, it was a great thing for the Arizona Chamber of Commerce.

H.F.   It made you quite a celebrity. Did you find your fame difficult to deal with?

K.H.   No! Not difficult. I just took it like an everyday job. Yet, everyplace I went — from the gas station to the market — people seemed to recognize me from the show. I had my name in the phone book. That's how naive I really was. I was thoroughly flattered and honored in June of 1962 when I was made an honorary citizen of Arizona by Governor Fannin.

H.F.   Much western TV work other than *Twenty-six Men*?

K.H.   I was in *Wells Fargo*, and *Sergeant Preston*, and *Cheyenne*. In one episode of *Cheyenne*, I had the honor of being killed by Clint Walker. I was a nasty bad guy in that one. I also went on location with MGM and did two pictures. In *Sergeant Preston* I had the distinction of having the dog "King" growl at me because I was the bad guy in that too.

H.F.   Some of the people you worked with who impressed you most?

K.H.   Oh, there were so many. But I have to single out Jim Davis, Doug McClure, Leonard Nimoy, Denver Pyle and George Keymas.

H.F.   You also did westerns in Europe?

K.H.   Yes! In the 1960s Lex Barker and I went to Germany and did two films based on novels by the German Zane Grey, Karl May. What is really interesting is that Karl May had never been to the American West, yet he wrote a whole series of western books while serving a prison term for forgery. The two films were in color and were produced by Arthur Brauner, President of Central Cinema Company in West Berlin.

H.F.   Were they filmed in Germany?

K.H.   No! They were dubbed in English and were filmed on location in Dubrovnik, Yugoslavia and Belgrade and Titograd. We left Germany before they were released, so for over twenty-five years I never got to see them.

H.F.   And you say that the writer of the stories had never been to the southwest?

K.H.   Not only the writer, but the producer as well. So Lex and I were called upon for lots of consultation. Actually the films were typical westerns with a decidedly European flavor. Actors and actresses from Spain, Italy, and France added to the international ambience.

An interesting story has to do with the casting of the Indians. The Indians were played by the Belgrade Ballet Company. They had peacock feathers in the Indian headdresses. We had to correct that immediately.

H.F.   You finally had a chance to see those two films twenty-five years later.

K.H.   It was a twist of irony. Gail and I moved to Ridgecrest and we met a local potter named Vera Schadow, a native of Germany. She told us about her relatives in Germany who might be able to find the films on video. What a great surprise when Vera's brother sent us the two videos. So, after all the many years we finally were able to see them.

H.F.   Was your work entirely in the western genre?

K.H.   Yes! I felt quite at ease in westerns, but never really had the opportunity to do other things.

H.F.   What did you prefer more, feature films or television?

K.H.   Oh I like TV much more than film-making. Feature films went real slow. It was kind of boring with the fast pace of television. In Arizona we shot a half-hour show in two and a half days. In one week we shot two shows.

H.F.   Some of your favorite western films?

K.H.   Well, there are the standards of course: *Red River, Stagecoach, High Noon*. And I'm going to add another which I am sure will surprise a lot of people. I loved a movie called *The Kissing Bandit* with Frank Sinatra and Kathryn Grayson. It was offbeat and kind of comical, but I enjoyed it. Besides, Kathryn Grayson was beautiful and sang like a nightingale.

H.F.   What about the films of today?

K.H.   I just guess that I'm an old timer now whose mind goes back to a better and slower pace, and different scripts. It's the nostalgia that we are trapped in, and we can't break out of it. It was our time and our era. This is new, and we don't accept the new too well, especially when it comes to westerns.

H.F.   You really have a passion for the American West!

K.H.   That I do. It's in my blood. Even my hobbies reflect this passion. I collect western oil paintings, do my own photography, and still practice with my guns. This is called "working the guns."

H.F.   You do a lot of film festivals now!

K.H.   As many as I can make when we are invited. I certainly enjoy meeting old friends and people who do remember. After being dormant for so many years, it's been real nice. I can thank my good friend Bob Ladd. He first told me about a show in Scottsdale a few years ago, and we've been having loads of fun at them for a few years now.

H.F.   Thanks, Kelo!

11

Robert Horton

The studio offered me a great deal of money. The catch was they wanted me to sign a contract for ten more years of Wagon Train. Fifteen years is a huge part of an actor's career. I had other things I wanted to do, some of which I've done...

As Flint McCollough in the top-rated *Wagon Train* series of the late fifties and early sixties, Robert Horton was perhaps the most dashing and romantic leading man of that wonderful TV western era. He was one of the wonders of the Wild West, a man's man and a heartthrob to the girls. Handsome, lean, rugged and fearless, he was the perfect sidekick to the rougher, gruffer, Ward Bond who played Major Seth Adams.

Wagon Train was a ratings smash and a critical hit. In 1961-62 the show dethroned *Gunsmoke* as the number one–rated TV show in the land. When Horton left the show after five years to pursue a career in musical theater, the ratings diminished. And while *Wagon Train* would continue through 1965, and account for two hundred fifty-two episodes, Horton's presence was sorely missed.

Show business seemed a natural entry for Horton. Born and raised in Los Angeles, he enrolled at the University of Miami, where he majored in dramatic literature. Described in his sophomore year as "six feet of red-headed dynamite," he won the University's Award for "Best Performance by an Actor."

Acting also satisfied a certain "rebel" inclination, a true departure from a family tradition of doctors, lawyers and educators. Transferring to UCLA, he completed his undergraduate work in less than three years, graduating with honors. From there it was onto Yale to pursue a master's degree in Fine Arts. He withdrew after one semester and enrolled instead in New York's finest professional school, The American Theater Wing, and earned his first salary in theater as a leading man in a summer stock company in Atlanta. Hollywood soon began bidding for his services, and within a few months he signed a long term contract with MGM. He appeared in such pictures as *A Walk in the Sun*, and *The Pony Soldiers*. However, the movie business was beginning to feel the challenge of television. In panic, the studios started firing young actors.

Robert Horton in *Wagon Train*

But Horton had all the physical requisites for a leading man. He also was extremely versatile. His "superstar" status in *Wagon Train* presents only part of the resume. A brilliant stage performance as Hal Carter, in William Inge's *Picnic* led to a new contract with Warner Brothers where he starred in the TV version of *King's Row*. The series failed, yet his outstanding and now familiar work on such television productions as *Climax*, *Studio One*, *Playhouse 90*, and *Alfred Hitchcock Presents* led Horton to *Wagon Train*, which soon became one of the most successful series in TV history. He later starred in a second series, *A Man Called Shenandoah* which included thirty-four episodes in 1965-66.

Horton's western laurels, of course, are well-known. Not so well-known is his success on the musical stage. His credits are many and impressive. Following his first Broadway audition, he was signed by Alan J. Lerner to do *On a Clear Day You Can See Forever*.

It was just the musical start. Over the years Horton starred in such standard musical classics as *Oklahoma*, *Guys and Dolls*, *Carousel*, *Pajama Game*, *Brigadoon*, *Man from La Mancha*, *Show Boat*, *Kismet*, *The Music Man*, and as John Adams in *1776*. In fact, he met his wife Marilyn when she was his leading lady in a production of *Guys and Dolls*. Together they toured the country for years doing a variety of musicals, the last being *I Do, I Do!*

In this second career, Horton has recorded for Columbia Records, he has worked as a troubadour in America's finest super clubs, and as a headliner on television variety shows in America, England, Germany, and Australia. A particularly proud moment was when he was asked to sing for the Queen of England at The Royal Command Performance. He was also honored by Ralph Edwards as the surprise celebrity guest in *This Is Your Life*. After a successful year's run in *110 in the Shade*, Horton was hailed as "A wonderful surprise," by one critic. "He not only sings a song, he acts it — A *Wagon Train* of talent," one critic said. Clearly, Robert Horton has touched every medium of show business. His work in television, motion pictures and the stage include *Golden Boy*, *All My Sons*, *Death of a Salesman*, and *Picnic*, and he's been equally adept at drama, comedy, and the musical stage.

It was for riding the range as Flint McCullough in *Wagon Train*, one of television's longest and most popular western shows, that Robert Horton was called "the sexiest thing on — or off a horse." In 1993 Horton was presented with the "Lifetime Achievement Award" at the Tuolumne County Wild West Film Festival in Sonora. And after more than thirty years, he still gets loyal fan mail from Britain and other parts of the world where the series is running.

Robert Horton and his wife Marilyn live happily at their ranch-style home in Encino, California. He likes fancy cars and flying. "I have eight cars including an Astin Martin, a Morgan, a '57 Thunderbird and a '57 Chrysler. I take them to auto shows and love showing them off." Still handsome, the years have been good to him. He admits to no longer wearing a thirty-two inch waist on his slacks. "Those days are gone forever, I guess." But he is quick to add that he still wears a size thirty-six. "Pretty good for a man my age," he says proudly.

H.F.   Bob, you came from Beverly Hills and your family was relatively well off. How did you first get started in show business?

R.H.   I got my first part in a play in my semi-adult life because I had red hair and freckles. I enjoyed it very much. I spent about twelve weeks rehearsing this play and about twelve weeks playing it. Normally, I never had a long attention span. But here, I was never bored. I guess to be truthful, I suddenly felt that I was involved in a love affair with the theater. I suddenly decided that this is what I wanted to do. I have never been bored yet. I was in the ninth grade in a junior high school in Los Angeles.

H.F.   Did you have any particular movie hero when you were a kid growing up? Somebody whose presence may have influenced you to change this interest into a career.

R.H.   I don't think so. But, when I was growing up if I had a hero it was Errol Flynn. But I don't think he was responsible for my being an actor. I'll say this though, once when I was doing a production of the musical *Kismet*, the critic who reviewed the production said I lent a certain "pizazz" to the part of Haj, which reminded him of vintage Errol Flynn. That was a very big compliment to me under the circumstances.

H.F. In 1945 you had a part in the film *A Walk in the Sun*, a particularly compelling war story.

R.H. Yes I did, and it was a good film. Great cast too: Dana Andrews, Sterling Holloway and John Ireland, I had about a half a dozen lines and became a member of the Screen Actors Guild at the time.

H.F. Were you under contract to a particular studio?

R.H. Yes! I was under contract with Selznick for a brief time. Then I was under contract with MGM for two years and Warner Brothers for one. And there were others. I was under contract with Universal for five years, to Richard Rodgers for one year and to David Merrick for a year. Then back to MGM, then to CBS.

H.F. What was your first western?

R.H. It was called *Pony Soldier* with Tyrone Power. I played the heavy in the film. I had never done westerns until then. I tested for a film at MGM which I didn't get. But I ended my contract with them. Then Fox borrowed me for a film called *The Return of the Texan* which was not a western in the classic sense. But it was made in Texas. Along the way I did a film for Warner Brothers called *The Tanks Are Coming*, which obviously was a war story. Steve Cochran was the star and I had a modest role.

H.F. How did you land *Wagon Train*, and did a lot of actors test for the part?

R.H. Well, I was doing quite well as a free lance actor. In 1956 I did about ten guest spots on television. By that time my name was above the title in programs like *Alfred Hitchcock Presents* and things like that. I had a very good role in a particular Hitchcock episode called *The Crack of Doom*. If I say so myself, it was a fine performance. The studio felt the same way and they decided to test me for *Wagon Train*. There were seven other fellows who tested. I was the smallest of the bunch.

H.F. Ward Bond played Major Seth Adams until his death in 1960. What do you remember about Ward?

R.H. Well, it was an experience. I'll say that. Ward and I had a fantastic chemistry on the screen. The nature of Ward was as a big, rough, macho fellow. I came along with a warm touch and a gentle smile, but I was not without strength. I think that the chemistry we had in *Wagon Train* has never been surpassed. It really worked marvelously well. Ward was a man of great personal charm, a very fine actor. I had become a fan of his when he played in *Gentleman Jim* with Errol Flynn. It was a great role. He was really fine.

H.F. His politics were said to be rather right wing. He has been criticized for this in certain circles.

R.H. Well you are right. His politics were rather extreme. In the late 1950s, he proclaimed with great pride that he thought Joe McCarthy was right. But at least you knew where he was coming from.

H.F. Where did you do most of the filming for *Wagon Train*?

R.H. Most of the filming was on the set of Universal. We did a lot of location work, too, in the Canao Valley which is about an hour's drive west of Hollywood. We did some location work — but every little — in Arizona. And we did some in a small area between Bakersfield and Los Angeles.

H.F. Who were some of your favorite directors on the show?

R.H. That's a tough one. Virgil Vogel did some nice work. A man named Earl Bellamy was a very good director. So was Richard Thorpe who did some work as an actor. He directed some episodes. These are some of the names who come to mind. It was a long time ago.

H.F. *Wagon Train* did so well, and you were very convincing in a western role. Did you have any prior training such as riding a horse and using a gun?

R.H. No, I really didn't. I learned to ride a horse when I was a boy. My father liked to ride and I used to ride with him. But I didn't know until I started to do *Wagon Train* and work with horses everyday that I had the tools to become a very good horseman. I spent a lot of time on the weekends going out riding. I improved greatly and extended my use of the horse and my ability to ride him and to do what I wanted with a horse.

H.F. The series made you a real heartthrob with the girls. Were you aware of your appeal and popularity?

R.H. Funny, that's what I hear. But I didn't know this until Virgil Vogel told me recently about the inordinate amount of fan mail I would receive, and just how popular I was on the show. I never really knew it.

H.F. You mean the studio never let you know?

R.H. Surprisingly, no! They are not interested in informing you. They were afraid you'd get after them to rewrite your contract. If I was doing *Wagon Train* now and it enjoyed the success it did back then, I'd probably be making a quarter of a million dollars an episode.

H.F.   You didn't make anything like that back then?

R.H.   Oh, no! Five thousand dollars was — and is — a very fine salary. But in today's market five thousand dollars is nothing.

H.F.   *Wagon Train* always had such great, big name guest stars. Any particular one come to mind?

R.H.   Yes, there were some wonderful actors. I was really most fortunate to work with people like James Mason, Raymond Massey, Lee Marvin, Bette Davis, Barbara Stanwyck, Dame Judith Anderson, Ernie Borgnine. Most, if not all, of them were Academy Award winners.

H.F.   What was Lee Marvin like?

R.H.   Lee Marvin and I had a very special relationship because Lee Marvin married a girl who was my sweetheart when I was going to college. We became very good friends and remained so until he died. As you know, Lee passed away a few years ago.

H.F.   He started out big as a cop named Frank Ballinger on the TV series *M Squad*.

R.H.   That's right! As a matter of fact, if you really got into the bookkeeping of Universal Pictures, I think you'd find that *M Squad* and *Wagon Train* put Universal Pictures on the map related to television. Then, of course, Lee did so many good things. Remember he did what I thought was a very risky performance when he did the musical *Paint Your Wagon*. But he did it quite well. He was a very good actor and a strong actor.

H.F.   He was also supposed to be a very tough guy.

R.H.   Lee Marvin was not tough in my eyes. He had a certain image that he was perfectly willing to maintain. He was most gentlemanly and respectful to my wife. One night we had a party at my house, maybe about a hundred people, and Lee was there with his wife, Betty. Lee had a little too much to drink. I came up and told him he had a little too much to drink. I said, "Lee, I think you kind of better take it easy." He looked at me and said, "I'm going to tear your head off." I didn't move an inch. I told him a second time that I think he better "cool it" and sit down with Betty. He looked at me, put his hands down, walked over and sat down. That was the end of it.

H.F.   With *Wagon Train* so enormously successful, and your career going so well, why did you leave the show?

R.H.   The studio offered me a great deal of money. The catch was that they wanted me to sign a contract for ten more years of *Wagon Train*. Fifteen years is a huge part of an actor's career. There were other things I wanted to do, much of which I have now done, although maybe without all the success I'd like to have attached to it.

H.F. You followed *Wagon Train* with another western series, *A Man Called Shenandoah.*

R.H. Yes I did. It lasted a year. There were about forty episodes. But I was not totally pleased with it. I did the pilot which was really a half-hour western. It was an excellent script, well-directed, and with an excellent cast. The show just sold like that, immediately. When we went on the air with it, we were number one in the ratings. Then we were preempted, and that hurt the show a great deal. We were also black and white on ABC, and the number one shows on CBS and NBC were both in color. That is a tough thing to fight. We had a good share of the audience — thirty-five to thirty-seven percent. The head of MGM where the show was produced was just stunned when it was canceled on the last day of its option. We all were.

H.F. But you say that you were personally unhappy with the show?

R.H. Well, first let me review the plot. It was the story of a man who had amnesia. He didn't know who he was, and was searching the West for his identity. Too many of the shows started with me walking into a bar, someone supposedly recognizing me and accusing me of murder or of being a bank robber. The sheriff arrests me and I'm thrown in jail. You'd then played the whole show with nothing more than that, and that is not enough.

But as the show progressed, they started showing a sequence or two where the viewer was not confronted with the problem immediately, and would get into it as the show advanced. Recently I saw three episodes and as I watched them closely, I thought that the show had a wonderful, melancholy, tormented quality which worked very well. I revised my estimate of the show, it holds up well today.

H.F. How did you make your way into musical theater? That's a long leap from the covered wagon.

R.H. Well, as you have seen I started in film and television. But along the way I decided I was interested in musical theater. At the time I was doing *Wagon Train*, so I decided to study voice. *Wagon Train* really gave me the impetus to start in musical theater. I liked it very much. As far as I'm concerned, it is the most exciting area of the theater I have worked in. When the overture goes on, it really gets your attention.

H.F. How did it start?

R.H. I went on Broadway with *One Hundred and Ten in the Shade.* The show was very successful. But truthfully it was overwhelmed by *Hello Dolly*, and by *Funny Girl* which was down the road. But is was a great musical season.

The show was successful and ran a year. I was asked to do it in London, but I chose not to. However, it gave me an entree to musical theater which is what I did almost exclusively from 1960 to the late 1970's. I worked in dinner theaters all over the country. You can earn a wonderful living, but in terms of national publicity your profile is enormously diminished.

H.F.   How did you get so interested in musicals, at least to the point that it overshadowed everything else careerwise?

R.H.   Well, I did *Guys and Dolls*. It was my first musical. I played Sky Masterson. My leading lady was a girl I fell in love with and eventually married. We've been together for the past thirty-four years. Marilyn was a gifted singer who was just starting to move from roles in summer stock to the Broadway stage. She was on Broadway in the chorus of several great shows. Marilyn also had a close friendship with Richard Rodgers, who automatically put her in his shows.

H.F.   What were some of your favorite musical roles and had you done much singing as a boy?

R.H.   I was interested in singing, but I really didn't do a lot of singing until I met Marilyn. Then I took it as a serious part of my career, and it remained so. As to my roles: I was Curley in *Oklahoma*; Billy in *Carousel*; Tommy in *Brigadoon*; Sky in *Guys and Dolls*. I was John Adams in *1776*. I also did *Zorba*. I'm fortunate. I had some wonderful lead roles.

H.F.   You sang before Queen Elizabeth II in London?

R.H.   Yes, that was 1960 at the Royal Command Performance in the Palladium. That was a nervous evening. I was singing with Nat Cole, Sammy Davis Jr., Liberace was one of the guest stars. It was an evening of pomp and ceremony and tradition. What a wonderful evening. I met the Queen after the performance. It was a very exciting evening and one which I will never forget.

H.F.   The high points of your career, Bob?

R.H.   Well, during *Wagon Train* one day there was a knock on my front door, and to my astonishment I opened the door and there was Ralph Edwards saying, "Robert Horton, *This Is Your Life!*" That was a very exciting moment. Opening night on Broadway in *One Hundred and Ten in the Shade*, was another. Being part of the Broadway scene, in the company of kings and queens, Richard Burton, Alec Guinness, Mary Martin, Barbara Streisand. That year is filled with a montage of memories.

H.F.   How do you feel about the film industry today?

R.H.   I have no negative comments about that. There are some excellent films. Of course, what is happening in society alters the kind of things being made. But there are certainly some excellent films coming out.

H.F.   Would you name a few?

R.H.   Last year I saw some good ones. *Unforgiven* won the award as Best Picture of the Year. I can't say that I thought it was the best film of the year. I thought it was a very good film. Clint Eastwood is a very popular figure in Hollywood. That has a lot to do with the awards.

I thought *Basic Instinct* was a better film as an overall picture. I thought it was a first class picture. There was a very small budget film called *One False Move*, and it was a wonderful performance by actors I had never even seen. Going back a couple of years I thought *The Crying Game* was a first class picture. *Dangerous Liaisons* was a wonderful film. So was the remake of *Of Mice and Men*. It was very well-made. That remake of *Cape Fear* was a wonderfully done movie. Robert DeNiro gave a brilliant performance. But I totally felt that Al Pacino deserved the award as Best Actor for *Scent of a Woman*. I thought he was just great, maybe the best performance I've seen anybody give anywhere.

H.F.   Any great disappointments or things you may have done differently?

R.H.   I was very disappointed after I left *Wagon Train*. I auditioned for a musical which was supposed to be a collaboration between Richard Rodgers and Alan J. Lerner. It was called *I Picked a Daisy*, and was to be directed by Gower Champion. I had left a show where the ratings showed me to be one of the top people on television. I left the show on my own volition and auditioned for the most highly-anticipated new Broadway musical in years. Then Mr. Rodgers and Mr. Lerner decided they didn't work well together. The show was postponed and resurfaced later with a different title called *On a Clear Day You Can See Forever*. After the show was postponed four times I withdrew from the show, and when David Merrick offered me *One Hundred and Ten in the Shade* which is the musical version of *The Rainmaker*, I felt it was a very good move. It was a very good show, but did not stand up to the super hits which were on Broadway at that time.

H.F.   Anything particular in the future?

R.H.   No, I have nothing going. I am very satisfied with what my achievements have been in this business. They may or may not be over. But if they are, it's OK. I spent most of my life in the fast lane. I have no complaints.

H.F.   Congratulations on your Lifetime Achievement Award here in Sonora.

R.H.   Thank you!

12

Will Hutchins

> *Sugarfoot was unique. Like my wife says, he was the Shirley Temple of cowboys. What made Sugarfoot unique was the comedy we had in there. It wasn't tongue and cheek or verbal. There was a lot of visual stuff. Like my love for Harold Lloyd. I tried to insert as much of his spirit into the show as I could.*

Will Hutchins is a rarity in the entertainment business. Not only did he achieve TV immortality as Tom Brewster in *Sugarfoot*, Hutchins is also one of the most astute students of movies and performing in the entire industry. As Tom Brewster, a law student who headed west for adventure, he proved himself so inept as a cowboy that he was nicknamed *Sugarfoot*, a step below being a *Tenderfoot*. During the show's four year run, (1957-61), Hutchins won over legions of devoted fans who still remember him fondly more than thirty years later.

Born in Los Angeles on May 5, 1932, Will Hutchins became a movie buff even before he started kindergarten. At Marshall High School he began acting in school plays. One of his high school roles was that of George, in Thorton Wilder's *Our Town*. It remains one of his favorite plays and favorite roles. Following high school it was off to Pamona College where he became the first Drama major in the history of the school.

After an obligatory tour of duty with the United States Army, Hutchins used the GI Bill to go to graduate school at UCLA where he specialized in cinematography. Soon he started getting small roles which would soon lead him to Warner Brothers and *Sugarfoot*. He can also be seen in such films as *No Time for Sergeants* with Andy Griffith, *Clambake* with Elvis Presley, and *The Shooting* — an offbeat western where he shared the camera's eye with a young actor named Jack Nicholson.

Hutchins would go on to star in two more television series: *Hey Landlord* (1966-67), where he played the naive owner and landlord of a rundown New York brownstone; and then in 1968 as Dagwood Bumstead in the TV adaptation of the popular comic strip *Blondie*.

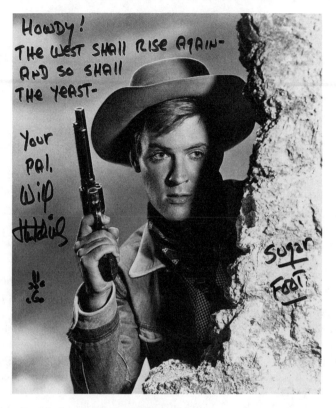

Will Hutchins

With roles less plentiful in the ensuing years and eager to try something new, Hutchins joined the circus as a ringmaster and a clown performing in California and around the entire country. Will Hutchins still works occasionally, and has recently appeared in the film *Maverick* with Mel Gibson, Jodie Foster and James Garner, the original Brett Maverick of TV fame.

I first met Will Hutchins in Marie's Coffee Shop in Sonora, California, in 1992. What started as benign friendly chatter, resulted in three hours of lively and riveting conversation. Will Hutchins knows film, he loves the movies, and he understands film-making at all levels. Rarely without an opinion or a personal conviction, he is also a veritable encyclopedia of movie trivia. His stories of a young boy growing up in Depression era Los Angeles, and who fell in love with movies, is a total delight. In 1993 the Tuolumne County Wild West Film Fest honored Will Hutchins with its Television Fame Award. It was an honor and well-deserved.

H.F.   Will, you were born in Los Angeles during the Depression years. The movies must have filled a real void in your life. Can you say something about these early years?

W.H.   You are right. The movies sure filled a void. I was born in Los Angeles in 1932, so my first memories were of the Depression. And interestingly, I still live on the very same street. My dad was a dentist, and his house is just a couple of blocks up the street from where I live. It is in a state of disrepair right now, but it's still there.

When my folks got divorced my mom and I moved around a lot. We wound up living right across the river from here in Atwater. It's a community between the LA River and the Glendale railroad tracks. It was a great place to grow up. One of the big reasons is that it had Griffith Park for a back yard. Griffith Park is one of the great municipal parks in the world. And it seemed a lot bigger in those days when there were no freeways.

The river was a lot stronger too. When the floods would come, we had to move to higher ground. One of the people we visited was Al Gilks, who was one of the top cameramen at MGM in those days. Whenever the floods would come, we'd stay at their house for a few days till the water subsided. Eventually the engineers came and filled the river in and made levees. I can also add that as a result I became an entrepreneur at an early age. I sold Kool Aid to the workers.

H.F.   And you had an infatuation with the movies as a young boy?

W.H.   Yes, I sure did. That was because of my grandmother. She'd pick me up after grammar school when I was in kindergarten, and every Thursday we'd go downtown or to Hollywood. If she took me to Hollywood, we'd usually go to the Warner Brothers Theater. They showed these wonderful Warner Brother movies such as *Ceiling Zero*. When I see it now, it is still a great movie. Movies like this made a strong impression on me. They got into my system and helped form me. I would see a Jimmy Cagney movie and I'd come out and be Jimmy Cagney for a week or two. Most of the movies today just bounce off me because it's too late. I've already been formed. They just don't affect me.

H.F.   So those old movies still affect you?

W.H.   Oh yes! It's funny the way movies begin to change as you change. For instance, when I was a kid I saw *Bank Dick* with W. C. Fields. I didn't think it was too funny. I see it now and I think it is a masterpiece, one of the great movies of all time. If you change, the movie changes before your eyes.

H.F.   And you saw lots and lots of movies as a kid?

W.H.   Like I said, my grandmother got me into the habit. Then on weekends we crowded into Mr. Worley's car. He was the richest guy in Atwater. He made $200 a month during the Depression. He was a liquor salesman and liquor never lost its popularity during the Depression. So he was able to buy a new Chevy every other year. On Saturday we'd pile into that Chevy and he'd drive us all to Glendale. We'd go to the Capital Theater and see the movie. What we really wanted to see, however, was the serial.

H.F. Any favorites?

W.H. Sure. The first one I saw was *Flash Gordon* with Buster Crabbe. They played it every Saturday so we would always come back. We'd go home and act out the serials, then we'd show up at the movie theater on Saturday for more. I grew up loving a lot of action in my movies, a lot of visual stuff which I think has stayed with me.

H.F. What was Hollywood like when you were a kid?

W.H. You see I lived in Atwater, so Hollywood seemed like a long way from me. It was exciting, not seedy like it is today. When I got a little older, my mother let me take the Asbury Rapid Transit bus into Hollywood on Saturday. I would either go with my buddies or I would go by myself. I'd walk up and down Hollywood Boulevard looking in the windows. First I would haunt the magic stores. I wanted to be a magician. I'd buy some magic tricks then go to a major motion picture theater like Groumans. They really were like palaces. Then I'd go across the street to *The Hitching Post Theater* and see the B westerns. So I grew up liking expensive movies and B movies alike. I liked them both.

H.F. What were the B westerns like for you as a kid?

W.H. Well, the first western which really knocked my socks off was *The Lone Ranger* serial, the one with Lee Powell as the Lone Ranger. I'd go to the Gateway Theater in Glendale to see Chief Thunder Cloud who played Tonto. He was a real Indian and I used to sit up close. I always sat up close and the screen seemed so big to me in those days. I was just a little kid and *The Lone Ranger* would come riding down those rocks. It looked so real. They shot a lot of them in Long Pine.

H.F. So you developed a real appreciation for westerns at an early age?

W.H. Sure! I especially liked Hopalong Cassidy. The only thing I didn't like about Hoppy was that he was so nice, he didn't kill many of the bad guys. They'd shoot it out for almost twenty minutes and no one would fall. In later years I began renting them in the video shops and took to liking Hoot Gibson a lot. One of the reasons I think was that the wranglers at Warner Brothers would call me "Hoot" all the time. I don't know if they were being sarcastic or what, but I think that *Sugarfoot* does resemble Hoot Gibson a bit. The wranglers were the guys who handled all the livestock and doubled as stunt men.

H.F. Did you still see as many movies in high school? Lots of guys drop everything for sports!

W.H. Oh sure! I was always a movie buff. I'd go to films more than most of my pals. My friends usually went on Saturday, but I'd go on Sundays too. They cost a dime, and a nickel for candy. So for fifteen cents I could go to the movies. My mom gave me fifty cents a week allowance, so I was a rich guy. I'd guess you'd say I was a little spoiled.

H.F. Which films impressed you most?

W.H. To me the movies of the thirties are still the best movies ever made. The early forties were great, but then they started to taper off, and after the War they lost a lot of their punch for me. I was at Warner Brothers in the 1950s and I think our TV product was better than most of their feature films. I think that's where they made most of their money. Then in the sixties, they just got kind of weaker and weaker.

H.F. Which films of the thirties best stand out in your mind, films which may have influenced you?

W.H. My grandparents lived next door to Foxy Lloyd who was Harold Lloyd's father. He was a great old guy and liked to talk to me. His garage had one of these big Harold Lloyd posters pasted on the wall, like a big circus poster. When you look at them you'd say, "Hey, I can't wait to go to the movies this weekend." So I always liked comedians. I think it grew out of knowing Fox Lloyd and getting to know about Harold Lloyd.

My grandmother took me to the Paramount Theater in downtown LA. One big thing about going downtown was that you had vaudeville too. There were all those great theaters. We had the Paramount, the Orphia, the RKO Hill Street. So you could go to vaudeville which really got you your money's worth. You'd see one or two features. You'd see all the short subjects and you would see the vaudeville show. If your parents sent you to the theater on a day when there was vaudeville, you would be there all day.

So back in about 1938, I saw *Professor Beware* with Harold Lloyd. That was the last movie his own company produced and that he starred in. It did not do all that well, but I just loved the movie. There were great visual gags. Years later when I was at UCLA Grad School on the GI Bill taking motion picture courses, I made a movie down at the beach called *It Happened in Pismo Beach*. I swiped the main gags from *Professor Beware* which Harold Lloyd in turn swiped from a silent movie called *For Heaven's Sake*.

The gag is that the hero is trying to get people to help him rescue his girlfriend off the yacht. She is being held captive by the bad guys. So he goes all over town and gets people mad at him. He goes up to a painter at lunch time and puts the painters brush right across his sandwich. The painter starts to chase him. Then he finds a shoeshine parlor and starts painting all the shoes.

Everybody there chases him. He keeps doing all those things to get people mad at him. They all chase him and he leads them to the boat where everyone has a fist fight with the bad guys, and he saves the girl. So I did it all in the finale of Pismo Beach. The only thing is that I had a sea monster come out of the ocean. The sea monster was played by John Shaner who is now a movie producer. He was just Herman Shiner in those days, so I had him play the sea monster.

He came out of the sea all covered with seaweed, grabbed the fair damsel and started carrying her back to the ocean. So I had my hero get all nervous and excited. He kicked sand all over everyone's sandwiches, getting all the people mad at him. They chase after him and help him rescue the fair damsel from the clutches of the sea monster.

H.F.   You did some acting in high school?

W.H.   Yes! I went to Marshall High School here in LA. You could only be in two plays your senior year. Incidentally, Marshall High was named after an ancestor of mine. My real name is Marshall Hutchinson. I was named after John Marshall, the great Supreme Court justice. I got into *Our Town* my senior year. I played George, the role William Holden played in the movie with Martha Scott. That is still about my favorite play of all time. That's a wonderful play. I played him a few times after high school. I remember all summer long I fretted because I knew I had the part, but I knew I would have to kiss Emily in front of all those students. Boy, was I embarrassed! Nowadays that wouldn't be anything for a kid. But in those days times were different and I really fretted about that.

H.F.   Do you still remember the young lady's name? Sometimes you never forget those things.

W.H.   Well, we had double casting, so there were two. One was a tall blonde. The other was shorter and a brunette. They were both good in their own way. But I don't remember their names. What I do remember is that I fell in love with the girl who played my sister. Her name was Noel Oliver. I really fell in love with her. Her father was the drama critic of the *Los Angeles Herald*. I had one date with her and I was very stupid and shy. It was a double date. I called her up again and asked her to go to the Rose Bowl, but she had another date. It turned out he was the guy she married. He was a folk singer who was very popular in the fifties.

H.F.   Did you have a real ambition to be an actor when you were a high school kid?

W.H.   Oh, I had this ambition to be an actor from day one. I never thought much about making a living from it, but it was my main interest. In high school though I filled up with sports. I never thought much about sports before then. But I was a real sports nut when I went to high school.

H.F. Did you play any high school sports?

W.H. I was on the track team but I was terrible. I was a shot putter and was about the last man on the team. But I got into one track meet and all my buddies cheered for me. We had the third best team in the city that year. We came in third in the City Championship Meet. Track doesn't draw the big crowds that it once did in high school. We had some great track meets back then.

H.F. Any more plays in high school?

W.H. I did one called *Ramshackle Inn*. I played the bad guy in that. I wasn't particularly good in that one. ZaSu Pitts played in it on Broadway. Years later I got to work with ZaSu Pitts and what a great thrill that was. Al Gilks, the guy who worked for MGM, would go to all the plays at school and knew of my love for acting. He had me try out for the part of Jody in *The Yearling*. I tried out and they liked me. But I was the wrong size.

H.F. Claude Jarmon Jr. got the part in the film!

W.H. I actually tried out earlier. In this one Spencer Tracy was going to play the father, but things didn't work out. A few years later they did it with Gregory Peck and Claude Jarmon Jr. did the part, and did it very well.

H.F. After high school, what happened?

W.H. I graduated in 1949, Then I went to Pamona College. I was the first drama major in the history of Pamona College. I was going to major in English, but they brought drama in as a major, so I switched. But truthfully, my main reason for going to college was to keep out of the Army. It was during the Korean War and I didn't want to get killed. I just knew I'd get killed if I got drafted. So I became the first drama major at Pamona College. Robert Taylor and Joel McCrea both went there too. They were in plays and were discovered. But there was no drama degree back then.

H.F. And you did lots of plays?

W.H. Yes! In fact I was the first guy ever to make it into *The Maskers*, the first half of my freshman year. I got two leads which was very unusual. They usually bring you up slowly through the ranks. I played the lead in *Ah, Wilderness!*, which was Will Rogers' last endeavor. Will Rogers was my all-time hero. I played the part Elisha Cook Jr. played on Broadway. It was written by Eugene O'Neil, who wanted to prove he could write a comedy. It starred George M. Cohan on Broadway. I also played Demetrius in *A Midsummer Night's Dream*. I'll never forget that because in those days my legs were so skinny that I had to wear suspenders on my tights.

H.F.   Did working on the stage help you a lot in your film and TV career?

W.H.   I think stage work gives you a lot of confidence. I think it's harder to work on stage and to do a good job on stage. Maybe I'm wrong, but a long list of great stage people don't do well in the movies and vice-versa. The Lunts come to mind. They only made about one or two movies. As great as Helen Hayes was, she was much better on stage than on screen.

H.F.   But she did win a couple of Oscars!

W.H.   Yes she did. She won a Best Actress Award in 1932 for *The Sin of Madelon Claudet*, but became discouraged after a couple of bad films and went back to the stage which was her real love. Then in the 1970s, she won a Best Supporting Actress Oscar for *Airport*.

H.F.   Any westerns in the thirties and forties which stand out in your mind?

W.H.   Yes! The best was *The Westerner* with Gary Cooper and Walter Brennan. Recently I bought a hat which looked like the one Gary Cooper wore in *The Westerner*. I bought it to wear at Iron Eyes Cody's ninetieth birthday party. It was one of these dressy western affairs. I saw some pictures later, and I can say one thing for sure. Unfortunately, I don't quite look like Gary Cooper in those pictures. But the hat looked great. I do remember *The Westerner* and it was one of the great ones.

During the 1940s John Ford's westerns made quite an impact on me. I'm thinking about the Cavalry trilogy in particular. I remember seeing *Fort Apache* when I was about fifteen. It was at the same Gateway Theater where I used to see *The Lone Ranger*. I loved that one. I remember we went around singing the melody which was one of the main themes in the movie (humming the theme for emphasis). I always loved John Ford westerns.

As I grew older I have learned to appreciate *My Darling Clementine* more and more. I remember once working with one of the guys in John Ford's Stock Company when I was doing a *Sugarfoot* episode. He was John Qualen, and he played the part of Muley in *The Grapes of Wrath*. Well, this particular episode of *Sugarfoot* I felt was one of my worst. I didn't like myself in it. I was very discouraged. The last day of shooting John Qualen came up to me and said, "John Ford would have liked you. He would have liked to work with you!" That was the best compliment I ever got.

H.F.   Did John Wayne make a great impression on you?

W.H.   The John Wayne movie I remember is *The Flying Tigers*. Of course that was during World War II and we were all so patriotic. I still like watching it. It was probably made on a shoestring but it had lots of quality to it. I have had arguments with people who don't think Wayne was a very good actor. I just say to them that they should watch one of his movies at home sometime, and when he reads a line of dialogue, to say it right after him. Then see if you could say it half as good as he did. I would also remind them that John Ford is considered by a lot of people to be the greatest American director and look at all the pictures that he put him in. And Ford never messed around with mediocrity.

H.F.   After college what did you do?

W.H.   Toward the end of the Korean War I tried to get into the Navy or the Air Force, but it was too late. I didn't want the Army because I really didn't think we were trying to win that war. So I got a job as a bus boy in a cafeteria about a block from where I lived, and was a bus boy until I got drafted.

H.F.   So you ended up in the Army after all?

W.H.   Yes, and luckily I had a great time in the Army. I got into the Signal Corps and got to spend some time in San Francisco at Fort Mason. I loved it up there. It was beautiful. I had never been to San Francisco before, and spent lots of time there just walking around at night. The only trouble is that it was where they shipped the troops off to Korea, so I was a little skittish. One day a guy said to me, "Do you want to go to Paris?" I said, "Sure!" It seemed they needed a guy to go to Paris. A lot of the guys were a little square and did not seem too enthusiastic by it. I said, "That's for me!" So I volunteered and got sent to Paris and I had one of the greatest times in my life in The Signal Corps doing cryptography. I got to see a lot of Paris. I loved it so much that at the end of my two-year hitch, I was ready to re-enlist. But I heard they were going to send us all to Germany. I had already been to Germany, and even in the late fifties, things were in bad shape there. Most of the cities were still bombed out. They hadn't built things up yet. I didn't want to go to Germany, so I decided to take my chances and go back home.

H.F.   Did you go right into acting?

W.H.   I went to Graduate School at UCLA on the GI Bill. I took a course in cinematography. We had some great teachers there. One of those teachers was the great director, Jean Renoir. Another was Arthur Ripely who directed some of the W. C. Fields and Mack Sennett comedies like *The Barber Shop* and *The Pharmacist*. He also directed Harry Langdon and worked with Frank Capra. He wrote *The Strong Man* which I think was Harry Langdon's best movie. He was a wonderful teacher. He thought I was good and gave me lots of encouragement.

H.F.   How did the professional career begin, Will?

W.H.   Well, I was at UCLA and they did an all-points bulletin for college kids to try out for *Matinee Theater* at NBC. It was a live show with a different story every day. It was coast to coast — no taping. So I went over there more interested in film editing than acting. But one of my friends talked me into trying out. I had been tired from working all day, and when we got there there were hundreds of kids trying out for parts. So I crawled under the piano and fell asleep. When it got down to the last few people they woke me up. I remembered from my days in speech tournaments in high school that you had a better chance of winning, because the judges would wait until all the contestants were through before they would really do the scoring. And if you were fresh in their memory, they would tend to give you a higher score. Since I was the last guy to try out, it helped me a lot and I got the lead. In my first venture I played the murderer. I was a college kid who was a psychopath. I did four of those and Warner Brothers saw me and signed me to a contract. So I was at Warner for five years.

H.F.   You made some films for Warner Brothers?

W.H.   Oh, yes! I made a lot of films. I was there from 1956-1961. The first thing I did was *Lafayette Escadrille*. That was William Wellman's story about himself and his buddies in World War I. I think it was unique because William Wellman Jr. played his dad in that one. And his dad directed it. I think this was the first time that happened. Jody McCrea was in it. He was Joel McCrea's son. Clint Eastwood and David Janssen were in it too.

H.F.   So you worked with Clint Eastwood early on?

W.H.   He was not under contract at Warners. I even had billing over him. That is how times have changed. We went up to Santa Maria, California, and used the same airport they used in *Spirit of St. Louis*. Getting back to Clint, he was a very quiet guy in those days. He and David Janssen were roommates. I was kind of the comedian in the movie. William Wellman really took a shine to me. He called me up one evening and said he would give me a lot more in the picture to do. He used to call me Shelly because I had a real mop of blond hair. My hair was pretty wild and reminded him of Shelly Winters' hair. It was a real treat, one of the truly great directors William Wellman taking a shine to me. Marcel Dalio, one of the great French character actors, played our drill sergeant. What a thrill for me.

H.F.   If Clint Eastwood and David Janssen were not big stars yet, who played the lead?

W.H.   Tab Hunter had the lead role. He didn't seem to be too happy at Warners. Then I didn't think anyone was. He was a very good looking guy. In fact when I was in the film I had blond hair too, because when I was in *Matinee Theater* they bleached my hair blond to play Gene Raymond's son.

H.F.   What other films did you do at Warners?

W.H.   I was in *No Time for Sergeants*. I played the pilot of the plane that got lost toward the end of the movie. Jamie Farr who gained fame in *M*A*S*H* was my copilot in the film. Actually I did a scene from *No Time for Sergeants* for my screen test. Warner Brothers actually wanted me to play the lead role because it would have saved them a lot of money. But Mervyn LeRoy would have none of that. They used Andy Griffith.

H.F.   This was a young Andy Griffith. What do you recall about him?

W.H.   He was an easy-going, friendly guy. I'd see him at certain times after the filming, and he'd always say "Hello." He was a very talented guy.

H.F.   Did they keep you quite busy when you were under contract at Warner Brothers?

W.H.   What they did was to let you do test scenes when you were not specifically working on a film, and they wanted to keep you working. I did a test scene for Jimmy Stewart in *Spirit of St. Louis*. I played him going down Fifth Avenue in the ticker tape parade. This allowed the studio to test the back screen projection and everything. I did a test scene for Robert Mitchum testing as one of his sons in *The Sundowners*. They gave it to Michael Anderson Jr. I tested for Clint Walker in *Yellowstone Kelly*. That was kind of fun. Gordon Douglas directed those great scenes and he was fun to work with. He was also one of the very nice guys I ever worked for. I guess his big film was *Them*, the film about the giant ants.

I also did *Bombers B-52*. But that was kind of disappointing for me. They were going to use Jimmy Cagney. That guy is like a god to me. He might have been the best of them all. During his career he did every and any part And not only did he never give a bad performance, I've never seen him do a bad scene. He was always perfect. He was just great. He was going to be the lead and then he didn't do it. However, they brought in Karl Malden who is not the most exciting actor in the world in my opinion, especially when you were hoping to get Jimmy Cagney. It was directed by Gordon Douglas and I had only a small part. But I had a lot of fun. I had to yell, "Sir! The plane is on fire!" and we all had to bail out. Of course it was all done on the sound stage, so after we crashed all the B-52 rocks, as we called them at Warners, we scrambled around after the crash; these giant paper mache rocks just scrambled and broke. So any time we'd shoot in the back lots, especially the westerns back then, we'd say, "We will meet you out at the B-52 rocks" because that is what they were originally.

H.F.   How did you start with *Sugarfoot*?

W.H.   Well I did a series for Warners called *Conflict*. It was an anthology series that alternated with *Cheyenne*. *Cheyenne* was the first big hit Warner Brothers ever had.

H.F. It made Clint Walker a star!

W.H. Clint was the guy who put Warner Brothers on the map in the TV division. *Conflict* was the alternating show. It had all kinds of stories. They used Natalie Wood, Tab Hunter, all the contract players at Warners. I got the lead in the first one I did. It was called *The Magic Brew*. It was with Jim Backus and was about a traveling medicine show. They come to this rural pass and I am the farmer. I fall in love with his daughter, and I want to go off to join the medicine show. But I realize that the country needs farmers, so I stayed behind and they went off.

H.F. And *Sugarfoot* grew out of that series?

W.H. I played in three or four episodes of *Conflict*, and I always played kind of a rural character. The next year they didn't have *Conflict* any more. They had *Cheyenne* and *Sugarfoot*. I guess *Conflict* was a little higher budget. Jack Warner was interested in saving money, I think.

H.F. Did they write the Tom Brewster character in *Sugarfoot* with you in mind?

W.H. No, because it was based on *The Boy from Oklahoma* which was a Will Rogers movie. It was similar to *Destry Rides Again*. So they rewrote the script, shortened it to an hour, used a lot of scenes from the original, and that is how *Sugarfoot* came about. I was already at Warner Brothers under contract doing these country bumpkin kind of parts. So the two factors just melded.

H.F. It was quite a successful series. What do you recall about making *Sugarfoot*?

W.H. I remember the first year was great because they put a lot of money into it. But then they started expanding their television division and brought in a lot of new shows. Consequently they spent less and less money on *Sugarfoot*. That's why Clint Walker took a hike for a couple of years. They started to cut down his budget too and he hated it. So did I. It really hurt your feelings because the show wasn't as good as it could be.

H.F. Was that because of the quality of the writing?

W.H. They had excellent writers the first year. I'm not saying the others were not good writers, but some of the scripts were not suited for me. They were like discards for other shows like *Cheyenne*. So I found myself miscast in my own show sometimes.

H.F. Are you saying that you were miscast as Tom Brewster?

W.H. Yes! Very often I was. It was disheartening. Sometimes though they would hit a winner.

H.F. But you seemed to fit the role so perfectly!

W.H. Well, *Sugarfoot* was unique. Like my wife says, he was the Shirley Temple of cowboys. What made *Sugarfoot* unique was the comedy we had there. It wasn't tongue-in-cheek or verbal, there was a lot of visual stuff, like my love for Harold Lloyd. I tried to insert as much of his spirit into the show as I could.

H.F. Were you paid well?

W.H. It suited me. We bought a house and lived nicely. But then it was nothing like we should have been paid. We also should have shared in the money when we did personal appearances, but they didn't share it with us. They could be pretty cheap.

H.F. Kelo Henderson who did *Twenty-six Men* helped you with your gun work, I heard.

W.H. When the show was sold, I went over to see Kelo at his house. He taught me a lot of roping tricks, and taught me a lot of fast draw stuff. Kelo was terrific with the guns and has always been a very nice guy.

H.F. And the series lasted for four years?

W.H. Yes, from 1957 to 1961. The ratings were pretty good. But after *Cheyenne* left, they brought in *Bronco* with Ty Hardin. Ty and I alternated for two years and then *Cheyenne* came back. Then the whole thing became *The Cheyenne Show* with *Sugarfoot* and *Bronco*. We didn't do as many shows the last year. Then I left and it became *Cheyenne* and *Bronco*. The whole TV department started to fall flat.

H.F. What happened when you left the show?

W.H. Right after *Sugarfoot*, I did a play in Hollywood that ran about six months. That led to the play I mentioned earlier with ZaSu Pitts. Then I did *Mister Roberts* with Hugh O'Brien and Vincent Gardenia. I played Ensign Pulver. We did it all over the East and I loved it. Since I was out East I tried out for *It's Never Too Late* and got the Orson Bean part. I played that all over the country in the National Company with William Bendix and Nancy Carroll. When that closed they had me come back to New York and replace Orson Bean on Broadway. I did it there with Dennis O'Keefe and Martha Scott. Remember, too, that it was Martha Scott who won an Oscar nomination as Emily in *Our Town*. It had been her first picture. That's also how I met my wife Babs.

H.F. How did that happen?

W.H. She came to see the play one afternoon in 1964. We've only been married for six years, but we have known each other for thirty years. We both had gotten married to other people. When we met she had just graduated from high school and we started keeping in touch. It's an interesting story, would you like to hear it?

H.F. Sure!

W.H. Well, she came to see the play with her girlfriend. Her girlfriend liked me more than she did. But her girlfriend was very shy, something Babs never was. She came up to me and said, "Hello, Mr. Hutchins!" I said, "Just call me Will!" She told me her name was Barbara Torres and she was a "natural thespian." Well, I got married in 1965 and Babs said it would never last. She was right! It never did. It lasted three years.

H.F. Was your first wife in show business?

W.H. No she wasn't, but her sister was. She still is. She's Carol Burnett. We have one daughter, Jennifer. She'll be twenty-nine this year.

H.F. You went on to make two pretty good pictures in the sixties, one with Jack Nicholson and one with Elvis Presley!

W.H. As I said, I got married in 1965 after *It's Never Too Late*, and we went to Nassau on our honeymoon. When I was there, I got a phone call that they wanted me to do this movie, *The Shooting*. I was a pal with Jack Nicholson. We had hung around the Hollywood scene together. I was also pals with Warren Oates. Both Warren and Millie Perkins were also in the picture. The same woman wrote it who wrote *Five Easy Pieces*, for Jack. Her name was Carol Eastman, but she used the name Adrienne Joyce for *The Shooting*. So our honeymoon continued in Utah. My wife came along and we did it in three weeks. We could have shot it in two but it rained. It's a cult film now, a very strange western, very strange.

H.F. How do you recall Jack Nicholson in those days, and did you recognize immediately the extent of his talent?

W.H. Well, he was nice and easy-going then. A funny guy, very funny and very smart. He was very intelligent too. But all that great talent wasn't obvious to me back then. But he was a good actor to work with. When I saw him in *Easy Rider*, I got the inkling of how good he really was. The film *The Shooting* was a lot of fun to work on, very strenuous. The director made us do everything over and over again. The director was Monte Hellman. It was very hard dialogue to memorize. It was written in a strange poetic vernacular, and I've never seen that kind of role again.

H.F. You did so much work. Any favorite part?

W.H. I liked doing Dagwood Bumstead in the *Blondie* series. I liked the *Sugarfoot* shows that were funny. I like the *Canary Kid* episodes. I liked working on *Clambake* with Elvis Presley. Not because I was so great in it, but because the director let us go crazy and we made up a lot of stuff that wasn't in the script. It was like the way movies used to be made, when you don't follow the script word for word. It was really exciting working that way, and Elvis was terrific at it too.

H.F.   How did the critics like it?

W.H.   Well, a lot of critics put it down. But Tom Hanks speaks highly of it and I believe Tom Hanks more than I believe the critics.

H.F.   What do you recall about working with Elvis?

W.H.   Well, I wasn't much of an Elvis fan in those days. I had my own taste in music. I grew up in the Big Band and Jazz era. So I always liked jazz. I wasn't much for country in those days. I have changed my tastes and have broadened since then. Now I can appreciate how really good a singer he was. In the movies it was just fun working with him. He'd toss the songs off. He was really a very good dancer. He'd pick up everything very quickly. He'd do everything in one take. He was a natural, a real talent.

H.F.   So many great talents like Elvis end up blowing their lives on drugs and alcohol. Any feelings as to why?

W.H.   I'm not that sure. I think a lot comes from fear. We go to a religious science church sometimes. And one thing I've learned is that you either come out of love, or you come out of fear. Hate comes out of fear. You make so many wrong turns in life because you are just scared. Looking back, it seems to me that he was a little depressed because the Beatles had come along and changed the whole sound of music. I think that bothered him. I asked him who his favorite singer was and he said Tom Jones. Of course, Tom Jones imitated Elvis and the Beatles didn't.

H.F.   That's when he started performing in Las Vegas.

W.H.   I think that recharged him. He started to perform in public again. I remember one day we shot a scene from *Clambake*. It was about the first scene in the movie, and we shot it in a gas station in the San Fernando Valley. Not much of a crowd showed up. I was surprised. I expected a lot more.

H.F.   It's the late sixties and things are starting to change, particularly in the movies. How do you see this era?

W.H.   I grew up in the censorship days and everyone talks about how awful that was. But in a lot of ways it was good because you had to use your imagination more. They couldn't spell everything out. I'm glad that I never got to see Katharine Hepburn naked or Lauren Bacall naked. I can't believe that all the big stars are taking their clothes off now. Its getting to be a cliché.

A lot of old timers won't even use bad language on the screen. We grew up with more rules, and I think we followed them. We learned a lot from the movies. Now there are no holds barred. It's harder for kids to develop some code from going to the movies.

H.F. Some of the great westerns, Will! How about *High Noon*?

W.H. I was not that crazy about *High Noon*. I didn't like it much. It didn't get me. I heard that John Wayne didn't like it. That's why he made *Rio Bravo*. He didn't like the western townspeople portrayed as a bunch of cowards. Personally, I'm not the biggest Fred Zinnemann fan. I don't think he knew how to direct a western that well. The rhythms were all wrong. In fact, story has it that it was a flop originally. They edited it and added music. That's what did it. But then no two people see things the same way. Yet, the fact that they re-edited it and added the music is common knowledge.

H.F. Tex Ritter sang the song in the film!

W.H. To this day, I think he did the best job on the song. As good as Frankie Laine was in the hit recording, Tex Ritter was a real cowboy, and nobody has sung it better.

H.F. You feel then that without the music the film would not have worked as well?

W.H. No, it wouldn't have. You have to have good music. John Ford always knew how to use music. He had music on the set to help get everybody in the mood.

H.F. Gary Cooper's performance was outstanding.

W.H. I thought he was ten times better in *The Westerner*. But Gary Cooper was a great actor. Stanislovsky said he was the best in the world. When someone reminded him that Cooper didn't use his method, Stanislovsky said, "He doesn't have to!" I think Gary Cooper in the thirties was the greatest.

H.F. But he won the Oscar for *High Noon*.

W.H. I know. I'm no longer a voting member of the Academy because my votes never come close to what wins. The last one I won on was Jack Palance in *City Slickers*. That's one I agreed on. And I don't think stars should accept Oscars for supporting roles. You see originally there weren't any supporting actor roles. I'm very strong on this point. Then they gave the award to supporting actors to help them in their careers. Originally I believe they gave them scrolls. After that they gave them a tiny Oscar. Then after that they gave them full-sized Oscars.

H.F. Walter Brennan won three Supporting Actor Awards. He was truly a supporting actor and a great one.

W.H. You're darn right! But if you get your name over the title, then to me you are no longer a supporting actor and you shouldn't compete in that category. At one time there was a demarcation point between actors and supporting actors. Later they let it go haywire and let you vote the way you want, and it became a big political thing. I don't like it.

H.F. You have always spoken about *Shane* with the greatest esteem?

W.H. I love the movie *Shane*. A lot of critics put it down now. It gets me angry. It is a marvelous movie. They put down George Stevens, and George Stevens made three of the greatest movies I'll ever see as long as I live. I don't know many directors who directed three giant movies like *Shane*, *A Place in the Sun*, and *Gunga Din*.

Getting back to *Shane*, I remember when I saw it I was in the Army. I was up in Fort Mason and it cost me twenty-five cents to see it on the base. I was always an Alan Ladd fan, and I think that is where his career should have been all the time. He had the talent and was always one of my heroes. I got to go to his house a few times and meet him. What a thrill for me. But he was a tragic character. You could tell it. He was a real sad guy. In fact, I saw him once when I was in high school. I always went to Griffith Park on my way home, and there he was on his horse. My friend was a big fan and just gulped. But I said, "Hi!" and he said, "Hi!" It gave me a thrill I'll never forget.

H.F. He was underrated as an actor, wasn't he?

W.H. Oh yes! He should have won the Oscar for *Shane*, and he wasn't even nominated. But he had left Paramount and they gave the Oscar to William Holden. Just ask anyone who knows anything about movies, *Shane*, or *Stalag 17*, which is the one that's going to last forever. *Stalag 17*, is just a good stage play made into a very good movie. Holden was good, but he had done a lot of better work. *Shane* is a classic. So is Alan Ladd's performance. I'd like to know what George Stevens did, because Ladd was never the same after that. Why couldn't other directors have gotten those same things out of him?

H.F. You are so knowledgeable and have seen so many westerns, can you pinpoint the two or three performances which best stand out in your mind?

W.H. Alan Ladd of course in *Shane*. Gary Cooper and Walter Brennan in *The Westerner*. I just loved Henry Fonda in *My Darling Clementine*. I love it more and more every time I see that picture. It's very subtle. He was also terrific in *The Return of Frank James*. He did a great scene in that one. It was directed by Fritz Lange, the fine German director. It is something people don't talk about, but I just happened to notice.

He had a scene where he was chasing the guy who killed his brother into the barn. He goes into the barn and it's dark. He's looking for the guy who killed his brother. The guy's finally dead when he finds him, but he doesn't know it. But he doesn't have the gun at the ready. He just has it calmly down on his side. I always thought it was terrific because so many directors always had me overdo things. They would have me holding the gun up too tense. But he was perfectly relaxed. I liked that a lot.

H.F.   And your favorite director?

W.H.   I want to stick up for George Stevens all I can because of these dumb critics nowadays who are putting him down. Pauline Keil is one; I've written blasting letters to her. There was a wonderful letter in *The New Yorker* recently by Norman Mailer. He really puts her down.

H.F.   A favorite director among those you worked with personally?

W.H.   Monte Pittman was my all time favorite. He was the one who created The Canary Kid Shows at Warner. He was a genius. Robert Altman was at Warner Brothers at the same time. And as good as he was, Monte Pittman was better. Monte died soon after I left Warner Brothers.

H.F.   Warren Douglas, who wrote for so many of the great western series, said you were just a natural for *Sugarfoot*. That Will Hutchins and Tom Brewster were totally compatible.

W.H.   That's nice to hear. Warren Douglas wrote the best *Sugarfoot* I was ever in. It was called *Apollo with a Gun*. If we had more scripts like that, the show could have been that good week-in and week-out.

H.F.   Can I throw a few names at you for comment?

W.H.   Sure!

H.F.   Ben Johnson.

W.H.   Oh yeah! He seems authentic. There is nothing phony about him. There is a sense of danger about him too. You don't want to mess with him.

H.F.   Hoot Gibson.

W.H.   I love his work now. At the time I was doing the show, I didn't know anything about him. Since then I have acquired some of his films and have seen him on television.

H.F.   Roy Rogers and Gene Autry.

W.H.   Oh, I have always been a big fan of theirs. You know Roy Rogers has adopted kids of every ethnic group. My wife is half Puerto Rican and when she was a little girl, she wrote Roy Rogers asking him if he would adopt her. I don't know if her mom and dad ever found out about that. All she got out of that was an eight by ten glossy [laughing]. I liked Gene Autry a little better than Roy, only because when I was a kid Gene was the "King of Cowboys." When the War came along he went off to the Air Force and that's when Roy took over. I always had a hankering for Gene.

H.F.   By the seventies the westerns had seen their popularity wane. What about your career?

W.H.   We get into the seventies and I'm sitting by the phone waiting for my agent to call me, which drove me nuts. I could get a job here and a job there, but I didn't like that. So I joined the circus and became a clown. I traveled around the West Coast with the circus, the mountain states and Pacific states. It was very hard work by the way.

The next year I became a ringmaster and traveled around the United States and Canada. I was in Boston at the Boston Gardens when I got a call to come out to Hollywood to do *Magnum Force*, one of the Dirty Harry films. So I flew all the way from Boston to Frisco. I paid my own air expenses and paid my own room and board for three days on *Magnum Force*. I was paid about $400. Then I went back to the circus in Boston. To this day I get residuals for *Magnum Force*. I played a cop and just a couple of weeks ago I got another residual from it.

H.F.   When the parts stopped coming in, was it tough emotionally?

W.H.   Just the natural phasing of events. That's how life works. It didn't bother me. I never believed my publicity anyhow. Then for four and a half years I worked as a clown in the city of LA. We put on shows for the city. It was the best job I ever had. But the thing that I was really proud of is that I formed a clown troupe out of actors: Bob Shayne and David Arkin who gets top billing in Robert Altman's *Nashville*. I got them all to be clowns. Our best audiences were the poor kids, the black kids, the Mexican kids. We didn't talk. The whole forty minutes were just visual. I wish we could have taped it.

H.F.   Any film work recently, Will?

W.H.   Well I'm in *Maverick*, the motion picture with Mel Gibson, Jodie Foster and James Garner. I'm only in one scene, James Coburn's gambling boat. All the old cowboys are in that scene.

H.F.   Do you miss the acting game?

W.H.   Well, I might as well get a plug in for my video tape I did last year. It's called *TV's Western Heroes,* and it's put out by Good Times Video. It's doing great business all over the country. I've gotten letters from people all over. We did it at the Autry Museum and I hosted and narrated it. It has clips from all the old westerns.

H.F. *Sugarfoot* aside, what TV westerns did you enjoy most?

W.H. I liked Clint Walker a lot in *Cheyenne*. I got to be pretty friendly with John Lupton, so it was really a shock when I heard he had died. We see Robert Horton from time-to-time. He was one of Babs' heart throbs. We see George Montgomery from time-to-time too.

H.F. This has been great, Will. Thanks for sharing these many thoughts and stories with us!

W.H. Always good talking about the movies, particularly the westerns. Thank you!

13

Ben Johnson

Everybody in town is a better actor than I am, but none of them can play Ben Johnson as good as I can. I've been able to play Ben Johnson and make a living out of it.

For nearly fifty years Academy Award winner Ben Johnson has been an actor of compelling substance and merit. From the reluctant trail boss in John Ford's small scale 1950 masterpiece *Wagonmaster*, to his Oscar-winning performance in the highly-acclaimed 1971 film, *The Last Picture Show*, Ben Johnson has lent a special dignity and integrity to his roles.

Born in Foraker, Oklahoma, on June 13, 1919, his early rodeo work and superb horsemanship served him well in the movie industry. He came to Hollywood in the early 1940s, working mainly as a stuntman and a wrangler, before John Ford signed him for a series of westerns. Soon he became one of Ford's most appealing proteges, working as a stuntman in *Fort Apache*, then making his acting debut in *Three Godfathers* (1948), a slight but quite personal John Ford Film. A remake of an earlier silent work called *Marked Men*, *Three Godfathers* was made as a dedication to the great screen star Harry Carey who had died a year earlier, and starred John Wayne, Pedro Armendariz, and Harry Carey Jr. as "the Kid."

Johnson's first lead role was opposite Terry More in *Mighty Joe Young* (1949), a timeless fantasy about a cowboy hired to help transport a giant ape from his African home to the Hollywood stage. Next it was *She Wore a Yellow Ribbon*, arguably the most sentimental of all Ford westerns and the second in his cavalry trilogy. As Tyree, an ex–Confederate officer now scout in the Yankee cavalry, Johnson's air of authenticity was so apparent, that Ford cast him as the lead role in *Wagonmaster* the following year.

This fine film — Ford's personal favorite some say — is an old-fashioned and dignified homage to the pioneer spirit, replete with a series of beautiful images and traditional western songs, and is considered by many to be Ford's finest film. As Travis, the soft-spoken wagon master, Johnson, and Harry Carey Jr. lead a Mormon wagon train on its westward trek to Utah, encountering along the way, outlaws, hostile Indians, and errant nature. In the final fade-out,

Ben Johnson in *The Last Picture Show*

they reach "the promised land," and Johnson even manages to snag the affections of a pretty Joanne Dru as well.

Over the next three decades Ben Johnson would appear in some of the best-known westerns ever filmed: *Rio Grande, Shane, One-Eyed Jacks, The Wild Bunch, Junior Bonner, The Rare Breed, Major Dundee, Will Penny, Cheyenne Autumn, Chisum, The Train Robbers, The Sacketts, The Shadow Riders,* and *My Heroes Have Always Been Cowboys.*

"No one has ever looked better on a horse than Ben Johnson," says longtime friend and fellow actor Harry Carey Jr. His reputation as the finest horseman in the movie game was clearly recognized by everyone, including Gordon MacRae, who immediately turned to Ben Johnson to teach him to ride when MacRae landed the part of Curly in the hit musical *Oklahoma*.

In 1953, the same year he became World Rodeo Champion, Johnson was hand picked by Director George Stevens for the part of Chris Calloway in *Shane*. An immensely beautiful film, splendidly acted and stunningly photographed, Johnson again is near perfect as the ornery hired hand who makes the surprising transition from "bar room bully" to "unlikely hero" with typical ease. The barroom fight between Johnson and Alan Ladd (in the title role) remains one of the very best in American cinema.

Through these many years, Ben Johnson has amassed one of the most impressive records of any western film star and was recently enshrined in the Hollywood Walk of Fame. Like John Wayne, whom he has appeared with in six films, he has created a persona all his own. And like John Wayne, he can display different facets of this persona to fit a variety of roles, western and non-western alike. "He has that "Ben Johnson" technique and is a much more versatile actor than a lot of people realize," Harry Carey Jr. reminds us. "He is not a one dimensional artist. He can go many ways. For instance, he can play one of the scariest villains you can ever want to encounter but is all cowboy inside."

In *Dillinger* (1973), Johnson adds a menacing touch to the role of *G Man* Melvin Purvis. And in *Hustle* (1975) an exciting Burt Reynolds action caper with many fine character performances, he steals the screen as a distraught and disturbed father who is trying to come to terms with his daughter's violent death.

Ben Johnson is the last true western hero. Perhaps not in a historic sense, but certainly in a cinematic one. Like John Wayne again, his roles are emblematic of the past and a world which has long since disappeared. The film industry clearly acknowledged this fact in 1971 when Ben Johnson captured all the major awards — The New York Film Critics Award, the British Academy Award and a well-deserved Oscar as Best Supporting Actor for his riveting performance in *The Last Picture Show*.

And he can still rodeo. At age seventy-five he rides and ropes like a man forty years younger. Just ask the folks who saw him in Sonora, California, the past two autumns. He has done it all. From the carefree young man eager to ride, laugh and fight in those marvelous John Ford westerns, to his Oscar-winning role in *The Last Picture Show*, to his touching performance as an old rodeo star rescued from a retirement home by his son in *My Heroes Have Always Been Cowboys*, Ben Johnson has ridden the trail to film stardom with few stops. And along the way he managed to become something of a rarity in the picture business — a true screen icon.

I interviewed Ben Johnson in Sonora, California. That distinctive Oklahoma drawl and commanding presence are as real in person as they are on the screen. He spoke candidly about his career in film, his many roles, the directors and the stars, the movie business today and the future of the western film.

H.F.   Ben, you were born and raised in Oklahoma and made your way to California in the late thirties or early forties. How did that happen?

B.J.   Back in 1939, I was working on a cattle ranch in Oklahoma and Howard Hughes was making a movie with Jane Russell called *The Outlaw*. Hughes came to California to buy a carload of horses for the movie. They brought them off the ranch where I was working. I had shown them the horses and they hired me to bring the horses out to California. That's how I got there.

H.F. So it was Hughes who put you in the movies?

B.J. Yeah! I was a stunt man and wrangler for my first few years in the business. Then I went under contract with John Ford. I was with Ford for about six years and got to be in a lot of good movies with a lot of good people — Joel McCrea, Jimmy Stewart, Gary Cooper, Bill Elliott — a lot of the oldies.

H.F. Your father-in-law was Fats Jones?

B.J. That's right. Fats Jones was my wife's, Carol's, father. The Fats Jones Stables along with the Hudkins Bros. Stables were the two biggest suppliers of horseflesh back then. Fat's stable was way out in the northeast San Fernando Valley. In those days it was really considered to be out in the sticks.

H.F. You soon became part of John Ford's marvelous stock company? In *She Wore a Yellow Ribbon* you played John Wayne's scout, and boy, could you ride. Was that the first film you did for Ford?

B.J. Yeah! That was *Yellow Ribbon*. It was a good one all right. But the first film I did for John Ford was *Three Godfathers* with Duke, Pedro Armendariz and Dobe (Harry Carey Jr.). I also did *Rio Grande* and *Wagonmaster* around the same time. Dobe and I made quite a sensation with our Roman Riding in *Rio Grande* with young Claude Jarmon. Actually, Ford first really noticed me when he saw me double John Agar in *Fort Apache*. He turned to Duke and asked "Who's that kid doubling Johnny?" Duke told him I was married to Fats Jones' daughter.

H.F. How many films did you do with John Ford?

B.J. Golly, I don't know for sure. But really not that many. I did make a lot of movies though. You see, I was under contract with Ford so he'd loan me out to a lot of people. He made the money and I didn't make any (laughing). But after I got out from under that contract, I started making some money. I've been in more than three hundred movies over the years, a lot of good one — *Shane*, *The Wild Bunch*, *Dillinger*. Lots of good ones.

H.F. You worked with John Wayne quite a bit when you were with Ford!

B.J. Oh yeah! With Ford at first, then later with others. Ol' Duke, he was real good to me. He helped me a lot in the picture business. He was real good to work with. Anybody who would try, he'd put up with them. If they didn't work well they didn't last long.

H.F. You were an integral part of that John Ford troupe who worked together in lots of films — people like Ward Bond, Harry Carey Jr., Victor McLaglen, George O'Brien. Was there a special bond between all of you?

B.J. Oh yeah, we were all good friends. You had to be back then. If you weren't like I said, you didn't last long.

H.F. How good a director was Ford?

B.J. A very good director. He was kind of a mean old son of a buck. But it was like Duke said, "He's my son of a buck." If you listened to him, he was a good education. He was good for me. I learned a lot from him.

H.F. Ben, you're so totally natural in front of a camera. It's almost like Ben Johnson isn't playing a role. Yet you've played some wonderful parts which required fine acting.

B.J. That's where I've been so fortunate. I've been able to play Ben Johnson and make a living out of it. Everybody in town is a better actor than I am, but none of them can play Ben Johnson as good as I can. And fortunately, people accept my character. So, I'm lucky. I'm the only cowboy that ever won a world's championship in the rodeo and won an Oscar to boot. Like I was telling someone awhile ago, I don't know if that means anything at all, but it's a good conversation piece.

H.F. Watching your work in *Shane* is a real treat. Alan Ladd was just great, but you were also a standout as Chris Calloway, his adversary in the film.

B.J. Yeah! "Pig farmer," "sodipop," and all that.

H.F. As Chris you made the transition from the heavy to the hero particularly well.

B.J. I liked that role a lot. It was a good one.

H.F. That fight scene in Grafton's saloon between you and Alan Ladd. There has never been a better one.

B.J. Well, you're right. It was very good. But George (Stevens) took a lot of time with it. It took about seven days to do that fight scene and he shot it from every direction. Of course, Fred Guiol, our second unit director, had a lot to do with that too. He was a good director.

H.F. What about George Stevens?

B.J. Oh, him and I got along great. I thought he was a great guy. So was Fred Guiol. But getting back to George, he did *Giant*, and *The Greatest Story Ever Told*. Lots of fine pictures. He was so capable. He never rushed anything, not a script, not a scene, not anything. He took the time to get the meat out of it. So it made it pretty easy to work for him. I sure liked him.

H.F. How about Alan Ladd? He was quite an underrated actor. And he did just a superb job in *Shane*. In fact, Stevens himself called Ladd's performance one of the best by an American actor in a screen western.

B.J. Alan did a wonderful job. I'm the first tall guy that Alan Ladd ever let work in a scene with him. It was George Stevens that made him let me in there. What they did was build a platform up about yea high for Alan to work around on. And I'm down in this hole.

  H.F. Is that how the fight scene was filmed?

  B.J. That's right. That's how the fight scene went, and that's why it took so long to do. Because Alan is up on this platform and I'm down in this hole and we're looking eye to eye.

  H.F. "Sodbuster" and "sodipop!"

  B.J. Yeah [with a smile]. But really I liked Alan. He was a good actor. He was an underrated actor — a very underrated actor. Alan lived acting, but had some personal problems. He was very capable and a good friend of mine. I liked him a lot.

  H.F. There were so many fine performances in *Shane*, Van Heflin and Jean Arthur. But it's Jack Palance who really comes to mind.

  B.J. [Smiling] Yeah, yeah. He was so mean that he had everyone scared of him. As Wilson he was so bad that in one scene even the dog walks away from him.

  H.F. Then there was the kid, Brandon DeWilde! His was one of the great child performances ever.

  B.J. Well, that's kind of a sad affair. He died you know. He got on that old dope and stuff. It's sad. If they get out of the limelight for awhile, nobody pays any attention to them. They can't handle it.

  H.F. Too much, too soon!

  B.J. Too much too soon. My thinking has always been if you got something to do, you can survive the picture business pretty good. If you haven't, you don't survive it. First thing you know you'll be on the jug or be on something trying to ease the pain. I've always been so fortunate in having something else to do. I either did rodeo or I went hunting or fishing. There was always something else I could do.

  H.F. Did Stevens hand pick you for the part of Chris in *Shane*?

  B.J. Yes! And that was really a big deal for me because George Stevens was such a big man in the picture business. To have him say that I was the man to do Chris Calloway was a big honor for me. So I worked pretty hard on it. And if I say so myself, I think I did a good job.

  H.F. You did a hell of a job. Did you ever take acting lessons along the way?

  B.J. No, no! Never did!

H.F. Just drifted into it?

B.J. Just read the part and said, "How would Ben Johnson do it?" And fortunately they let me do it that way.

H.F. Did you know you had a real classic when you made *Shane*?

B.J. I did. I felt we did because everything about that thing was so real. It was made with a lot of integrity, and you had so much respect for some of those guys. Every individual had an individual role which was different. Like Palance, he was a terrible son of a bitch in the picture. And then mine. I was a terrible character at first, but wound up being a goody at the end. Stevens directed the film real well.

H.F. How does it feel to look back at the film today?

B.J. To give you an idea, when it hits the air now, it still plays as well as it did forty years ago. It was so real, it's just indelible. It stays with you. I was in it and I still like to watch it.

H.F. What about Sam Peckinpah and *The Wild Bunch*? The film can best be described as beautifully violent.

B.J. Peckinpah was different. He was a fatalist.

H.F. Yet the film had a folkloric quality all its own, and the cast was just tops. You and Warren Oates were outstanding as those wild and raucous Gorch Brothers.

B.J. Yep! I was old Tector. We had a lot of fun making the movie. Everyone was awfully good in it — William Holden, Robert Ryan, Ernest Borgnine, Robert Ryan, all of them.

H.F. What kind of director was Peckinpah?

B.J. He was a good director. Only thing was that he was so violent. He was very violent. I made *Junior Bonner* for him. Then I made *The Getaway*, with Steve McQueen. Like in *One-Eyed Jacks* I wasn't a very nice guy in that one.

H.F. That film too was very violent. Was this in his nature?

B.J. Yeah. It was. I think so. He was a fatalist all the way. He tried to kill himself for forty years before he ever got it done. Drinking that old whiskey and taking those pills and stuff like that.

H.F. In *The Last Picture Show* you put it all together. Sam the Lion was one of the most memorable movie roles in the past thirty years. Lots of people feel that way. You ran away with all the awards, including an Oscar for Best Supporting Actor.

B.J. That picture changed my whole life, you know. After I won that old Oscar everybody thought I knew something. I didn't know any more than I did before I won it, but they thought I did.

H.F. Did Peter Bogdanovich pick you especially for the role, like George Stevens did in *Shane*? It's safe to say that no one else could have done the part of Sam like Ben Johnson.

B.J. Actually it was his wife, Polly. She brought that picture together. She handled the wardrobe and called the shots. She did a great job. Also, John Ford encouraged me to do it. I didn't want to use all those dirty words at first, so they let me clean up my part of the script and I won all them. Awards anyway.

Actually, Peter Bogdanovich and his wife Polly showed up when Ford was making his last film *Cheyenne Autumn*. They were both pretty young then. Peter wanted to do an article on Ford for some big magazine. I was in that picture too. That was the first time I saw the two of them. Little did I know that a few years later this young couple would give me my greatest role, and I would win that ol' Oscar.

H.F. Did you know you had something special with that picture?

B.J. I really didn't know much about that until the first showing. Then everybody was so crazy about it that I thought that well, maybe it was that good. As I said, it changed my whole life.

H.F. When you look back at all the roles and all the pictures, which one sticks with you most?

B.J. Well, I don't know. I've done so many that I consider good movies and good characters. But I think *One-Eyed Jacks*, I think *Dillinger*, I think *Yellow Ribbon*, I think *Rio Grande* and *Wagonmaster*. The last two with John Wayne, *Train Robbers* and *Chisum*. And, of course, *Shane* and *Picture Show*. All of those characters in those pictures were good characters to play.

H.F. Who was the best director you worked with?

B.J. Oh, that would be tough. You've got to say John Ford, and you've got to say George Stevens. Then there's Peckinpah, and Bob Totten did a good job in *The Sacketts*.

H.F. What about that *Bonanza* remake which appeared on TV.

B.J. Well, it was cast with the offsprings of the old actors like Michael Landon Jr., and Hoss Jr. I'm Ben Cartwright's oldest and closest friend when he died, so he left me foreman of the Ponderosa. When I feel that these young people are capable of taking over the Ponderosa, then I die out and go fishing.

H.F.   The future of the western, Ben. Is it ever going to come back?

B.J.   No! I don't think it will ever come back to the magnitude it was. But if we can get things like *Bonanza* back on the screen, and get something real out there, and not having all those hippies running around using all their dirty words in front of our women and children, then we've got a chance.

H.F.   How do you feel when you see what the movie industry is today?

B.J.   It makes me mad. I don't like to see anyone getting up and using their dirty words in front of your family or my family. I stay in hot water a lot, because I cuss 'em out all the time. I don't like it. I'm old enough and have been around long enough to say what I want to, and I just don't like it. You know, as a youngster, I was lucky enough to have parents who taught me the real meaning of three words: "honesty," "realism," and "respect." I try to live by them.

H.F.   And you feel that strongly about what's coming out today?

B.J.   I sure do. You know if they're not capable of expressing themselves without using four-letter words, they ought to stay home. My version is that those kind of people didn't get the right kind of milk when they were little [laughing].

H.F.   Ben, thanks so much.

B.J.   You bet. Thank you!

14

Sue Ane Langdon

Westerns aren't really a woman's genre. They are almost always in the background, like Amanda (Blake) in Gunsmoke. It's an action medium. But I think it's a shame because there are so many wonderful stories about women of the west. It's hard to get the audience interested because they want it to be High Noon, *the shoot out, or whatever.*

Although she has done everything from Broadway musicals, to top flight movies such as *The Cheyenne Social Club*, to numerous TV shows, including a Golden Globe Award for the television series *Arnie*, Sue Ane Langdon is every bit a woman of the west.

The winner of the 1994 "Woman of Western Fame Award" at the Tuolumne County Wild West Film Fest, Sue Ane Langdon has appeared in such hit series as *Bonanza, Gunsmoke, Tales of Wells Fargo,* and *Wild, Wild West.* On the screen she has played opposite Jimmy Stewart, Henry Fonda, Glenn Ford, and Sean Connery. She has also been in two films directed by Gene Kelly, *The Cheyenne Social Club,* and *A Guide to a Married Man.*

Born in New Jersey, she spent her summers in Oregon. It was there that her love for the West began, a love which has lasted all her life. At an early age she learned to love horses, and has remained an accomplished horse woman. She has a natural flair for performing. While most of her roles have been in a comedy vein — she once appeared on the cover of *Life* with Jackie Gleason — there is a penetrating and serious side which illuminates any interview. She gives a penetrating account of the film and TV industry and an insight, professional and personal, to the great stars she has worked with — Jimmy Stewart, Henry Fonda, Gene Kelly, Glenn Ford, Sean Connery, Shirley Jones, Barbara Stanwyck, and Elvis Presley. Sue Ane Langdon and Jack Emrek, her husband of thirty-five years, continue to live in the Los Angeles area.

H.F.   Sue Ane, how did a girl from New Jersey evolve into a woman of the west?

S.A.L. Well, as you indicated I was born in New Jersey, but my mother and I moved around a lot. My mother was headed for an operatic career. When she had her chance to debut at the Met she was very pregnant with child. So she was unable to make her debut. I was born and my daddy died two years later. She sold everything and went to New York to continue with her career. However, she decided that was not the best way to raise a kid. So she received her masters degree at the University of Michigan. She never remarried and proceeded to become an instructor in voice. We moved around a lot according to where the jobs were — West Virginia, Iowa, Ohio, Connecticut, Texas, Idaho.

H.F. And you developed this love for the west along the way!

S.A.L. I did. We spent summers in Oregon and that's where I began my love of the West, and that love has lasted all my life. I live and dress western! We live on a ranch with horses and white board fences and our home is decorated totally western, even to the extent that I have the same furniture as one of the world's greatest "for real" cowboys, Will Rogers.

This furniture is called Monterey, crafted in the late twenties here in Los Angeles and is now antique and highly collectible. As a matter of fact many "cowboy" and other movie stars had it in their homes, such as Buck Jones, Gene Autry, Roy Rogers, Leo Carrillo, Rex Bell, Charles Bickford (we have some of his collection), Clark Gable, Edward G. Robinson, Valentino, Bela Lugosi, to mention a few. It was also used to furnish many "dude" ranches throughout the west.

H.F. When did you start riding?

S.A.L. I always had this thing for horses. I learned to ride well before I was ten. I had a horse in West Virginia named Sheik. I just loved that horse. Because mom moved around a lot as a teacher, we ended up in Kingsville, Texas. Mom taught at Texas A & I. The King ranch was there, the largest in the world. I had a second horse from the King Ranch named "Wishes Come True." It was a kid's dream to be around that kind of place. I finished high school there. I started college at North Texas State Teachers in Denton, Texas, for a little while. Then I went to the University of Idaho briefly, before deciding to go back to New York to pursue a career.

H.F. Had you actively pursued a show business career while you were growing up?

S.A.L. Well I did my first part when I was five in one of the musicals my mother was involved with in college. I was one of the kids in the show. I grew up around it. I think my mother pushed and encouraged me into show business. When I got to high school, I kept doing this all along. Lots of musicals and dramatic plays.

Sue Ane Langdon

H.F.   What happened when you got to New York?

S.A.L.   I went to all the auditions. In New York you could do that. They have a newspaper that prints all the auditions for the chorus, and replacements. My mother had been in the chorus at Radio City Music Hall. That's the first job I got, Radio City. I sang in a trio. We sang "Mr. Sandman." Then I did a little bit of stock and some Broadway shows.

H.F.   Remember your first Broadway musical?

S.A.L.   It was called *Ankles Away*. I understudied Jane Keane. Later we owned apartment buildings next door in West Hollywood. I was in a show called *Copper and Brass*. I got fired because Nancy Walker didn't like pretty ladies. There were no pretty ladies in the show. I did *Most Happy Fella*. I played Cleo both in stock and in the National Company in Washington, D.C. with Robert Weede and Art Lund. I used to stand in the wings and swoon over Art Lund's voice, and Weede's too.

In the late sixties, I went back to Broadway and starred in a show called *The Apple Tree* with Alan Alda and Hal Linden, and directed by Mike Nichols. In my four early years in New York, I actually did quite a bit. I did lots of TV: *The Bilko Show*, *The Perry Como Show*, *The Steve Allen Show*. I was with the Ray Charles Singers conducted by Nick Perito who is my neighbor now. He's still conducting for Perry.

H.F.   But you are still a few years away from westerns?

S.A.L.   Well kind of far. I got a job in Las Vegas at the Riviera. I was doing a comedy sketch with a comedian named Dickie Henderson. Jane Morgan was the headliner. One evening after the show, this guy named Jack had come to see Jane about doing a show in Hollywood. He had worked with her in Maine in summer stock. She introduced me to Jack Emrek. He came on pretty strong. He asked me out. I told him I'd go out with him if he wanted to get up early in the morning and go riding. Somewhere during our ride he said, "Come to Hollywood, I'll make you a star." He was a director. So when the show closed in Vegas I drove to Hollywood to meet Jack. He introduced me to his agent. Nothing much was going on then. It was Christmas. So I went back to New York. He kept calling and calling. He had his agent tell me there was a job for me. So I headed back to Hollywood. When I hung up the phone, the agent turned to Jack and said, "Now I have to get her a job, she's coming out."

H.F.   Did you get a job?

S.A.L.   I should say! He set up an interview. It was for a starring part opposite John Cassavetes in *The Lux Playhouse*. I got the part. Three months later, on April 4, Jack Emrek and I were married. Then I did *The Andy Griffith Show*, *Coronado Nine* which Bill Witney directed. I did lots of television, but I couldn't seem to land a western until I did *Bonanza*.

H.F.   What do you recall about the show?

S.A.L.   The first episode I did was great fun. I really enjoyed it. The second episode I did was kind of stupid. I think I enjoyed the first one because for starters it was written quite well. It was done with a lot of comedy, and I worked a lot with Dan Blocker. Then there is the fact that it was the first one. I had finally landed a western!

H.F.   Did you work with the entire *Bonanza* group?

S.A.L.   I worked with Lorne Greene, Dan Blocker and Michael Landon. Pernell Roberts was not in the show when I worked *Bonanza*.

H.F.   What do you recall of Lorne Greene?

S.A.L.   He was very professional and really a very nice person. I found him cooperative and congenial. He was a gentleman. I do remember that I really loved Dan Blocker. I just loved working with him.

H.F.   Was it difficult making that transition from sitcoms to westerns?

S.A.L.   Not really. I had been doing an awful lot of television. Things like *Bachelor Father*, *The Dick Van Dyke Show*, *Surfside 6* and *77 Sunset Strip*. Remember, too, I had been doing leading parts in Hollywood. So the transition was actually very easy. I came out here thinking I would do a lot of westerns. I had long hair. They could do a period style hairdo. I could shoot a gun.

I knew how to ride a horse. There was no problem at all changing over to westerns. They were mostly in a comedy vein too.

H.F.   Did you have any preference between the stage and movie/television?

S.A.L.   Well, I liked the stage because you get instant reaction. With film you are sitting and waiting for set ups. Unfortunately, the stage doesn't reach as many people and it doesn't pay as well. I think for performing, stage is the best show business there is.

H.F.   At this point was the work pretty steady with the westerns?

S.A.L.   No, it was off and on. Westerns are not really a woman's genre. They are almost always in the background, like Amanda Blake in *Gunsmoke*. It's an action medium. But I think it's a shame because there are so many wonderful stories about women of the west. It's hard to get the audience interested because they want it to be *High Noon*, the shoot out, or whatever.

At first I had this wonderful agent. He handled John Russell who did *The Lawman*. When he hung up the phone and said, "Now I have to get her a job," he meant it. He was really good and helped me out a lot. Then an agent could call directly to producers and directors, they still can, but now so much goes through casting people. Nowadays it's hard. The casting people have to know who you are and call for you directly.

H.F.   At what point did you start feeling that people really knew who you were?

S.A.L.   Maybe they got to know me a little more when Herschel Bernardi and I did a series called *Arnie* and I was given a Golden Globe Award. In Robert Taylor's *Detectives* I was a French girl. In *McHale's Navy* I was a Russian commander. I did the show *The Apple Tree* on Broadway and played four different people. I wore a lot of wigs and did different accents.

When I did *The Rounders* there was a stagehand on the show who didn't realize he worked with me in another picture. He didn't know I was the same person. So a lot of people didn't even realize they were seeing me because I did so much that was different. Some say that's the sign of a good actress. But it's not the sign of an identifiable personality. Nobody gets to know you because you don't identify as a type. I think a lot of directors and producers thought of me only in terms of the last production they saw me do. They did not realize that I could go in another direction, and that's been a problem in my career. They don't know the scope of your talent. If they saw you do a western, then they'd say, "She has a Texas accent. We can't use her because we need a girl who sounds like she comes from Brooklyn"— even though I used that accent as Billie Dawn in *Born Yesterday*.

H.F.   What you are saying then is that it is better that you have separate identity?

S.A.L.   Sure, but that is only if you have an identity that is workable. If you have an identity that nobody wants, then you are in trouble. I have a theory about acting that there is a certain scope that you can go. In other words you can go only so far. You are somewhat limited by the way you look, and the quality you project. Mine has been mostly the perky, light-hearted comedic roles. It doesn't mean I haven't done some dramatic roles. It doesn't mean I can't.

It's harder to be a heavy or dramatic actor and then try to do comedy, because comedy is much more difficult. You have to have a comedic ability or timing. A lot of dramatic actors don't have it. That's just the way it is. But most of the time a good comedian is a very good dramatic actor. That usually is just the way it seems to work. Except Chuck Connors. Remember he was *The Rifleman*. A stern guy, a real man's man. But Chuck had the most wild sense of humor. Just a crazy, loose guy. I think he could have played comedy very well.

H.F.   Did you ever do a part which you feel was beyond your given reach, as you say?

S.A.L.   The musical *Gypsy* was probably the most difficult reach for me. I'm not an Ethel Merman. I don't sing like that either. It was hard, and a little beyond my type. In a movie called *The Evictors,* I played an old woman in a wheel chair. This was when I was much younger. Again, I had a wig. It was a tough reach but one I handled well.

H.F.   You did some nice western movies.

S.A.L.   That's true and I really enjoyed doing them. But they were not like the old westerns. By the sixties the westerns were starting to wane.

H.F.   *The Cheyenne Social Club* comes to mind. It was quite a good picture with a wonderful cast.

S.A.L.   Yes it was, and Gene Kelly directed the film. But before I did *Cheyenne Social Club*, I had done another film Gene directed called *A Guide to a Married Man*, which has almost become a classic, so I had already worked with Gene before. But what an amazing group of people to work with in this business: Jimmy Stewart, Henry Fonda, Shirley Jones, and of course, Gene.

H.F.   What do you recall of Gene Kelly?

S.A.L.   We did a PA tour, Jimmy, Gene, and myself. It really was a wonderful opportunity because I got to know both of them well. Gene actually tried to get me to do the Shirley Jones part in *Social Club*. But Jimmy wanted Shirley in the role. He didn't think the role should be a perky brassy lady, but a more subdued one.

Gene is a fine comedy director. When we did *Cheyenne Social Club* we went up to Utah for the premier of it, and it was one of the funniest movies I have ever seen. The premier audience was rolling on the floor. It was so very, very funny. When I saw it the next time, something was missing. Gene told me it had been re-edited. It didn't fit the Jimmy Stewart image. It was still funny and still cute. But it was not as raucous, wild and funny as it had been before. More folksy — in the Jimmy Stewart tradition.

H.F. So the film which was premiered was not the same film that was released. Is that correct?

S.A.L. No! It had been tamed down, and I spoke to Gene about it later. I thought Gene did a wonderful job. It was still cute and charming, but it was certainly more funny the first time. It was not typical of a Jimmy Stewart film. Jimmy has that homespun humor and he is adorable. I so much liked working with him. Nevertheless the picture was charming and people enjoyed it.

H.F. You worked with Henry Fonda a couple of times?

S.A.L. Yes I did. I worked with him in *The Rounders* too. I didn't work opposite him as much as I did Glenn Ford. In *Cheyenne Social Club* it was more Henry. Henry was a fine performer. He was a little more distant than Jimmy. Jimmy loved to tell stories and jokes. Like Gene, Jimmy was loose. Henry was more subdued and quiet. I think part of it was that when we made *The Rounders* he was falling in love with Shirley, and all his concentration was on her. He'd go to the trailer after the scene, and wouldn't hang around. But I can't say enough about his professionalism.

H.F. It must have been great working with these very top people.

S.A.L. Oh, it was. Sean Connery is another I worked with. He's certainly one of the greats. It was the first thing he did after all the *James Bond*s. The film was *A Fine Madness*, with Joanne Woodward and Sean. The audience wasn't ready for this new image. He played a carpet cleaner who's a wild poet. It was such a far reach from the gallant James Bond. I did a crazy, wild segment with Sean and a foaming carpet cleaning machine, and we landed in *Playboy*! I also landed on the cover of *Life* with "The Great One," Jackie Gleason, when I did Alice in *The Honeymooners*.

H.F. You worked with Glenn Ford!

S.A.L. I really love Glenn. He's always been so very warm and kind to us. We've seen him socially since then. Peter Ford (Glenn's son) and Peter Fonda both came up when we were shooting *The Rounders*. Later I did a movie called *Hawken's Breed*. It was sort of a western and Jack Elam was in it. He's about as western as you get. He was a joy to work with — loved to joke — but it was a terrible movie.

H.F.   Glenn Ford is a fine actor. Audiences just took it for granted that he'd do good work. Yet, he never won an Oscar nomination.

S.A.L.   I think he is a fine actor, although I don't know about the Oscar nominations. He's gone through so much recently. I knew he drank but I never saw him loaded, but in later years he had big problems with that. But when I worked with him I thought he was wonderful. A very generous guy. We had a horse and he offered to let us keep it on his land in Malibu.

H.F.   Why do so many in the business seem to ruin their lives by drinking? Is it part of the show business terrain?

S.A.L.   I have no idea what drives anybody to drink. I think drinking can give you a feeling of confidence sometimes, and God knows people in this business need to feel confident. I would assume it gives you strength to do something, but it runs you down afterwards. I guess that's the same reason anyone drinks. But I don't know if there is any more of that in the entertainment industry than in any other industry. I think you just hear about it more.

H.F.   How about Shirley Jones? She's done so well in musicals and yet won her Oscar for strictly a dramatic part in *Elmer Gantry*.

S.A.L.   Shirley's a very sweet lady. I see her from time to time. She had a penchant for marrying kind of crazy guys. Jack Cassidy treated her pretty badly. She had quite a career, and she is a pretty and very warm lady.

H.F.   You made some movies with Elvis Presley!

S.A.L.   That's right. I did two films with Elvis, *Roustabout* and *Frankie and Johnny*. I haven't seen all the Elvis movies but I think *Frankie and Johnny* was one of the best movies he ever made. He had a good back-up cast. We were all excellent in it! It was colorful, he sang good, and he seemed to be relaxed in the movie. It was really a nice, cute movie. It had Harry Morgan and Donna Douglas.

H.F.   Your impressions of him?

S.A.L.   I think I did *Roustabout* first. At the time I found him to be a very sensitive guy. You didn't want to say anything to offend him. He always said, "Yes Sir!" or "No Sir!" He was brought up to be a polite southern boy. He liked to laugh and he always had that group of guys around him. He gave all the guys Harleys when we made the first movie. I think Barbara (Stanwyck) was too strong a lady for him. I loved her, but Elvis was very sensitive. I don't think she cared one way or the other about being in an Elvis picture. She did not try to hurt him or anything, but she didn't mince any punches.

It was really one of the very sad times in my life when I heard of his death. He was kind of scared to break out of his cocoon. But then again, it was a tremendous load he carried. I never realized what enormous magnetism he had until I went to Vegas and saw him on stage in person. He had a magnetism like other stage stars such as Merman or Gwen Verdon. Again, when I went backstage after the show he always had the guys around.

H.F.   Of the western films you have seen, which stand out?

S.A.L.   I really liked *Tombstone*, mainly because of Val Kilmer. I thought he was fantastic. I liked *Dances with Wolves*, even though I don't particularly care for Kevin Costner. I remember I liked *Shane*. Ben Johnson was in that too. He certainly has done a lot for an old cowboy. I also loved Hopalong Cassidy as a kid. "Hoppy" was one of my real favorites. I liked Roy Rogers and most everything with Gary Cooper — loved "Coop!"

H.F.   The industry today, Sue Ane?

S.A.L.   The business today is relatively impersonal. I don't think we grow to love any of our stars. They are not projected as lovable people for the most part. There are no charming men. There is far too much emphasis on violence. There is little warmth or innocence on the screen today and that is sad.

H.F.   Thanks so much, Sue Ane, for a great interview.

S.A.L.   Thanks, Herb!

15

Pierce Lyden

*When I look back I thank God I was typed as a badman,
because badmen could work all the time. Every picture had
a badman. You see them in all the pictures. But good guys
can only work as a star.*

Today they cheer him at western film festivals across the land. But in the golden age of the B western, he was booed and hooted each and every Saturday afternoon. Pierce Lyden is the elder statesman of the B western badmen, but a nicer guy you will never meet. Born in Nebraska, more than eighty years ago, Pierce Lyden began acting in high school and studied dramatic arts at the University of Nebraska. He began his professional career on the stage, then moved to Hollywood in 1932 when the advent of the talkies put a crimp in his stage career.

Raised on a ranch in Nebraska, Pierce Lyden brought to Hollywood all the tools of the western trade. He could ride, he could fight, he could handle guns and horses. He found his movie niche as a B western badman, and remained so for nearly thirty years. Working with the likes of Johnny Mack Brown, Hopalong Cassidy (Bill Boyd) and Wild Bill Elliott, Pierce Lyden's career represents a vintage slice of film history: those beautiful B westerns which lit up our Saturday afternoon screens, and a better bad buy there has never been.

In the following interview Pierce Lyden talks about his over sixty years in show business. He relates some little known facts and anecdotes about the film *Red River*, Howard Hawks 1948 classic western where he himself had a small part. "I was a darn good chess player and had lots of matches with Duke Wayne during the filming. I never won once." He also talks about his good friend, former stuntman turned actor, Richard Farnsworth, who according to Pierce, never did receive his proper due.

After his acting career was over, Lyden worked many years as both a stagehand and property manager for the Shipshead and Johnson Ice Follies. He also wrote a regular column for *Classic Images* magazine. Married for more than fifty years, he and his wife Hazel lived in Orange County, California.

Retired? Yes! but in his own words, "busier than ever." Pierce Lyden has also authored his own multi-volume work on the B western and his long career in film (edited by Mario DeMarco).

H.F.   You spent so many years wearing a black hat in western films, Pierce, do you regret being typecast as a badman in your film career, and how did badman casting begin?

P.L.   Well, I was working on the stage before I came to Hollywood in 1932. I starved to death for a couple of years until I found out that they had one Clark Gable and didn't need two. That's when I started making a living as a cowboy. Everybody was making westerns in those days, all of the studios. So it was easy to get a job. I was born and raised on a ranch in Nebraska. So it was easy to go back to it again. I knew how to ride. I could fight, I could handle guns and horses and everything.

I just played one too many badmen. Then all of a sudden I'm a badman and I'm a cowboy. Once Hollywood would type you, that's where you stayed. If you wanted to stay in Hollywood, you had to settle down and do what they wanted you to do. So I made the best of it. I spent nearly thirty years playing badmen and enjoyed every moment of it. I had a good time working with a lot of good people. It was lots of fun.

H.F.   Did you aspire to be an actor as a youngster?

P.L.   As I said earlier, I was on stage before I came to Hollywood. But I can't say that acting was always on my mind. I had a couple of plays in high school where I did the lead. There was this girl in high school who talked me into going to the university to study dramatic arts. I was working as a night operator on the railroads my last two years of high school. She talked me out of that, so I went down and studied in college for two years and worked my way through the University of Nebraska.

But things were tough in those days, so that after two years I had to quit. I got a job on the stage and that is how my acting career began. I stayed with it and became a leading man. That was during the era of the silent pictures. When the talkies came in during the 1930s, naturally there was no more work for stage actors. If you wanted to stay in the business, you had to go to Hollywood. That is what I did in 1932.

H.F.   You were typecast early on as you said. Would you have preferred it any other way?

P.L.   No! Not at all! When I look back I thank God I was typed as a badman, because badmen could work all the time. Every picture had a badman, and they moved around all over the west. You see them in all the pictures. But the good guys can only work one or two years. They could only work as a star.

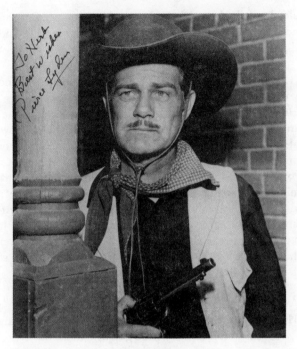

Pierce Lyden

I worked twenty-two times in a row with Johnny Mack Brown, and I could hit along ten or twelve pictures with Hopalong Cassidy. We could always double our work and do a few stunts for extra money. It turned out to be a great life and a great career. As a leading man I may have played a couple of roles and would have been washed up in a few years. That would have been it.

H.F. Any westerns you did particularly stand out in your mind?

P.L. I always liked to do the Johnny Mack Browns. And I liked to work with Bill Elliott. But to me the westerns were all alike except the one I did with John Wayne. I only worked with the Duke once. That was in *Red River*, and I enjoyed it very much. I think it was a very underrated western. It was a fine western.

H.F. Yes, it was. You mentioned Duke Wayne. What about Montgomery Clift? It was his first or second movie role.

P.L. That's right, it was. Clift was a New York actor. Howard Hawks had been in New York and had seen him in a stage show and liked him. Hawks wanted him to come to Hollywood, and of all things he put him in a western. Well, he had to be trained for everything. They were fortunate in getting a friend of mine, Richard Farnsworth. He looked just enough like Monty Clift so they could shoot all close-ups. He taught Montgomery Clift how to roll a cigarette and how to ride a horse. He made Montgomery Clift, and he should have played the part.

H.F.   He later became a fine actor. He did such an outstanding job in *The Grey Fox* in the early Eighties.

P.L.   He was also outstanding in *Comes a Horseman* with Jane Fonda and Jason Robards a few years earlier. But at the time Richard Farnsworth was a professional stunt man. He never thought he'd be an actor, although he did read lines once in a while. He had just about retired, then he got this part as *The Grey Fox*, and he was an overnight sensation — a real overnight sensation. He was nominated for an Oscar and I really thought he would get it. But someone else did. Richard was an old fishing buddy of mine. We went out in the ocean, sat and spit tobacco, and fished. We had a lot of fun together and did a lot of pictures together. He's a great guy. Gene Autry and I were the only cowboys who were there last year in Hollywood, when they put a star for him on the Walk of Fame. Richard Farnsworth now has a star there.

H.F.   What about Howard Hawks?

P.L.   He was producer and director of *Red River*. He was a great man, but I never got to know him. I was a little guy who made my living in B western pictures. I caught a break and had the opportunity to go there and play a scout in *Red River*. I was a scout for the wagon train, and when John Wayne tries to pull out I try to stop him. I didn't have too much, and what I did have was pulled out except for a couple of lines which are still in there. If you look fast, you can still find me in the prologue of *Red River*. I met Howard Hawks. We rehearsed a couple of times together with John Wayne, and I found him to be a very nice guy. After that it was back to my B westerns. Just rehearsing my lines dialogue with John Wayne was one of the great thrills of my life.

H.F.   When the heyday of the B western was over, what happened to your career?

P.L.   Well, I was still in good shape physically, but I didn't want to keep bucking the business when I couldn't make westerns. I spent five years trying to get a stage hand's card and finally did. I worked the theaters. Then I went down to Disneyland and worked there as a stagehand at the Horseshoe Theater for two years. Then I went on the road. I finished my working career on the road with Shipshead and Johnson's Ice Follies. I was their property manager. I took care of a million dollar show. That was a great career. I enjoyed it very much.

H.F.   You write a very nice column for *Classic Images*, a publication I am also associated with. How did that start?

P.L. Sam Rubin was the head of *CI* at the time, knew my work, and had read my books. He asked me to write something for him. When Rubin left I continued on with Bob King the present editor.

H.F. Any regrets in your career?

P.L. Wouldn't have it any other way. It was the greatest career in the world.

H.F. Are you fully retired now?

P.L. I am retired. But I am busier than I have ever been. My wife, Hazel, and I make a lot of these film festivals. Since we live in Orange County, we are in a good location.

H.F. All told, how many films do you estimate you were in?

P.L. Oh, I'd have to say almost four hundred movies. I also appeared on lots of television shows and serials, first as a free-lancer and then after signing with Columbia studios. Again, I never got the girl, I lost every fight, I played opposite Roy Rogers, Gene Autry and Hopalong Cassidy. I've been on the receiving end of punches thrown by Wild Bill Elliott and Sunset Carson. Lots of times I would wake up black and blue, but I worked all the time. I was never anything but a heavy and a bad guy. But I made a good living out of it.

16

Beth Marion

I never got close or knew any of my leading men real well, even though I was always the romantic lead. They were all nice people I recall. I didn't see the side of them that I heard others talk about.

For much of the 1930s, pretty Beth Marion was one of the B westerns premier leading ladies. During a period of six years she played the romantic interest to such slugging cowboys as Johnny Mack Brown, Buck Jones, Ken Maynard, Bob Steele and Kermit Maynard. Her career came to a sudden halt following her marriage to Cliff Lyons, one of the industry's leading stuntmen.

Born in the mid-west to a theatrical family, Beth Marion attended Northwestern University in Evanston, Illinois. She became part of a singing trio performing at the famed College Inn in Chicago and with Paul Whiteman at the Edgewater Beach Hotel along Chicago's lake front. When the singing trio broke up, Beth Marion performed on the stage before coming to Hollywood in 1934 at the age of twenty-two.

One of life's biggest surprises is how well she is still remembered by avid film buffs, since the advent of the western film festivals across the country. Although she has lost touch with many in the industry — each of her nine leading men are gone — she has renewed her friendship with Eleanor Stewart, another of the thirties western queens, and keeps in touch with Audrey Canutt, the widow of the great stuntman Yakima Canutt.

Married to her second husband for forty years now, Beth Marion lives in Jacksonville, Oregon. She is an accomplished artist and at the request of film historian Boyd Magers, Beth Marion has painted an oil portrait of herself, surrounded by her nine movie leading men.

H.F.   Beth, you were born into a theatrical family, weren't you?

B.M.   I certainly was. I was born in Clinton, Iowa, way back in 1912. My father and mother had a vaudeville act called *The Laborer*. I was traveling with them until I was five years old, so I literally came up in the trunk. My mother would put me in a drawer in some of the places.

But getting back to my mother, she had gone on the road when she was only eighteen years old. How she got permission from my grandma and grandpa, I don't know. She was with a Shakespearean Repertoire Company. She traveled in a stagecoach and all those things. She used to kid around and say she played Shakespeare to a bunch of blanket Indians.

My dad was a would be actor and formed the George Paul Company. That was my dad's name. But when they divorced, my mother decided she could not depend on that to make a living. She went to school and worked on other things, then became a secretary.

There is also an interesting sidelight to the story. I had a half brother whom I had not seen since he was a baby. It seems I was seeing the name George Paul on the *Today Show* credits. I wondered if it could possibly be my father's little boy. Well, I checked it out and he is the same person. Today he is the director of *20/20* with Barbara Walters and Hugh Downs. Previously he had been the director of *The Today Show* for many years.

H.F.   Did you have a fascination with movies as a youngster?

B.M.   Oh yes! With both the stage and the screen. I recall sending away for something called the *Blue Book of the Screen*. I sent in and got as many pictures of the stars as I could. When I grew up I always loved Ingrid Bergman. I would have loved to have met her, but I never did.

H.F.   You were also quite involved with the theater!

B.M.   Oh, always. I always had kind of the lead in our high school plays. Then I majored in speech and drama at Northwestern University. You see, my stepdad legally adopted me after my mother remarried. He was an attorney named Lloyd Heth and the two of us were very close. I didn't see too much of my own father once my parents were divorced.

I did some shows at Northwestern. Two other girls and myself had a trio. We called ourselves "The Coeds," and we sang at the Edgewater Beach Hotel with Paul Whiteman on College Night. We also sang at the famous College Inn at the Sherman House in downtown Chicago and at the Blackhawk Supper Club. In those days young women didn't travel on the road alone, so if we'd go to a place like the Wisconsin Dells to perform, our folks would come with us.

H.F.   And how did this lead to Hollywood?

B.M.   Well, our trio was singing on a matinee show on WBBM in Chicago, and I was modeling and doing some commercial photography around town. But the other girls weren't interested in the theater and entertaining any longer, so I came out to California when I was about twenty-two years old.

Beth Marion

H.F. Were you a little naive coming from the Midwest to Hollywood back then? In those days there was a real difference in the two cultures.

B.M. I think I was. I had a certain Midwest provincialism. I had a lot of sad things happen out there that I would have rather not have happened. For one thing I missed out on a real good screen test at MGM because of an agent.

H.F. Did you go right into westerns?

B.M. No, I didn't. I did some legitimate theater for Charlotte Greenwood for her Company Show. I did a comedy with Percy Kilbridge. We worked Chicago, New York, and lots of other places. I loved doing those. There really wasn't too much going on in New York then. Most of the dramatic plays were imports from England. When we were on location in Pennsylvania, I got a call to come in for a final reading of *Stage Door*, but I couldn't make it in time. That might have changed my career because the girl who got the part was Ginger Rogers.

H.F. But ultimately you became a western star. Did you have any background for this?

B.M. Nothing specific. What happened is that I returned to California and got hold of an agent. His name was Jimmy Stanley, and he started getting me in these western deals. I did two with every star I worked with. I worked with Johnny Mack Brown, Tom Tyler, Bob Steele, Ken Maynard, and a couple with his brother, Kermit. There was one man, George Houston, whom I really don't remember much at all. I've seen the pictures but I don't really remember him.

H.F.   Johnny Mack Brown was one of the best. What do you recall of him?

B.M.   Johnny Mack was a former all–American football star, and a very nice person. We did a movie together called *Between Men* which received some very nice reviews. It's also available on video. I remember it was my first movie. We did it up in Lone Pine, California, and worked twenty-four straight hours one day. That was before they had the Screen Actor's Guild. Bill Farnum was in that too. I think it was 1935.

Actually, I had no problems with any of the men I worked with. I did worry some when I went to work with Ken Maynard because I heard some real tall tales about him. He was kind of a wild one, the type that purposely shot out the lights there at Lone Pine and stuff like that. I also heard he was a bad womanizer so I worried quite a bit. But he was really very nice to me.

I never got close to or knew my leading men very well, even though I always had the romantic lead. The first film I did with Buck Jones called *Silver Spurs* I had the second lead. They were all nice people as I recall, although I didn't see the side of them that I heard others talk about.

H.F.   Then you married Cliff Lyons.

B.M.   That's right. I worked on these pictures until I married Cliff Lyons in 1938. Cliff was one of the movie industry's biggest stuntmen. He and Yak (Yakima Canutt) were at the top of the list. I was married to him for sixteen years, and tried to get away a number of times. He just didn't make a good husband. He was quite a heavy drinker. You had to be in those days, because most of those guys were drinkers. When I think of it, Cliff was probably an alcoholic and it wasn't an easy road.

Anyhow, once I married Cliff, my career was over because he was a very jealous person. Cliff Lyons was a very fine stuntman but a terrible father and husband. By that I mean he was mentally cruel, very mentally cruel. Boyd Magers recently suggested what my career may have been had I stayed in the industry. Sometimes I have to wonder too. But I always feel that things happen a certain way because they were meant to be.

H.F.   So your career just came to a halt in 1938?

B.M.   Yes, it did. I did nothing after that except have sixteen bad years. Then later I remarried a wonderful man and we've been married for forty years now.

H.F.   Obviously you had a very nice voice, did you sing at all in your western films?

B.M.   No, I didn't. But I do recall that Ken Maynard always wanted to play his fiddle in his movies. I was always the romantic lead, the good girl all the time, but I didn't sing. The thing is that I had a natural seat in the saddle. I learned to mount and to dismount. They cut the inserts down shorter and shorter because I didn't ride. But I'll say this, it remains a mystery to me that the B westerns have hung on so long. It's been years and I think the foreign market has helped the B western survive. They always enjoyed those films.

H.F.   Any westerns that you list among your favorites?

B.M.   To tell you the truth, I never cared much about westerns, even when I was making them. I don't favor them today either, Herb. I think it's due to Cliff. I just turned off to cowboys. I don't think the cowboys would like me too much for saying that, but then not very many of them are around any more. They were very much into this macho thing.

H.F.   But you did enjoy your work?

B.M.   Oh I enjoyed working, especially in the stock company. I would have liked to have done some comedy. I had a bit of a chance when I did one of the Tom Tyler westerns. Funny, once I did a reading for a drama coach at MGM and he complimented me because my emotions are very close to the surface and I could bring them up quickly. I get touched very easily by sentimentality.

H.F.   How did you feel about being a recognizable star?

B.M.   I never really thought so, but I guess I was. I just always enjoyed theater and acting. I went to Northwestern University with Eleanor Stewart. She came out to California to do some westerns. She and I saw each other at the Memphis Film Festival, and we keep in touch. She just got married again, and is having lots of fun.

H.F.   Tell us something about your paintings?

B.M.   I started painting about eight years ago, and today my art is my big thing. I recently did an oil painting of myself and all my leading men. Boyd Magers asked me to do it. All the leading men are on it: Johnny Mack, Buck Jones, Bob Steele, the Maynards, all of them. I'm quite proud of that painting.

H.F.   You've been sort of rediscovered after all these many years, how did this happen?

B.M.   It's a strange story. I had a fan in Michigan who finally located me. He had seen *Between Men* and some of my other movies and wanted to get in touch with me. He wrote to the Screen Actors Guild who wrote him back saying they didn't have any data on me. All they could tell him was I had married Cliff Lyons. So he wrote Cliff, but Cliff, of course, had passed away. Then the Screen Actors Guild sent the letter to Cliff's brother and he knew where I was. Well, he sent me the letter from Mr. Collins in Michigan. From then on I was in that so-called circle. I started getting fan mail galore. Then they started asking me to film festivals. It's been quite a while now.

H.F.   Are you surprised by all this attention?
B.M.   I'm surprised that people even know us now. It's been so long. Most all the men are gone. I guess I'm a survivor. But I've enjoyed all the shows we've been to. They even gave me the "Key to the City," in Raleigh.

H.F.   Thanks so much!
B.M.   Thank you, Herb!

17

Jan Merlin

I preferred doing westerns, because they are more natural. You didn't have to worry about make-up, and the stories always had an American moral. To work with people I had seen on the screen and idolized as a kid, was a wonderful experience.

Jan Merlin is just another one of the many nice guys who excelled when playing menacing heavies on the screen. An Emmy-winning actor and a writer, Merlin has appeared in fifteen hundred television shows, numerous films and two successful series, *Tom Corbett, Space Cadet*, and as the star of the ABC series *Rough Riders*.

Born and raised in New York City, Merlin joined the Navy in 1942. Acting as a career never really occurred to him until he became intrigued with the Japanese Theater, when he was part of the American Occupation Force following the destruction of Hiroshima.

Returning to New York he studied at The Playhouse School with another aspiring young actor named Eli Wallach. Soon he was doing Summer Stock which led to stints on the Broadway stage, where he debuted in *Mister Roberts*. Then came television and the role of Roger Manning in the series *Tom Corbett, Space Cadet*. Universal Pictures discovered him and soon twenty-six year old Merlin was off to Hollywood to do the film *Six Bridges to Cross* with Tony Curtis. The westerns soon became his calling, where more often than not he was cast as the villain. In the ensuing years he would work with Dale Robertson in *Day of Fury*, while he and Audie Murphy became close friends and worked together on many projects. In 1963, he appeared as the man behind all the masks in John Huston's taut thriller *The List of Adrian Messenger*.

I interviewed Jan Merlin at the Lone Pine Film Festival. He talks candidly about his foray into acting, his films and television series, his personal and professional friendship with war hero/movie star Audie Murphy, the state of the industry — especially western films — past and present, and his present career as a writer. His first novel, *Brocade*, was published in 1982.

Jan Merlin

H.F. Jan, you were born and raised in New York City where Broadway was king, but you never entertained any ideas of an acting career as a youngster!

J.M. No, not really. You see, I was born in an apartment which was in the basement section of a Russian Orthodox Church on the lower East Side. My mother and father were caretakers. In the back of our apartment was an auditorium with a stage. They would put on plays in their own language, and as a kid I would sit and watch those plays. But I never had any conception then of being an actor. I went to PS 15 in New York City and then to a church school for boys. I joined the Navy in 1942 intending to make it a career. I was in the South Pacific for four years, and that's where I got my first inclination for the entertainment industry.

H.F. How was that?

J.M. Well, we were the first group to go into Hiroshima after the Japanese surrender. We were fighting on Okinawa when the bombs were dropped to end the War. There was still some semblance of life going on in areas not totally destroyed. While I was there I saw some Japanese Theater. Each day I watched little children training to be actors. I realized that even in the midst of all this destruction, theater had a meaning to those people and I wanted to be a part of it.

When I got out of the Navy in 1946, I decided to make acting a career. I went back to New York and entered The Neighborhood Playhouse School of Theater. It was a fine school, and people like Martha Graham taught there. We had a heck of a class. Eli Wallach was one of our group. We were all characters, we were out of service, and here we were learning to act. Soon I was doing summer theater, and landed my first role on Broadway in *Mister Roberts*.

The show had been running on for six months at the Alvin Theater. The Director was Josh Logan and he was having a casting call for a new show he was going to do. The show he was casting for was the musical *South Pacific*. Well, I was up there on the stage with four or five other guys, when Josh Logan walked on the stage. He looked at me and announced that he had a young fellow playing in *Mister Roberts* who was about to leave the cast. He asked me which show I would rather be in, *Mister Roberts*, or *South Pacific*. I was just stunned. I looked at Mister Logan and said, "*Mister Roberts*, because I can't sing." So I replaced the kid in the play, and stayed with the production for two years.

Henry Fonda played *Mister Roberts* as he later did in the film, and David Wayne was Ensign Pulver. He was sensational. David then did the musical *Finian's Rainbow*, and every time he had to leave the cast briefly, they would ask me to replace him as Ensign Pulver. This was certainly far away from the heavies I later played in the movies.

H.F.   Your stage career was going so well, why did you leave?

J.M.   I left it to do a live television program called *Tom Corbett, Space Cadet*. I played Roger Manning in that and he was a troublemaker. It was a lot of fun and I stayed with it for three years.

Tom Corbett was in the days of live television and it was aired coast to coast. Roger Manning was kind of a cocky guy but he really wasn't a heavy. We went on the air with everyone just crazy because we were missing one of our actors. He wasn't dressed and we were trying to work without him. Well, we had this situation when Captain Strong was floating around in space. The guys wanted to go out and help him. Roger didn't want them to go out. He wanted to go back to the Space Academy to get some help. He had a long explanation to give. The cue was, "You mean you are going to leave Captain Strong out there to die." Then I'd go into this long explanation.

Well, we went on the air and here's Captain Strong floating around,. The actor playing Astro turned to me and said, "You mean you are going to leave Captain Strong out there to die!" Well, I just couldn't remember a word from my line, so I said, "Why not!" From that day on they wrote Roger Manning as a real stinker. That carried over. From that point people started thinking of him as one of those heavy nasties. *Tom Corbett* ran longer than I was with it. I was there about three and a half years, I think the show went five.

H.F.   How come you cut it short?

J.M.   I decided that I wanted to do some real acting. I was doing an off

Broadway production called *The Rope*, when somebody from Universal saw me and called me about doing a film called *Six Bridges to Cross* with Tony Curtis. I was signed to play a part of a sixteen-year old kid. I was twenty-six years old then but looked real young. We went to Boston to shoot that portion of the film, and when the character grew older they took me to the coast to finish the film.

H.F.   And that was your first taste of Hollywood!

J.M.   That's right! I came to Hollywood to finish the picture. I really thought that Hollywood was beautiful. The sunshine. The palm trees, everything. It was real clean at the time and wasn't crowded. I thought I could make a living here so I decided to stay. Once I started working, I worked every week as a free lance actor. Sometimes I worked two pictures at the same time. Most of the youngsters were good looking boys who were trying to be leading men. I was kind of a feisty guy who was always playing mean, nasty parts.

H.F.   What were some of your early roles?

J.M.   I was in *Six Bridges to Cross*. The second one was *Illegal* with Edward G. Robinson. Imagine that! As a kid I had seen him in *Little Caesar*, and here I was working with him in a picture. In the first scene, I was to pick him up and bring him to my boss. So we were rehearsing the first scene and I walked up to Mr. Robinson and put my gun under his nose and started to laugh. Well, Eddie looked at me and said, "What are you laughing at?" I said, "Geez, I never thought I'd be sticking up Little Caesar!" Well, he broke up. We were friends from then on. I worked with his son later on. His son was one of the soldiers in *Screaming Eagles*.

H.F.   Tell me about your work in western films.

J.M.   Well, I did a film called *Day of Fury* with Dale Robertson and Jock Mahoney. That's when I finally had to learn to ride a horse. Heck, in New York I didn't even have to know how to drive a car, no less ride a horse. But I did learn. I did *Guns of Diablo* with Charles Bronson and a young Kurt Russell. It was actually edited from two episodes of the TV series, *The Travels of Jamie McPheeters*.

Then I did a lot of work with Audie Murphy. We played in the TV series *Whispering Smith* together. He was usually the hero and I was the villain when we worked together. It was Audie who felt that maybe I couldn't play the heavy all the time. So in a film we did together called *Gunfight at Comanche Creek*, he insisted that I be cast as his best friend. So I got killed very early in the picture. I really preferred being the heavy. That way you lasted throughout the picture.

I preferred doing westerns though, because they were the most natural. You didn't have to worry about make-up and the stories always had an

American moral. It was also a pleasure because that is what I watched as a kid. To be in one and work with people I had idolized as a kid was so shocking and such a wonderful experience.

H.F.   Again, you are a very nice guy. Was it difficult to play the heavy? You could be real mean and nasty.

J.M.   On the contrary, it is really easier to play what you are not, then to play what you are. Because when you play what you are, you are really revealing yourself. It's difficult. You get embarrassed.

H.F.   But do you put a part of your real self into each role? Is there at least a bit of Jan Merlin in each role you play?

J.M.   Well, let's say I always play a facet of myself. I don't see how you can do it any other way.

H.F.   What was Audie Murphy like?

J.M.   Audie was a quiet guy. He knew what he wanted and what he wanted to do. I don't think he had any formal training. He knew his limitations and what worked for him. He didn't try to stretch himself beyond what he could do. The very first time we met he was playing the hero and I was playing the heavy. We hit it off immediately. We really liked each other and worked very well together.

Audie was a genuine war hero. The most decorated soldier of World War II. But he never discussed it with me. We both had the same reaction to the War. When we came home we just didn't want to talk about it. Actually, I was surprised when he made the film *From Hell and Back*, which was the story of his life and his wartime heroics. His death in a plane crash hit me very hard. It was a real shock. He had asked me to work with him in Texas. I was expecting to get together with him shortly.

H.F.   Can we talk now about *The List of Adrian Messenger*? It has been said that Kirk Douglas did not do all those roles, but that Jan Merlin was actually the guy behind all the masks?

J.M.   That was the only time that I did a part which was not me at all. And you are right. I was the guy behind the masks in *The List of Adrian Messenger*. Kirk Douglas did not do those roles as he would like people to think. It's no secret. John Huston has already revealed that. A lot of people know that I did it. A lot more have read it. Actually I worked on the whole thing almost from the beginning. I was a year inside the make-up, in the whole process of making up those different masks. Kirk Douglas did a couple of the scenes, and he did the ending when he took off the mask.

H.F.   How were you signed to do it?

J.M.   I was approached directly by the studio. They needed an actor who could do a variety of things and I had a good reputation. I also had a look that was a little similar to Kirk. Kirk has sort of a Slavic look as I do. I thought Kirk and I were going to get together, but we never did. I never had anything more to do with him after our initial meeting, so I never got to know him well. But looking back, I think the project was a big mistake.

H.F. Why do you say that? It was a showcase for your talent!

J.M. I tell you why. Because I was a hot actor then. I was working all the time. When I stepped into that it was kept a secret for almost a year. Nobody knew what I was doing or where I was. I could walk in and out of the studio, but I was in a mask.

H.F. Did you ever aspire to be a leading man, or were character roles more to your liking?

J.M. No! Really I didn't. I don't think leading parts were as interesting. The leading man only reacted to what the heavy did. As a big heavy, you could be all kinds of characters. You could be psychotic if you chose. You could play someone who appears very nice at first, and then come out totally evil due to the nature of the part. So overall I was most pleased to be known as a heavy for most of my career, because they were the most interesting parts.

Still there were films where I was not the heavy. I already mentioned *Gunfight at Comanche Creek* with Audie. Then in *Screaming Eagles*, I was a very nice lieutenant leading a bunch of guys during the Normandy Invasion. It was an unusual part for me because I never had the chance to do the leading man hero-type of role. Then in the series, *The Rough Riders*, I also had a chance to do that. The series lasted thirty-nine weeks.

H.F. What directors did you work with?

J.M. Oh, a lot of the old timers. Guys like George Wagoner, Bill Witney. I did several things with Bill. Also, I got to work with John Huston in *The List of Adrian Messenger*.

Huston was an interesting man. If you read the book, *White Hunter, Black Heart*, I don't mean the movie, but rather the book, you could almost predict what he was going to do the following day, depending on who he was deviling at the time. Because he was exactly like the book. It was a remarkable portrait of the man. When I made *Adrian Messenger,* he never got to see me in my face. I would get up in the morning and put on full make-up. When we broke at the end of the day, I'd go back to the make-up room and painfully take it off. It would take sometimes two or three hours. So I never got to see Mr. Huston in my own face.

H.F. Jan, let's look back. Who do you feel was the major western movie star?

J.M. John Wayne, without question! The Duke absolutely! Then, if you go back before him there was Hoot Gibson, Tom Mix, and people like that. But once John Wayne hit his stride, he dominated so thoroughly that he became an icon, and all the people who preceded him kind of get lost a bit, although we have great love and admiration for them. But John Wayne was a fine, fine actor. Films like *The Quiet Man*, and *Red River* which is my favorite. I thought he was fabulous.

H.F.   The future of the western! Is it coming back?

J.M.   It's coming back in a different form. We had almost the pure western story. Good guys and bad guys. When you went to the theater you knew how it was coming out. Audiences could have the myth unfold as they knew it. Today, they are getting so introspective and psychological that they don't even seem like real westerns anymore. The one difference now is that they are bringing different groups into the westerns. When we made *Rough Riders* we didn't have one black person in it. There were too many political pressures back then, and we didn't have the power to do so.

H.F.   Is it possible that there is a tendency now to revise too much? I mean to go over too far to the other extreme?

J.M.   Absolutely! In the attempt to do so, you are not only rewriting history, you are rewriting reality. That's not good. Today you would have trouble showing a Chinese who in the old days did laundry to make a living in the movies, do such a part. The same with other ethnic groups. This is silly. Don't destroy a movie because you think the part demeans you. It's only a part. It always seems to be the extremes that prevail. It's no good for movies.

H.F.   Your feelings toward the movie industry today?

J.M.   Almost comical. People get bored seeing shows because they look like recycled scripts. You keep seeing the same people over and over again. This is especially true in television. They go from one series to another series. And they recycle scripts from a third series to make a new series. It just does not work. It's dull. It's boring!

H.F.   Do you see a lot of films today?

J.M.   Very few. The good ones though are so good and so exciting that the impact is double.

H.F.   A couple of examples of those good films you mention?

J.M.   I liked *Unforgiven*. It had a reality about it. It was real, but yet the flavor was still right. It was a wonderful marriage of the old entertainment we had with what could be. I loved *Dances with Wolves*. The only problem I had was that Kevin Costner's voice did not match his character. I was shocked by the timbre of his voice. It didn't match his character and that bothered me. I loved what he did, but I wish he had a deeper voice.

There are a lot of good actors around, but they can't do much without a good script. But the caliber of the people brought into the industry don't have what they had before. Before the lives of the stars were kept so private that the public didn't know a hell of a lot about them. That was great, because that was the image you went to the theater to see. There was a mystery. It was like the old Greek Theater where a god came out of a cloud. Today these people think they have to tell you every little thing about them. In doing so they have lost their magic. I might add that the same thing is happening with the scripts. The scripts are becoming so commonplace that the next one is just like the one you were watching.

H.F.   Are things going to turn around?

J.M.   Never totally. I don't think so. There are less plays in New York than there ever was. The Golden Days of the 1940s and 1950s is over and the theater is dry. The Golden Age of motion pictures began to die when television blossomed. Originally the motion pictures did not want anything to do with television. Then they absorbed it and took it over. But in the process it lost that kind of attention to detail that existed in the studios that were building the stars. Making them grow into actors. Training them. That training does not seem to exist anymore.

The only trained actors anymore are not those who are often "trained" in college. Those drama classes are always saying the theater is art. The theater is show business! And, if it doesn't go at the box office, the actor better know that he is out of work. They get this idealized kind of training in school and colleges. The one thing Sanford Mizener said when we left the Neighborhood Theater was, "Forget everything I taught you and go out in the real world."

H.F.   What do you remember most about the films you watched when you were a young boy growing up in New York City?

J.M.   For one thing, the musicals of those days were marvelous. You were thrilled by the actors. During the Depression, the movies could grab the audience by the gut and take away the problems we were living. We may have been poor, but we could feel rich because we had magic. I used to have a nickel and I would take it to the store and sit on a box and watch a movie. The first movie I ever saw was Lon Chaney in *The Hunchback of Notre Dame*. I was so stunned by it. I would have loved to play that.

H.F.   And some of your favorite westerns, Jan?

J.M.   Well, I'd say *Stagecoach*, *Red River*, *Dances with Wolves*, because it was bringing us back to what westerns should be. Then there was no way you could beat those great B westerns you saw every Saturday at the movies. They were great entertainment. We saw what we wanted to see. They were absolutely fabulous. And I can't forget *The Searchers* and *Shane*. *Shane* was a wonderful movie. I just loved it.

H.F.   You go to a lot of these western film festivals. Are you surprised by their great popularity?

J.M.   I find it almost unbelievable that anybody really remembers. These are the real film buffs, and younger people who are watching the old movies. When they talk with you, you almost feel like you are back in the business. You are that young guy you used to be. It's kind of an advantage to still retain some of the youth. I've been lucky. I haven't changed as much as some of the others. It's amusing but sad.

H.F.   What are you doing these days, Jan?

J.M.   I write books. I wrote a book which was published in 1982 which dealt with occupied Japan. It's fiction, but actually based on what I experienced when I spent a year there after Hiroshima. I put together a book about the enormous prejudice the Japanese had against the children born from American servicemen.

H.F.   Thanks for a great interview and good luck!

18

John Mitchum

*I wrote "America, Why I Love Her" in just twenty minutes.
When you hobo across the country, when you walk across
half of it, you sleep in culverts, and you're a little kid of
fourteen, my God, it was awe inspiring. People who fly over
it in four hours have no idea what this country is like.*

He's an actor and an author, a songwriter, singer and poet. John Mitchum's
resume and credits could fill the pages of a Captain's log. As versatile as they
come, John Mitchum's life reflects the life he has lived and tasted. Like all fine
poets, he is not ashamed to share his feelings, the bittersweet and the hurtful,
the mirth and the magic. He is a masterful storyteller. His poetry, his stories
and his homespun presence, makes him a particular favorite at western film
festivals. An accomplished actor and westerner himself, at age seventy-five, he
recently won the celebrity fast draw contest at the Sonora Film Festival.

His movies are many, well over sixty in number. He has worked closely
with John Wayne on many projects, and with Clint Eastwood, where review-
ers lauded his performance in *The Enforcer*. He has worked with the likes of
Ernest Borgnine, Robert Taylor, Robert Ryan, and Charles Bronson. And with
Lee Marvin and Clint Eastwood again in the musical *Paint Your Wagon*. He
has also appeared in four movies with another Mitchum, a guy whom he likes
to call "Brother Bob." He has written the autobiographical book, aptly titled
Them Ornery Mitchum Boys, an anecdotal account of one of movie land's most
remarkable families.

His life-long love affair with music and singing is well-known. He sang
the classics with the Roger Wagner Chorale. He sang country western with
the late Ray Lanham, and has sung in nightclubs, state fairs and film festivals
across the land. Indeed, one would have to go a long way to hear a better rendition of the song "Amazing Grace" than hearing it done by John and Bonnie
Mitchum.

John Mitchum wrote the album John Wayne recited on RCA "America,
Why I Love Her." He wrote the stories the late Dan Blocker told on the RCA
album, "Our Land, Our Heritage." He sang his own songs backed up by a

John Mitchum

twenty-six piece symphony orchestra and the Ken Darby Choir. Mitchum is also busy putting together a video series of twenty-six segments called "Songs of History" for schools and television broadcast.

John Mitchum has appeared in hundreds of series episodes and more than sixty movies. He was honored in Sonora, California, in 1992 with its Wild West Supporting Actor Award. Mitchum, who now resides in Sonora with his wife, Bonnie, accepted the Award by interjecting some humor of his own. "I may have died in a lot of movies," he said after watching his demise recreated on a large video screen, "but at least I always did it well!"

Not surprising from a man who over his long career just seems to do everything so well. Few people can weave tales into such interesting yarns. His life has been interesting to the extreme. And in the following interview, John Mitchum shares many of those stories with us.

H.F.   John, I've read parts of your book and hope to finish it shortly. Is it true that early in life you wanted to be a concert and operatic singer, and really just drifted into films as an actor?

J.M.   That is very true. I did want to be an operatic singer, and was even studying music after the war. But I happened to be walking down Santa Monica

Boulevard, and an agent who had too much to drink tapped me on the shoulder, "Are you an actor?" he said. I replied, "No!" He asked me if I wanted to be one and I said, "Why not?" That's how my foray into acting started.

He took me up to a man named Frank Wisvar. He was a refugee from Germany who had made a film called *Maidens in Uniform*, which had been a big success in Germany before the War. He fled so he wouldn't be killed. He was doing a picture then called *The Prairie*, and he needed a big blustering fellow to play the youngest son. So he picked me. That was my first venture into pictures. About halfway through the picture he came up to me and said that he knew why my timing was so great. I asked him why. He replied that he found out that I had been a boxer. Actually, I had been boxing for years.

Frank Wisvar also did *The Fireside Theater* on television. He liked me well enough to hire me to do several shows for him. This was the late 1940s and early 1950s. I did several shows for him. Sometimes we did as many as three shows a week.

H.F.   So Frank Wisvar started you in the picture business. Was there anyone else along the way who really helped you along?

J.M.   Well I had a marvelous agent by the name of Bob Brandeis. He was absolutely the typical agent of fame. He smoked a big cigar and was very forward and aggressive. He never sent his "boys" as he called us out on interviews. He sent us to pick up scripts; he had already sold us. So it was a wonderful feeling to walk in and pick up your script and know you were going to start on Tuesday. Today you sit around for hours and wait and they say, "What have you done?" after you've already done hundreds of shows.

H.F.   Any acting lessons or drama workshops, John?

J.M.   No! I never had an acting lesson in my life. No, not at all. Like I said, I studied music and with that you should have a certain flair. I sang with the Roger Wagner Chorale for four years and Roger and I were very close friends. He hired me to be choral director for the Los Angeles Bureau of Music which I did for many years. He put me in charge of many youth choral divisions. So I learned a little artistry with Roger.

H.F.   Once you got interested in acting, did you have a particular bent for the westerns?

J.M.   No, not really. But I had some marvelous, marvelous experiences with people who were really good. In the early days I worked with Bud Osborne, Kermit Maynard, a consummate cowboy. Then I worked with Lenny Geer, one of the top stuntmen in the business. They are all gone now but they were sure good teachers.

H.F.   Any real riding experience before you began doing westerns?

J.M.   I'll tell you a funny story. I was on location on a serial. It was called

Perils of the Wilderness. Little Buddy Sherwood was the wrangler on the show. We were up in Big Bear Mountain, some nine thousand feet high. That is where we were shooting. He said to me, "John, I like you. So I'm going to tell you something. What the hell are you doing. You're getting on that horse and you ride him like a damn jockey." He said this because I was leaning forward like you see jockey's do.

Then he said, "Don't do that. Sit up straight, put your feet down in the stirrups, and act like you own that animal. He's yours. You are proud of him, and you are going to hang on to him and let him know who's the boss. You look like a monkey having sex with a watermelon," he said, laughing.

Well that shows you how well I rode. I learned that when you ride up in the mountains, don't feel too proud to hold on to that horse. If it gets rough, all cowboys hang on to the horse. If you are twenty miles away from home in the desert, and the horse stumbles and throws you, it is a long way back.

H.F.   John, you are clearly a man of the West, but actually you were born in the East!

J.M..   I was born in Bridgeport, Connecticut. My father was killed before I was born. My brother Bob is two years older than me, so because of that fact I had no father figure. My mother married again, but frankly, it was a disaster. He was an alcoholic and tried to kill her.

Years later though, she married the most marvelous stepfather a man could ever have. I was about nine or ten years old and she married an Englishman who was absolutely delightful. He did so many things, and did them so well. He sailed around the Horn about seven times on sail ships. When he was injured in Belgium during World War I, he recuperated and designed the observation balloons that the destroyers carried so they could see the submarine shadows. Later he became a spy for the British government, and barely escaped with his life during the first part of Hitler's failed attempt to take over Germany.

In World War II he pleaded to go back into the British Service. Churchill, however, knew his record and how bad he had been hurt. Churchill actually wrote him a letter saying the British Empire was in dreadful shape, but not so bad that they needed his services. Like I said, Churchill knew just how badly my stepfather had been hurt.

Then without telling us, he joined a Libyan freighter as a deck hand. With but two trips they recognized his abilities and made him the ship's first officer. With that under his belt, he joined the American Services as a ship's captain in the refrigerator barge. He made the Philippine invasion and the Okinawa invasion.

Now here's where I come into the picture. I was in an Army Boat Company during the War — the 361st Boat Company of Hawaii. All of a sudden I got a call to go to the main office. There was a major there, I was told, with all his gold braids who had put in for a leave for me. Of course that major was my stepdad.

"My boy, my boy," he was sobbing quietly, "I never thought I would see you again." When the other servicemen heard him they bought us drinks. Lots of drinks. So for a full week he went through that same routine. Well we had all the drinks we wanted and we didn't pay a nickel. He was a real character, but a wonderful man, and a great influence on me.

H.F.   Did you have an adventurous spirit from the time you were a young boy?

J.M.   Oh yes! Bob and I started hoboing when I was fourteen years old and he was sixteen. We rode the freights and hoboed to California. But he deserted me in Lake Charles, Louisiana, something which he denies.

There was big freight being made up in the morning and we got on it. It went about a mile or two miles an hour. It was a big thing — about one hundred and twenty cars. So I stopped at the water tank to get a drink of water, and as I pulled up from the water tank there was a thirty-eight in one eye and a forty-five in the other. There was the town constable and the railroad detective, each with a gun in his hand. They were both Cajuns. We were nervous and shaking.

"Don't move! Don't move!" they yelled. Bob said, "Come on, come on, they won't shoot." I stayed and he left. I finally found my way to California. I went about a thousand miles out of my direction. Well, I finally got to LA, where I promptly got arrested for "evading railroad fare." They had no juvenile halls then. So they put me in the drunk tanks with everyone else. There I was for three days. The little night judge simply said, "You are accused of evading railroad fare, are you guilty or not guilty! You are guilty! Three days!"

Well, I finally went down to Long Beach, California, where my sister lived. She had married a Navy corpsman. When I got there Brother Robert was taking a bath. And when I finally came in he said, "What kept you!"

H.F.   Any more freight trips along the way?

J.M.   I made another trip back east on the freights to see my grandmother, and came back the same way. Then I finished high school and got a job as a deck hand on small ships. The first ship I sailed on had been the camera ship they used on the film *Captains Courageous*. Talk about adventure. The cook was German and one time two of us went to a little beer bar. Three Mexicans came in, all wearing guns. All except the leader who, like Hopalong Cassidy, had a black outfit and two guns. Right off he started making derogatory comments about me, some real nasty things.

Well, in those days I really thought I could lick Joe Louis, so I punched him. Then I went over to him and said, "Get up!" He got up all right, and "bam" out came the two guns, hammers back, right in my eyes, not a smile on the man's face. He said, "Si!" Hmm, what to do, I thought!

So I slowly turned my back on him and stalked out of the Club Hollywood, never to return. Later I found out that he was known as "The Gypsy," and very famous in that area. He was the head "pistolere" for the governor of the province and two years later assassinated the governor. So as you can see, I was dealing with interesting folks. This was how my life had gone.

H.F.   Did you ever do any stage work, John?

J.M.   Yes I did. My wife has done a lot more, but I did quite a bit of stage work. I did a bit of everything you can do in the business.

H.F.   Once you began a career in the picture business, was there ever any doubt that this is what you wanted out of life?

J.M.   Let me answer this way. I'm just simply an entertainer, that's all! I felt at home with it. For me it's easy. It's just natural.

H.F.   Your poetry and your writing is excellent.

J.M.   That's nice of you to say. I've done a lot of poetry. For example, I wrote the only album that John Wayne ever recorded. I also wrote a book called *Them Ornery Mitchum Boys*. You can really find an awful lot of stuff about all of us.

H.F.   How did the John Wayne album originate, and how did you come to be associated with the Duke?

J.M.   Well, ours was a beautiful association. I worked with him way back in *Flying Leathernecks*. I didn't really know him too well back then, but we worked together for thirteen weeks on the picture. Later when we did *Chisum* down in Mexico, Forrest Tucker, who was also in the film, called me up and asked me to come down to his place in Durango. Forrest sang quite a bit, and mentioned that someone had written a song for him about Chicago which he didn't like. He said he was tired of doing the traditional and usual "Chicago, Chicago, That Wonderful Town" too.

He wanted me to hear the new song, and he could tell by my expression that I didn't like it. I told him I could write a much better song for him. So I went back and wrote him a song about Chicago. About four hours later I came back with it. He fell in love with it and used it everywhere. He said that he didn't know that I wrote. I replied that I did all the time.

Forrest asked to see some of my other stuff. So I recited a thing called "Why Are You Marching, Son!" for him. The next morning Tucker wheeled me in front of John Wayne who was playing checkers with my nephew, Christopher. He said, "Duke, listen to what Mitch just wrote." When I recited it there were tears in John's eyes. He was crying. So Tucker told Duke that if it meant so much to him, why doesn't he record it? So Duke just said, "I will!" Well, we had quite a time. We did the full album and Duke was marvelous, just marvelous!

H.F.　I played that album to my classes when I taught high school history.

J.M.　The truth is I wrote "America, Why I Love Her" in just twenty minutes. When you hobo across the country, walk across half of it, and sleep in little culverts when you are fourteen, just imagine what it felt to me to cross the Mississippi River for the first time. Imagine what it was like to see the Teton Mountains, the Rockies and the great American deserts. My God, it was right out of Zane Grey. It was awe inspiring to me. It still is. The people who fly over it in four hours have no idea what the country is like.

H.F.　You are obviously quite a patriot. How do you feel when you hear people constantly run down the country which you write about so beautifully. There has been a lot of that in the past thirty years.

J.M.　Well, that's the reason I wrote, "Why Are You Marching!" Actually, I wrote it because when my son was fourteen, he came in, put the newspaper down on the table and said, "Dad, you have to do something about this!" Now here I am in Van Nuys, California, and they are burning the American flag in New York City. So I wrote this:

> Why Are You Marching, Son?
> I really want to know.
> Is it because of Valley Forge, or perhaps the Alamo?
> Or of one if by land, or two if by sea.
> The trumpets call the will to be free.
> And what of the man who stood straight and tall.
> Who wept silent tears when we saw brave men fall.
> No matter, no difference, the Blue or the Gray.
> All were his brothers, and how often they'd play.

Now this kind of thing I feel very strongly about. And when I see these people who deride the country, I feel "my dear boy," or whoever the hell you are. Why don't you spend a few years in Guatemala, or Serbia, or Somalia? You might then have a fair idea of what you have. I feel strongly about this.

H.F.　You worked with John Wayne in *Chisum*. Were you in *The Train Robbers* too? And was Duke's presence just as strong in person as it was on the screen?

J.M.　I didn't do *The Train Robbers*. But I did *El Dorado* with him. I played the bartender. In *Chisum* I played a baddy. I got killed for my pains. As far as his great presence, very definitely! I'll put it this way. Someone once asked me if Duke really was the way he was personified. I said that I would tell him something about the man. If he tells you he is going to knock you on your ass, you better find a place to fall. He said what he meant.

H.F.   He matured beautifully as an actor too.

J.M.   Yes he did! Some people said he couldn't act. The hell he couldn't. His reacting was the best acting you ever saw. Of course he was a fine actor and a fine person. And he was a very sensitive man. This is a little insight into his sensitivity:

We were doing the recording on "Taps." The story of "Taps" is a beautiful story. It is how the two armies were so close together when they had a burial part. The Union soldiers would fire a volley over the dead. The Rebels would answer it with mortar fire and kill the burial party. So Colonel Butterfield, "Dan Butterfield," was a man of music as well as being a good soldier. He wrote out some notes for his bugler and said at our next funeral he should play this. Now on July 2, a cannoneer was killed and as they buried him you heard the strains of "Taps" for the first time.

So John Wayne comes in, and it has been almost a hundred years since that sound was born. He turns to me with tears in his eyes. "Mitch," he says, "aren't the people going to get mad at me for talking while they are playing that?" That's humility, my boy! Instead of saying, "I'm John Wayne, and I'm going to recite this," he questions whether people are going to be mad at him.

H.F.   During the Viet Nam war, he stood strong and took on the forces of dissent. He tackled those college kids and did a good job too.

J.M.   Well his idea was that if you were in a war, you are in a war to win it. And what's all this nonsense about appeasement?

H.F.   I have a couple of degrees in history, and I've asked that same question many times myself.

J.M.   Well, let me tell you another story. We were over at my brother's house one night, and Bob had a little too much to drink. My wife, Bonnie, had never seen him this way. At one point he had tears in his eyes, and told Bonnie that we Mitchum boys had to fight for everything we had. We don't fight to show off or to be tough. We fight to survive. So if we get into a fight we are going to win it, no matter how the hell we are going to do it. He was so intense about it that it made you back off a little bit. So that is how we feel about the whole thing.

H.F.   You worked with Clint Eastwood in some very good films!

J.M.   I worked with Clint in *Dirty Harry*, *Magnum Force*, and *The Enforcer*. I also did *The Outlaw Josey Wales*, *High Plains Drifter*, and *Paint Your Wagon* with Clint.

H.F.   Your work in *The Enforcer* received particularly good reviews. One critic lauded "A standout performance by John Mitchum."

J.M.   The thing is I played the same character in *Dirty Harry* and *Magnum Force,* too. I was Frank DiGeorgio, his partner. In *Dirty Harry* I was the one who couldn't climb the wall in Kezar Stadium. In *Magnum Force* I was the one who was up in the apartment house looking down at the pervert. I ran down to find that Mitch Ryan had been killed.

In *The Enforcer* I believe I got such good reviews because I was in control of the entire scene. I was in the warehouse, all the criminals were there, and I had my gun on them. Then when I get stabbed, I guess I played the death scene quite realistically. Quite frankly, the nurse at the hospital turned white when I was there. When they yelled "cut" after the death scene, she said she had been watching people die for twenty-four years, and this man "died! He died, really died!" Not all the spasms, and the grimacing and groping, yelling and screaming. "My God," she said. So I was quite flattered to die so realistically.

H.F.   Would you share your feeling about Clint Eastwood?

J.M.   Clint Eastwood is a complete motion picture entity. Not only as an actor and director, but as a total professional man. He's in control at all times. He doesn't go into anything halfway. He knows what he is doing. He never hovers over you, and is not superior whatsoever. He's just a perfect, perfect person to work with.

H.F.   How do you feel about his *Unforgiven?* There is some controversy about it.

J.M.   To tell the truth, we haven't seen it yet. But I've always enjoyed him. He is the consummate professional. You can't fault him in any way.

H.F.   Ben Johnson is another acknowledged professional?

J.M.   Oh, Ben! He's the most beautiful man in the world. I've known Ben personally for a long time. I found if you want strength, real strength, that's Ben. It's like watching the Mississippi. Inexorable. He's a superb man, just superb! There is nothing said about him that isn't said in that one word.

You were at the rodeo in Sonora and saw him ride. Have you ever seen anyone in more control? Bonnie says he is like a centaur on a horse. And as an actor he has a commanding presence, which is so rare. See the movie *My Heroes Have Always Been Cowboys!* He was marvelous.

H.F.   You were in the musical *Paint Your Wagon.*

J.M.   Sure! We did that in Baker, Oregon, and you had to go fifty-two miles into the mountains from Baker. The road was so treacherous that it took the buses three hours to go fifty-two miles. It was a very awesome location.

It went very smoothly, except the first two weeks old Lee (Marvin) was drunk out of his mind. He pulled himself together and did a real good job. His singing surprised me. His "Wandering Star" was very effective. Lee was tough. Don't kid yourself. He was a Marine and he went through the island campaigns in the Pacific. He went through holy hell. He was something else. Once I saw him kick his foot higher than his head so rapidly, you couldn't believe it. He had real heavy shoes on too. So if he wanted to take your chin off he really could.

I played a Mormon. I was the one who sold Jean Seaberg, a very foolish move. The singers were made up of the Robert Wagner Chorale. You probably didn't know that!

H.F.   Then the real motivation is to be a professional and just do good work.

J.M.   We were doing *Chisum* and Geoffrey Duel, a nice guy but small, who came up to Duke's abdomen, was arguing with Andy McLaglen who was directing the picture. He was wondering about his motivation. He told Andy he was in a real quandary because he couldn't get the feeling of a particular scene. Well, Duke heard enough of that. He walked over to Geoffrey, spread his wings out, all six foot four of him, and said "Motivation! Motivation! You're getting paid. That's your God-damned motivation!" He swung on his heels and walked away.

H.F.   You also played in the film *Hitler* with Richard Basehart in the title role.

J.M.   I sure did. I played Hermann Goering. The whole premise of the movie was a little ridiculous, to try to show the soft side of Hitler. It was a little weird, but it was fun. I had a friend who is gone now. His name was George Fargo. I met him through brother Robert. We organized a little scene. The director was very German, Stuart Heisler. We would walk down the cobblestone streets on the sound stage and give the Nazi salute, and we would sing some very funny songs about the entire Nazi Gang. He would scream, "Stop it! Stop it!" But the pronunciation was quite German [laughing]. Anyhow, we had a little fun with him.

H.F.   What directors stand out in your mind?

J.M.   Oh a number of them: Don Siegel, Earl Bellamy, Tay Garnett, Andy McLaglen.

H.F.   Did you ever work with John Ford?

J.M.   I did one thing with Ford. It was a very minor thing and I didn't get along with him. I had just gotten out of the Army. I had marched a lot, and if you excuse me for bragging a little, I became the heavyweight champion of my division. In the picture, *When Willie Comes Marching Home*, there was a group of soldiers waiting for Dan Dailey to get off the train. Ford was sitting there and yells at me, "You, you!" I said, "Me!" He said, "We're paying you to see your face, so let's see it." Now standing in front of me was a guy about six feet, two inches and two hundred twenty pounds, and he is shifting around like a horse to see that he gets the best advantage. So I got tired of dancing around him and said, "Sir, if you allow me to knock this big ape on his ass, you'll see my face." That didn't go off too well with John Ford.

H.F.   Any particular role or roles that give you great sentimental value, or that you consider to be your best work?

J.M.   Well, I'm a character actor, so there is a whole bunch. For example, in *The High Plains Drifter* I had very little to do, but I got one line that you don't get to say very often. I was a warden in Yuma prison. My deputy and I are holding shotguns on them as they are getting their guns back on. One looks back at me and says, "You know, we had three pretty good horses when we came here." I said, "What do you think you've been eating the past three months?" What a great line. You see little things stand out in your mind.

H.F.   How about Charles Bronson? You worked with him in *Breakheart Pass*.

J.M.   Well, my brother talked with him at great length and Bob is very perceptive. He said that Charlie is really a street guy and carried that Depression Era attitude with him. He's hard to reach. We had a little run in on *Breakheart Pass*.

The interesting thing is that the director said, "John, when you slap him I want it to look so real that you really have to throw a punch at him." So I said, "OK!" I threw a left hook at him with an open hand, but in a hundredth of a second I saw he wasn't rolling with it. He had this stern look and was really looking macho. Now I weighed about two hundred fifteen pounds, so I had to pull the punch or hit him full in the face. The director saw that and took me aside and wanted to know why I pulled the punch. I said that Bronson wasn't reacting, so rather than hit him, and I threw a hell of a punch, I had to pull it or hit him hard.

Well there is Bronson behind me, now in a fighting stance. He's coming in with his left hand by his left knee. So I said, "Yes, Charlie," and I took my stance, "here's how I do it." He took a look and backed off. The next time he took the punch beautifully, and I hit him with my right hand. My wife says she has never seen anything look so real.

H.F.   You really simulate those fights beautifully.

J.M.   Well, we have to. No one can take all those hard punches.

H.F.   The future of the western, John. Is it coming back?

J.M.   No, I don't think so. Unfortunately I don't. It's historical and nostalgic now, like watching *Mutiny on the Bounty* or shows like that. So much now has lost its reality. The western genre lasted for many years, well over twenty. And there are a lot of people alive and well who remember many of the people who worked in them. When you look at the characters they had, they epitomized what Americans would like to be like. But what are your new story lines going to be? What I do feel is that the western motif — if you will — will evolve more into a documentary thing. Go into the real history of it, and do it from that standpoint. I feel this will be well-accepted.

H.F.   Your feelings about Hollywood today?

J.M.   I can't handle it. You've got Arnold Schwarzenegger and Stallone, and they keep repeating themselves and repeating themselves, trying to be more and more violent. If they haven't killed everybody in the first reel, they are looking around for somebody else to kill.

Even to be on a commercial today is a real experience. Don't ever go. Your love for theater dissipates very rapidly. They are actually cattle calls. They bring in eight people for maybe one twenty second spot, and ask asinine things from everybody. When you see what the lust for money does to people's dignity and pride, it makes you say you really enjoyed the old bank robbers, because there was an element of danger in their job. But these people will do anything for a buck and I will not. It's as simple as that.

H.F.   A lot of folks say that when Bob Mitchum and Clint Eastwood pass from the movie scene, that a whole era of screen performers will be lost. They both have a remarkable presence which cannot be replaced. Do you see anyone around today with that strong magnetism and presence?

J.M.   No, I really haven't seen it. I really haven't. Look at Bob in *Cape Fear*, then look at the remake and try to beat the original he did with Gregory Peck. There was all that shouting in the remake with Nick Nolte and DeNiro. Bob didn't do that in the original. He underplayed it all the way through and it was much more deadly.

H.F.   How do you feel about attending these film festivals? They have become quite popular.

J.M.   Yes, they have. But I have a certain sadness. There is a sadness because they are trying to keep something alive which is destined to go. The people who are showing up are just getting older and older. Many are starting to die off.

H.F.   What are you doing now?

J.M.   I'm writing and putting together a series which is being funded and is called "The Songs of History." I've been working on this for a number of years. Each one of these songs has an enormous story behind it. Once you dig into it, it opens peoples eyes to their own history because the songs extend and reach all over the world.

For example, the little song, "Ring Around the Rosie" which kids have been dancing around the maypole for hundreds of years, is actually the story of the Black Plague. The "roses" were actually red spots around the body. The "ring" was actually the pus which formed around it. And when "they all fall down," they all fall dead. So you see what six hundred years of time has done to that memory. We've got twenty-six shows which we've researched. We've got six scripts that we researched, and we did a pilot for *The Battle Hymn of the Republic.* My wife, Bonnie, is part of the project.

H.F. The two of you perform so well together. How long have you been married?

J.M. This is my fourth marriage. I met Bonnie when she was doing a play in Hollywood and a friend of mine was in the play. My friend Will Hunter was a hell of an actor. The little theater they were in could afford the libretto, but they couldn't afford the music. So Will told them he had a friend who could write music. I went down there to teach the cast the music. Well, Bonnie was standing there and I'm like a pointer dog looking at her. I couldn't keep my eyes off her. We went to the cast party and Bonnie asked why I hadn't called her. I told her I thought she was married. She said she wasn't. That was nine years ago. She was a marvelous singer and a very strong stage actress.

H.F. About those ornery Mitchum boys, is your son acting too?

J.M. My boy is not the least interested in theater. But Bob's two boys are actors. And Bentley, Chris's son, is an actor too.

H.F. Thank you very much, John, for such an enlightening and informative interview.

19

Walter Reed

I liked the westerns because you were outside. I'll tell you
something else. As the film industry goes, they were the best
people to work with. I had always fantasized about being a
cowboy. In fact, I had wished I was one. But come to think
of it, I sure did a lot of westerns.

With a resume that includes more than four hundred television shows
and one hundred fifty movies, actor Walter Reed has worked with all the big
names. Born Walter Reed Smith, the brother of singer "Smiling Jack Smith,"
in Bambridge Island in Seattle, he moved to Los Angeles when his father retired
from a military career in 1923.

Walter Reed began his acting career as a leading man, playing opposite
such stars as Lucille Ball, Ann Shirley and Paulette Goddard. Unlike other
leading men, however, he made a rather remarkable transition to character
roles early in his career, soon becoming one of the best known and most successful character actors in the business. Reed has starred in such films as *How
the West Was Won, Cheyenne Autumn, Sergeant Rutledge,* and *The Horse Soldiers.* He has also been a familiar face on the small screen as well, with regular featured roles on *Bonanza, Wyatt Earp, The Deputy,* and *The Lone Ranger.*

As a man who came of age during the years of "The Great Depression,"
Walter Reed weaves some wonderful stories detailing his life both in and out
of films. He offers tidbits and anecdotes about some of the industry's greatest stars: John Wayne, William Holden, Alan Ladd, Dennis Weaver, Victor
Mature, and a different perspective on John Ford, who directed him in a number of pictures.

I interviewed Walter Reed in Sonora, California, recently. He knows the
movie game from top to bottom, and recalls his years in the business with
great fondness.

H.F.   Walter, people say you were quite an accomplished horseman at
an early age. I imagine that made you real fodder for screen westerns.

Walter Reed

W.R. It did and it didn't, because my early roles really weren't westerns. But yes, I could ride pretty well for an actor. When I was a kid, some friends had a riding stable. They used to let me take up the rear end in case anybody fell off. They taught me to ride. So while I wasn't a westerner in the traditional mold, I had ridden a lot and had learned to ride pretty well. Let's just say for an actor I rode rather well.

H.F. You were born in Seattle, and moved to Los Angeles at a fairly young age. Is LA where you got the acting bug?

W.R. My father was an Army officer, and when he retired in 1923, we moved to Los Angeles. I got to know a lot of people. There was a very famous comedian named Charlie Chase, and I knew him and his daughter. Harry Langdon was a great comic and I also knew his daughter. Someone told me that they were looking for people for a film called *Red Skin* with Richard Dix. I went on an interview and got a job as an Indian boy. It was my first picture. I was thirteen years old then. By the time I was seventeen I decided that I wanted to go on the stage. So I hooked my way on a train to New York.

H.F. You were just a kid. That had to be a real experience for you?

W.R. It sure was! Because I had run away they pulled me in for vagrancy and I was on a chain gang for three days in Texas. That was during the Depression. There were about two hundred of us on the train.

H.F.   And you got to New York finally?

W.R.   Eventually I did. I had a note to an agent in New York. He got me a job just a few days after I got there. They were doing some plays about a military school. I stayed in the east and did about sixty-eight weeks of stock, a different play every week. I really learned my craft.

H.F.   Then you returned to Los Angeles!

W.R.   That's right! I was seen doing a play in Kennebunkport, Maine. Some movie people saw me and took me back to Hollywood. I was staying at the Roosevelt Hotel. To get my name around and to get noticed, I would have myself paged all the time. I guess it worked. Eventually I signed a contract with RKO.

The first picture I did was something called *The Mayor of 44th Street* with George Murphy and Ann Shirley. George later became a U.S. Senator from California. In 1943 I was cast opposite Ann Shirley Again in *Bombardier*. I played her love interest in that one. Then I did a film called *Wednesday's Child*. Soon I was doing everything. I played Lucille Ball's fiancé in a thing called *Seven Days' Leave*. Victor Mature gets her away from me. I was Paulette Goddard's fiancé in *The Torch*, a picture we made down in Mexico. I played her fiancé and this time Pedro Armendariz gets her away from me, but she was very nice to me when we were filming the picture. So as you can see, I played opposite some great leading ladies.

H.F.   Were you working in westerns too?

W.R.   Sure, I played in three westerns with Tim Holt. Tim was a very nice guy, and a very good actor.

H.F.   You were working as a fairly successful leading man. Why the transition to character roles?

W.R.   To tell you the truth, I thought it was a good idea. I was getting a little older, like all of us. I looked in the mirror one day and said, "You are no longer a leading man!" I knew I wouldn't last too long like that, so I started doing character work.

H.F.   You did some great westerns as a character actor, many of them with John Ford.

W.R.   Oh, I did a lot of westerns. Like I said, I wasn't a cowboy, but I fitted in with them. I lived in the west most of my life and some of my good friends were cowboys. One of my very good friends was Chuck Roberson, John Wayne's double. He was a very famous stuntman. He did thirty-six pictures with Wayne.

Duke Wayne wasn't brought up as a cowboy. A lot of us weren't brought up as cowboys, but we learned. I felt very comfortable in westerns. I never owned a horse or rode all the time. But I actually did my own riding in films. Again, because of my early training, I was always good enough to do my own riding, although I never really had to learn to handle the gun that well.

You see, much of the time I would play what you would call a "smooth heavy." I was the guy who did all the evil brainwork, then I would have my stooges go out and do the dirty work.

H.F.   What westerns that you played in stand out in your mind?

W.R.   There was *Return of the Badman*, with Randy Scott, *The Eagle and the Hawk*, with John Payne and Dennis O'Keefe. Then, of course, I did those John Ford westerns, *Cheyenne Autumn, How the West Was Won, Sergeant Rutledge,* and *The Horse Soldiers,* with Duke Wayne and William Holden. But I think my best part was the lead in a film called *Seven Men from Now.* I was Gail Russell's husband, and I was killed in the last scene. It was directed by Budd Boetticher, and written by Burt Kennedy. Randolph Scott and Lee Marvin were also in it.

H.F.   You mentioned *The Horse Soldiers.* It was an interesting film. John Wayne and Bill Holden worked well together on the screen.

W.R.   I remember it well. I was the leader of Troop B. Duke headed the troop. Holden was the doctor. Ford was the director. Ford would say, "Now you lead this troop and go over the bridge," and I'd take off. I'd come back and Ford would say, "You sure did a great job!" One of the stuntmen told me, "You were so scared of the horses in back of you." He was right. If I went down, I'd have one hundred forty guys going over me.

H.F.   How was Ford to work with? Lots of people had trouble with him.

W.R.   I liked Ford. He was a tough man, but I'll tell you something. I had a heart attack and he put me in a film called *Cheyenne Autumn.* But he wouldn't let me ride. He gave me a job to get me money, but he never mentioned my heart attack. I was kind of in his stock company for the last three or four pictures he did. I really respected him for that. He gave me a job but he wouldn't let me ride. Remember in the days when I did *The Horse Soldiers* for him, we were on the horses every day, even Saturdays and Sundays for fourteen weeks.

When he'd come on the set, one of the guys would start playing some military music on the accordion. We'd all stand up and call him "Admiral." He'd been a Navy man. You'd play the part off stage too with Ford. But I liked him very much, he was a nice man. Yet, if he didn't like you, or if you were a horseman and you were cocky with him, he'd let you do dangerous stuff. But basically he was a nice guy. His real name was Feeney. He came from Portland, Maine, and they called him "Bull Feeney."

H.F.   Any other directors you particularly enjoyed working for?

W.R.   Well, I was in twelve pictures which Budd Boetticher directed. I did a fine war story, *The Red Ball Express* with Jeff Chandler. Earlier I mentioned *Seven Men from Now*. John Wayne was sorry he didn't take the lead role because it was his production company which produced the film. Oh, it was a real good show.

H.F.   What are your memories of John Wayne?

W.R.   I used to go to Duke's house. We would go there to drink with him and play poker. He was so funny. He was a good guy in a poker game, a good guy to drink with. He just loved to have fun. He really wasn't a ladies' man. he'd rather hang around with the guys. Whenever he was on a show, instead of going out, each Saturday night he ran an all night poker game, and everybody got drunk. He just plain liked that. But he wouldn't drink during the week. Just that one night, if he was working. Saturday night was his night to relax and to be with the boys. He loved it. John was brought up in Los Angeles. He and Ward Bond played football together in college. They were good football players, both of them. But he was not brought up as a cowboy.

H.F.   How was William Holden to work with?

W.R.   Bill Holden was one of the most wonderful guys I ever knew in my life. The way he died was startling to me. They say he was an alcoholic, but I never saw him loaded or anything. I had a few drinks with him, but I never knew he was that bad. He was a good actor and a sweetheart of a guy.

I can think of a funny story. When we were on *The Horse Soldiers* we were in this great big trailer. We were the Horse Soldiers and when they said something, we'd yell, "Yo!" Well, once Ford yelled in that raspy voice of his, "Bill Holden!" So Holden runs to the door and he says, "Yo!" like that. Then he turns around to us and says with a puzzled look, "What the hell am I doing that for? I'm making a million dollars on that picture and he's only making five hundred thousand [laughing]. What am I going 'Yo' for?"

H.F.   You mentioned Gail Russell earlier. She was a beautiful girl who met with a tragic end. She worked real well with Alan Ladd in a couple of pictures.

W.R.   You are right about Gail. I liked her very much. But let me tell you something about Alan Ladd. He had the most beautiful body for a little man you ever saw. He had an absolutely great build. Anyone whoever called him puny is nuts. He was a miniature strong man.

I did a training film in Monterey for the Army. Alan was there too. He told me he was going into a picture when he got back. It was called *This Gun for Hire*. Of course that was the picture which made Alan a star. I told him I was under contact with RKO and was going back too. He was happy for the both of us and we talked quite a bit. Then he became a big star and I never heard from him.

All of a sudden years passed and I got a call from my agent. He said that they wanted me for an Alan Ladd picture. He said they were giving me double my money. I said, "Really!" I was surprised. Well, I worked for four weeks on the film and I played his rival. The movie was called *The Deep Six*. I saw him afterwards and I said, "Alan, how did you do this?" He said, "Walter, I've been trying to find a part for you ever since we did that army thing." He was a good man.

H.F.   But like Gail Russell, he, too, had a sad life.

W.R.   Yes he did. He died an alcoholic. But I never saw him like that. He was a perfect gentleman and kept in shape. I didn't know him during the time he was an alcoholic. He was a handsome guy. But then you never know. Heck, I worked with Brod Crawford in those *Highway Patrol* episodes and he'd be so crocked. But he's stay sober for the scenes. Then he would fall apart. So you can't tell.

H.F.   How much television did you do?

W.R.   Oh, I did a lot. I think I did about four hundred television shows and one hundred fifty movies during my career. Most all the big westerns and much more. When we did things like the "Annie Oakleys" or "Buffalo Bill Jr.," we'd do two a week. We'd go up to Pioneer Town and do something like that. Come to think of it, I did a lot of westerns. Then I had a heart attack and I moved out of Hollywood because I thought it was going to kill me.

H.F.   How long ago was that?

W.R.   I had my first heart attack when I was forty-seven. I'm seventy-seven now. I've had a lot of health problems including a cancer operation about seven years ago. But I am still here.

H.F.   You're not a complainer, considering what you went through.

W.R.   Oh, no! I've had a wonderful, wonderful life. Many dear people. I quit pictures at about age fifty-five. I never mentioned the heart attack because in this business it could have meant the kiss of death. The picture business can be nerve wracking. Lots of stress. I did a couple of television shows and a few commercials since.

H.F.   Do you miss the acting game?

W.R.   Very much so. But I couldn't remember my own name now. I take something like eighteen pills a day [laughing]. They make you punchy. I don't care what anybody says. But I had a wonderful career, and worked very hard. When television first came in, we did two shows a week. We worked on Saturdays.

H.F. What were some of the shows?

W.R. I did *Matinee Theater*. I did *Front Row Center*. I did live shows, and things like *Wagon Train*. I played heavies in episodes of *Perry Mason*. I was Jackie Cooper's older brother in *Hennesey*. Once I became a character actor after I got out of service, I had a long career. You won't make as much money as a character actor, but you'll last longer. Unless you can hit it as a star in this business, then you'd better be versatile.

H.F. A lot of people in this business have huge egos. Did you find this a problem?

W.R. Well some of them certainly do. But I do have a funny story I like to tell. We got back from the service and were in a show called *Winged Victory*. Red Buttons was Aaron Schwatt in those days. Then in 1957 he wins a Best Supporting Actor Oscar for *Sayonara*. Well, I see him in the make-up room at Universal and I say, "Hi, Red!" He looks at me and says something like, "Oh, Hello, Walter!" I told him, "What are you giving me this crap for? I remember when you were a burlesque comedian." He answered, "You're right! Just give me a couple of days to get over this!" But he was down to earth. He just said he needed a couple of days for his ego to get over this.

H.F. Of all the people you worked with over the years, who stands out most in your mind?

W.R. The greatest guy I ever worked with was Dennis Weaver. He was my roommate in a picture I did with Victor Mature, Piper Laurie, and Bill Bendix. Dennis and I were forest rangers in the film, and I had a bigger part than he did. He was broke then and was living in a little house, paying one hundred twenty-five dollars a month and his son was sick. He said he was going to do a pilot called *Gunsmoke*. To make sure they remembered him, he said he was going to do it with a stiff leg. Dennis Weaver you know was almost an Olympic champion, but that limp routine made him famous.

There is still another interesting yarn concerned with that film. It deals with Victor Mature. Victor was in the next room, but didn't have a shower or a bath tub. I told him I'd leave the door unlocked from our side, and when he wanted to take a shower he could go in there. Well, soon he was not only showering, he was using my razor and other things. I told him that when he got to my toothbrush I was going to close the door and lock it. But I liked Mature. He was a real nice guy. He still is. We shot the film in Glacier National Park, and had a lot of fun doing it.

H.F. Is Walter Reed your real name?

W.R. Actually it isn't. My real name is Walter Reed Smith. My brother is Smiling Jack Smith, the singer. Well, RKO got me into the publicity department. They said, "We have this Smith kid here and we have to think of a name for him." One of the guys said he had the perfect name for me. The name he wanted to give me was Stark Nolan. Well, one of the girls began to laugh. She really started to laugh. Then she said she thought it should be Stark Naked. That did it. I just dropped my last name and became Walter Reed.

H.F.   You were very versatile and did so many different things over your career. Were the westerns your favorite?

W.R.   Definitely! I liked the westerns because you were outside. I'll tell you something else. As far as the film industry goes, they were the best people to work with. I always fantasized about being a cowboy. In fact, I wish I had been one!

H.F.   Thanks, Walter!

20

Bob Totten

It was Christmas Eve and we were shooting on the Green Set over at Fox Western. I got a call from my agent to phone Phillip Leacock at CBS right after the Christmas holiday was over. ... Well, it seems that one of the guys doing Gunsmoke *got sick, and Phil Leacock told me to report there for a multiple of three episodes. That was the greatest Christmas present anyone could get.*

Bob Totten is one of the most talented people in the industry today, pure and simple. He directs, he writes, he acts, and he produces. And he does each equally well. Yet, for all his remarkable talent there is not an inch of pretense or pomposity.

The winner of both an Emmy and a Peabody Award for Directing the television versions of *The Red Pony*, and *The Adventures of Huckleberry Finn*. Totten also directed *The Sacketts,* one of the true classic westerns of the past two decades. The film, which starred Tom Selleck, Sam Elliott and Ben Johnson, was named the Best Western of the 1980s (TV or movies) by the National Cowboy Hall of Fame. And his close association with *Gunsmoke* lasted ten years including many guest star appearances and directing.

Yet, Bob Totten will be the first to say how fortunate he has been as a film maker, to have had the opportunity to meet up and *learn* that art and craft of film production from some of the better known and talented directors in film making. Among those he credits with enhancing his later success are Delmer Daves, Don Siegel, Elia Kazan, and Henry Fonda.

Bob Totten is a native Californian, born in Los Angeles and raised in the San Bernadino and Riverside counties of Southern California. Totten never experienced college classes in "Film." After graduating from Eagle Rock High School in 1955, he continued his education at the Pasadena Playhouse of Theater Arts, and Los Angeles Valley Junior College. He was also a special music student in the Music College of Colorado Western State University at the tender age of twelve or thirteen. To top everything, he was the recipient of President Lyndon Johnson's "Most Outstanding Young Man of America" award.

Robert Totten

Totten's directing debut was a feature film entitled *The Quick and the Dead*. He was only twenty-two years old and working on a tight budget. But the film attracted the attention of Jack Warner who offered him a contract for his acting and directing services. So impressive was Totten's work that Delmer Daves, Mervyn LeRoy, and Morton DaCosta sponsored him for the Directors Guild Association.

In addition to his award-winning endeavors, *Huckleberry Finn*, *The Red Pony*, *The Sacketts*, and his ten years with *Gunsmoke*, Totten has directed and acted in such top shows as *The Virginian*, *The Gallant Men*, *Bonanza*, *The Road West*, *Mission: Impossible*, and *Magnum, P.I.* During the 1980s he continued directing multiple episodes of *Kung Fu* starring David Carradine, *Iron Horse*, with Dale Robertson, and *Hawaii Five-O* with Jack Lord. He has been recognized with "The Golden Lariat Award" for his twenty-five years in film making.

Bob Totten is a true man of the west. He loves the west and respects western films. He is a consummate filmmaker who is never too busy to lend a helping hand to others. His non-professional involvements include working with the California Department of Corrections and the High Road Drivers Education service.

Bob Totten and his wife Mikki live in Sherman Oaks, California. His typewriter is always chattering. If there is a true resurgence of the western film, bet your money that Bob Totten will head the pack. He is truly a "Man for All Western Seasons."

H.F. Bob, your life and career has been prolific to the extreme. How did all this begin?

B.T. Well, my love affair with the west was born at a very early age. I was born here in L.A. and shortly after birth I went clear up to the other extreme — to an area called Valley View in the San Bernadino Mountains. We were not people of means. There was no real money, property or prestige on either side of the family, the Tottens or the Barkers.

My family traveled a lot so I spent most of my first eight years with my grandfather, M. M. Barker. He was my mother's father. I must mention here my dear mother, Merry Florine Barker Totten. Among *all* the wifely and motherly gifts that she gave to my sister and my father, R.C. Totten, she worked with my grandfather and taught me to read at an early age. By age four I was already an accomplished reader. I thank my mother and grandfather for this early training. I didn't realize at that time just how *all important* this basic skill was for my learning future and my entire life

Because my folks traveled a lot, I spent much of my time with Grandpa and a little Boston Bull terrier named Patsy whom I will never forget. I never really knew how humble we were. We didn't have electricity or running water. Everything was done just like it is done in western movie-making.

I started working very young. Grandpa gave me one buck and two does and domestic rabbits, and in a year's time, I never had less than three hundred fifty head of rabbits. This became my business and it was a good business. It was well-organized and maintained by me, and Grandpa was a great teacher. Grandpa took me down to San Bernadino and signed me up for Social Security. So my social security number goes back to when I was nine years old.

H.F. Story has it that there was a link between your grandfather and your entry into show business. Can you explain?

B.T. Sure. Grandpa Barker had many odd jobs when we lived in the mountain country. He was an independent contractor and an expert in lots of different things. He looked after three or four beautiful mountain homes — perhaps estates would be a better term. One of those, now owned by the Episcopal Church in Westwood, was owned by Delmer Daves. This was when Delmer was a young and very hot sought after screen writer working all the time at MGM and Warner Brothers. Eventually with the film *Destination Tokyo,* he became a director.

Well, Grandpa and Delmer had a great relationship. He used to look after Del's cabin. He called it a cabin, but let me tell you we all wished we had a cabin like that. St. Albans owns it today and it is part of their youth program with the church. It's still just a gorgeous place.

H.F.   Did you have an interest in movies at this early age?

B.T.   Well if I did it was because of the close relationship between Delmer Daves and my grandfather. Del always called Grandpa "dad." Later I would learn that Delmer lost his father when he was very young, and Grandpa was sort of a replacement, a surrogate father to Del. But Grandpa had absolutely nothing to do with the movies except in knowing Del. He never showed any interest in being a participant in movie work.

It was when we'd go from the mountains down to the farming country that I really got the bug. The big, big entertainment thing for me was that once a week — if my chores were done right — I'd go to the nickel show at the Beaumont and see movies. I loved baseball too, and played baseball for Graves Malt Shop. It was a little ice cream store in Beaumont and was right next to the theater. By going to the matinee I became so fascinated with the movies, that after I played baseball in the morning, I'd stay in the theater all day. I really became fascinated by the movies. I was mesmerized by them.

H.F.   Any specific movies stand out?

B.T.   What I do remember is that I had some trouble with Gene Autry and Roy Rogers when I was a kid. For some reason, I had this bug for everything being authentic. I irritated a lot of people, even as a youngster, by insisting that things should be authentic — not just movies, everything.

Remember, I had this everyday knowledge of animal husbandry, horse and cattle, feed and grain, irrigation and all that goes with it. The type of farming I did was a marvelous education for me. So when I went to see a "Western Picture" it was pretty hard to fool this boy. But, regardless, my favorite picture shows were westerns, good or bad or indifferent. I was pretty comfortable with that. The idea and the fantasy of a guy and a beautiful gal. The hero is always trying to save people and protect them. It's always a survival story if you are making a good western. You'd better not forget about that.

I thought Wild Bill Elliott was just fantastic because he didn't try to sing while he was doing it. I never had anything against the musicianship of Roy Rogers or Gene Autry, but I wondered what the hell they were doing, stopping the story and singing when the gal was over there hanging for her life, the little kid was at the bottom of the well, and the bad guys were robbing the bank. And these guys were over there singing. So Bill Elliott was my favorite, and he had that brat kid running with him who was a lot like me. All those *Red Ryder/Little Beaver* pictures were my favorites. I could never get enough of them.

H.F.   So Delmer Daves was your early mentor?

B.T.   Sure. He was my first on-the-job teacher. My grandfather introduced me to him when I was a lad of six or seven. I didn't take hold of my burning desire to be a "filmmaker" until I was twelve years old. Grandpa took me to see Delmer Daves, to help me sort out what I was "dreaming" about, and to listen to his advice on a study program. I did what I was told by Delmer Daves. He kept a very close watch on me as I stayed in public schools and excelled in Theater Arts and Play Production. I might add that Delmer had this fantastic second house in the back which he called his study. That was where all his stuff was and where he worked on his writing and his preparation for making films. So I hung out a lot there. As the years went by and the older I got, the more time I spent there.

At Eagle Rock High School, I met Robert Rivera through the special efforts of the school principal, Bob Kelly. Robert Rivera taught and directed a mature and very exciting Play Production Program. The combination of the very active music program, as directed by Fred Rupp with the Theater Program of Bob Rivera's, *filled* my teenage years with my "work 4x4" and my social activities.

H.F.   You were the recipient of President Johnson's "Most Outstanding Young Man of America Award!"

B.T.   I had just finished my first picture which I wrote, directed and co-produced. It was a little World War II picture called *The Quick and the Dead*. Somehow Bob Rivera, my former teacher at Eagle Rock High, heard about it. He found out they were doing something like a "Who's Who Book of Potential Young People" endorsed by the President. Lyndon Johnson was President then. They put me in the book. That was the award I received.

H.F.   Can you say something about your first film, *The Quick and the Dead*?

B.T.   Again, as a kid I began working a bit for Delmer Daves playing some bit parts. I would just hang around with him making shows. Eventually, I had an opportunity to come up with a picture of my own. It was a real challenge. *The Quick and the Dead* was a World War II film shot on a real tight budget and schedule. It starred my old friend, Victor French. The film caught on pretty well and attracted the attention of Jack Warner.

H.F.   Did Warner Brothers sign you to a contract?

B.T.   Yes! Jack Warner had me paged and signed me to a term contract. In fact, Mr. Warner talked to Delmer Daves, Mervyn LeRoy, and Morton Da Costa, three of the top guns and most respected men in Hollywood, about sponsoring me into the D.G.A. (The Directors Guild of America). Mr. Warner also paid my initiation fees and my guild dues.

H.F.   So this was your advanced basic training in the movie business, so to speak?

B.T.   It sure was. I was able to do an awful lot of every kind of thing you can imagine. I did a lot of second unit stuff as they called it. I was a Second Unit Director there at Warner Brothers in the old days, when the Colonel was still the head man. I also got to play some bit parts. In those days Warner, and people like him, did a lot of public service films. I recall doing an awful lot of Community Chest films and military recruiting films. Warners needed a lot of that kind of work done.

Warners was also a pioneer in episodic film television, as they have been in so many areas of movie making. They were especially active in making those western series. There were over twenty hours of prime-time television a week taken up by Warner Brothers.

H.F. So you were associated with the big westerns like *Cheyenne, Sugarfoot,* and *Bronco!*

B.T. Well, I should have been, but I wasn't. I didn't like it at all. They started me off doing *Hawaiian Eye.* The reason for that was the cast was always squabbling. Bob Conrad was in it. So was Connie Stevens and Troy Donahue. It was the exact same format that was later done on *Hawaii Five-O* with Jack Lord, and even later on *Magnum, P.I.*

I was doing a bunch of those and complaining all the time. I kept asking why they weren't letting me do any of the westerns. "What the hell is this?" I would say, "I've never been to Hawaii. I could care less." Finally, somebody listened to me — or maybe somebody got sick — but I got a western. The show was called *The Dakotas.* It was about a group of federal marshals roaming the Badlands and finding trouble behind each and every bush. Each episode saw one or two of them find appropriate trouble, and that would be your one-hour episode. Chad Everett was the big name in the cast.

H.F. When you finally branched out from Warner Brothers, where did you start working?

B.T. When I left Warners, Andy McLaglen was hung up with too many *Virginians* to do. We were in the men's room at Universal one day and he said, "Little 'T', take me off the book." He told me to see Frank Price and pick up a script called *Bryn Mawr Hall* for the series. When you did a *Virginian,* of course, you might as well say you did a movie. It was a long experience.

So I did a *Virginian* episode which really had nothing to do with *The Virginian* or James Drury. It didn't have a thing to do with animal husbandry and all that. The whole thing takes place in a haunted house called *Bryn Mawr Hall.* So he really didn't do me any favor.

H.F. How did you begin your long association with *Gunsmoke?*

B.T. For starters, I was getting out and meeting people. My ambition had always been to get into *Gunsmoke.* I remember well what happened. It was Christmas Eve and we were shooting on the Green Set over at Fox Western. I got a call from my agent to phone Philip Leacock at CBS right after the Christmas holiday was over. *Gunsmoke* people took a Christmas hiatus. They never worked on holiday. Well, it seems that one of the guys doing *Gunsmoke* got sick, and Phil Leacock told me to report there for a multiple of three episodes. That was the greatest Christmas present anyone could get.

I'd like to add a bit more about Philip Leacock. He didn't mix up his directorial knowledge with his producing of *Gunsmoke* for CBS television. However, he would deal with me as another Director and Storyteller of equal status and work experience. I loved this man. He gave me more than he ever knew.

H.F.   Did you do both the half-hour and hour episodes of *Gunsmoke*?

B.T.   No. As a kid, when they started in the Fifties, I went there to try out for a kid role they had in the first episode they shot. I didn't get the part, but I always had this burning desire to be associated with the show. At the time I got my call to be an emergency replacement, they were into one hour black and white. I arrived on the show at the very time Dennis Weaver left. So I was right there when they discovered that they could take a marvelous character that Jay Simms wrote from *Have Gun Will Travel* called "Monk." The actor who played the part was Ken Curtis. Well, they got legal clearance to find a character for him in *Gunsmoke* to replace "Chester." The rest is history, because Ken Curtis now played Festus. Two years later the show went to color when it became a Saturday night one hour show.

H.F.   Did you both direct and write?

B.T.   Directing was my main function. Actually, I did a lot of writing, but nothing I could take credit for. I had a separate paycheck for being a writing consultant. Most all my work on *Gunsmoke* was directing and acting. As an actor in the series, I had all different kinds of character roles. I had a wide range, in fact. It was most enjoyable and challenging. The *Gunsmoke* leads that I played were really strange guys. I always said that I didn't give a damn for more publicity or screen credits. What I needed was more money. So I used to get paid pretty darn good. You'd think I was a celebrity the way they were paying me.

H.F.   Story also has it that John Wayne personally recommended James Arness for the role of Matt Dillon. Is that true?

B.T.   It's true! Actually, Charles (Bill Warren) really believed that John Wayne would take a real stab at it himself. They knew they couldn't use Bill Conrad who did it on radio. They were looking for a larger-than-life figure who could also match Conrad's voice. Well, they were talking about one guy, the one and only! So they went to John Wayne, and Duke didn't scuff at it at all. In fact, he once told me that they flattered him by coming to him that way, but that he knew a young guy who really needed a break. Television was new and so was Jim Arness. So Duke pushed for Jim, and you know the rest of the story. Duke did make a piece of the film when he introduced the *Gunsmoke* show.

H.F.   Let's talk about Tom Selleck. You first directed him in *The Sacketts*.

B.T.   That's right! Tom was a guy whom I met when we were doing the casting for *The Sacketts*. There were quite a few guys who were there the week we had tryouts. Not just for the three choice roles of the three Sackett brothers, but for a lot of parts in the show.

I didn't have actors come in to read scripts in the casting room. I didn't go to a studio or use video tape to tape them and let them make fools of themselves. That's how it's done today. Today, actors go to a casting call and make asses of themselves because they are not prepared. They don't even know what they are there for to begin with. The whole system now has gone completely berserk.

What we did with *The Sacketts* because so much was going to be demanded of these guys, was to work in some not-too-nice places. Nothing urban, it was to be super rural and I wanted the guys to look like they belonged there. So I went out to Randall Ranch and talked to Corky out there. We had the guys come out there for three days if they really wanted to be considered for one of these roles. They had to come out there and start with a horse who was naked. They had to saddle him up and then step on him. I had a little megaphone and I was up in a little bleachers stand. I would ask them to do different things. Nothing dangerous or silly. Just to see if they could walk him or take a lazy figure eight. I would surprise them a bit. Stop them in their track and things like that. Then I'd ask them to take him back to the wranglers and step off of him. And through it all I just watched and took notes in my little yellow book. Some, of course, didn't get past their automobiles to the corral, because right away it came across real quickly that they were scared to death of horses. That took them right out of the running. Sure, a lot of guys auditioned. But the three guys who played in it — Tom Selleck, Sam Elliott and Jeff Osterhage — didn't just have to show what great actors they were. They had to show how comfortable they were around horses.

H.F.   Your early impressions of Tom Selleck?

B.T.   Oh, he was a very nice guy who was very eager and more than willing to learn how to do things right. I remember his asking me if it was all right to put in some extra training. He said he had spoke to my wranglers and they would be glad to work more with him. I told him to go ahead because these wranglers were the greatest teachers he was every going to find. So because of Tom's eagerness and willingness to learn, and how teachable he was, he had a leg up on the rest of his competition.

He knew he would have to learn more about horsemanship and horses, how to behave around them. He also knew that his director chewed Red Man tobacco. Pretty soon he was doing that, too. I'll never forget he showed up one day and had his tobacco in a little leather pouch which he had someone in a shoe store make for him. He said, "Well, I'm trying to get over being sick, but

I'm not going to do it with the god damn licorice. I'm not going to throw up on your damn camera. I'm going to learn how to chew this crap and like it."

And he did! He was a real eager guy. Everybody loved this man. He had this gift. The same qualities that were necessary to play the part of Orrin Sackett. Just the way Louis L'Amour had written Orrin Sackett. Tom was the same kind of guy exactly.

H.F. Sam Elliott has done so much good work. Was there ever any doubt about him?

B.T. No! As a matter of fact, he was securely cast in his role a couple of days before Tom or Jeff were in theirs.

H.F. Jeff Osterhage did a heck of a job as Tyrell, the youngest Sackett.

B.T. He sure did. But things were a lot harder for him afterwards. But he's like me. He wouldn't change that name any more than I would change the name Totten. He was born with it and he will die with it. Not so much now, but for years, I thought that might be holding him back. I had even talked about it with his dad.

I didn't know Jeff, but I was watching a take off of *Rooster Cogburn*, the movie John Wayne made. Warren Oates was playing Duke's part and this kid had the part that Glen Campbell played so badly in the movie. Sandor Stern had sent it to me. As soon as I saw it, I picked up the phone and called Sandor. "Hey, Doc Sandy, [Sandor Stern was a medical doctor]," I said, "Who is that kid...." I didn't finish. He laughed and said he knew I'd like him. "Bring me that kid," I told him, "Where can I find him. I can make him Tyrell Sackett in a heartbeat."

I remember he came to the reading hall and all these different people were there. The big financiers I was trying to sell him on. I was ranting and raving about this kid whose last name I couldn't pronounce. Before I brought him in, I went outside to talk with Jeff. We went over there to the men's room. I said, "You're a pretty nervous guy, aren't you?" He said, "Wouldn't you be?" I said, "Yeah, I think I would be, but I am going to tell you how this thing is going to go." Then I asked him if he had been working on the reading. He said he almost had it memorized.

Then I jerked the papers out of his hand. "Now when you come in you're not going to have this on your mind. You're not going to have this in your hand, no script material. What you are going to do when you walk in is to take a full stance, absolutely starring me into the ground. I'm going to be standing there in the far corner of the room, and you just pick me out and keep starring. Then I'm going to talk slowly toward you, and when you think I get close enough I want you to pull your hand from your hip as though you are drawing a gun. To draw in lightning, snakelike fashion and gun me down right there."

He told me I had to be out of my mind. I reminded him that I was the director, and if I'm out of my mind it's going to be in an insane movie. So let's try it my way. Well, that's what he did and he got the part. I said, "Boys, if Elia Kazan was sitting here right now, he would say, 'Gentlemen, this man is going to be a star because he has promise of impending violence.'" That was exactly what Kazan liked. If Jeff Osterhage had come along at the time Paul Newman did when Kazan was in his heyday, then Osterhage would be a household name today.

We don't hear nearly enough about him now, but I can't give you the exact reason. He's just not as lucky as he might have been. He's still working but he is not playing those outstanding leading roles that I thought he would be.

H.F.   You thought quite highly of Elia Kazan, didn't you?

B.T.   I most certainly did. I worked some Second Unit Directing for him on *America, America*. He used to like my morning coffee. We talked mostly about acting and performance. He taught me a great deal about *casting* the best person in the role. I learned from Kazan that the requirement for a successful movie leading man is "The promise of impending violence."

H.F.   You worked with Ben Johnson in *The Sacketts*. He is so well thought of by everyone.

B.T.   Now you are talking about a man whom I know as well as I have known any other man, including that beloved Grandpa of mine. I first met him way back in 1953. I was still in high school back then, and Ben came to Eagle Rock with a kid from Oklahoma named Don Crow, whom he helped put in the same 4x4 Plan I was in. We would go to school for four hours, and then spend the rest of the day earning a living. Ben's wife, Carol Jones, was a Glendale girl. She was the only daughter of Fats Jones and was a tennis gal. She was a good looking gal also. When Gussie Moran was popular, they should have taken a look at Carol Jones. She was a dynamite red head and a real spunky personality. So it was always Uncle Ben and Auntie Carol. I was very saddened when Carol died recently after a long illness.

But back to Ben. Ben Johnson is a good example of the ingredients that are necessary for a motion picture personality to become beloved by the audience. Men want to be like him because they want to be handy like him. The want to be able to move and act — not meaning acting — like him. They want to be physically like, and do things with the ease he displays around animals, particularly horses, of course. And to be able to handle himself the way he handles himself. And, of course, women take to him and love him because he has that same boyish, shy charm that he always had. His dad before him had this charm. His mother, you know, is still alive and active.

H.F. How did *Huckleberry Finn* come about?

B.T. Well, that was one of the few times that through the system itself, I was asked to make a special for ABC Circle Theater. They wanted to make a show by blending ABC together with 20th Century–Fox. Steve North, the son of the great composer Alex North, was to be the producer. We started talking about doing *Huckleberry Finn*. He had a script he wasn't too happy with at the time, so I began doctoring it up with no name on it.

Now we were getting into winter and it seemed we should be doing something. I suggested that we didn't have to go south, that we could do it right here in California. Nobody wanted to be around the Mississippi River when it was being flooded out. So naturally big mouth me took them to Marysville along the Sacramento River. When it flooded out we lost all our sets, but we still got the movie made. It was really kind of a whim of mine because of the great success I had with the Howard family in a film for Disney called *The Wild Country*. So I decided to have all four of the Howards: Rance, Jean, Clint and Ron.

H.F. Ron Howard is a very talented guy, a fine director and, from what people say, also a very nice guy.

B.T. He's all those things. That's for sure. He is a wonderful guy. Of course, It's hard for me to think of him as a grown-up, mature man, because to me he's always been just R.W. When we were doing *Wild Country* he came up to me and said, "'T,' I really want to do what you are doing." Then he showed me his eight millimeter camera, and told me he had entered a contest. Well, he finished third and that kicked him off. So here I did one of "those go around/come around things." It seemed like just a few years before, I was talking with Delmer Daves the same way. I sponsored Ron Howard into the DGA of which I am very proud.

The show won an Emmy. Although I didn't specifically win one as "Directed by…" Steve North was very excited. It was his first producing effort. We had a big New Year's party to celebrate. Lots of people, including Henry Mancini, were there. We're talking now about some great musicians.

H.F. There are some conflicting stories about your role in the western film, *Death of a Gunfighter*, and the fictitious name of Allen Smithee which was used by the studio.

B.T. Well, I was fired off the job of directing it. Don Siegel, who had just finished doing *Two Mules for Sister Sara* was called in to finish it. It was very much against his will and against my will. After all, I was under contract.

The guy that was responsible and made everybody's life horribly impossible through the whole experience was the one and only Richard Widmark. What happened was that Widmark was given creative control of the picture through the studio and thought he was going to be making a picture with Siegel directing him. But the studio wanted Don Siegel to direct Clint Eastwood down in Mexico in *Two Mules for Sister Sara* with Shirley MacLaine. Well, the two pictures come up for production schedule at the same time. They were conflicting, and Widmark didn't have his director. Siegel suggested me and assured them that I could do the job. That's when they contacted me. At the time I was working at Paramount making *Mission: Impossible,* one right after the other.

Well, I went over to Universal and met with Widmark who promptly told me that he was part of the company which was doing the picture. Then he started off with, "You're not going to like this experience you know, because I wanted Siegel to make this picture. Who the f—- do you think you are? You're just some punk kid that does *Gunsmoke.*" That's how we started.

So I knew the writing on the wall. I contacted my agent, went back to Universal and upped my ante three hundred percent. I figured if they were going to stay with me on this thing, then they would have to really pay me. So it was the most money I ever made in my life and I stayed there too. When I was taken off the picture, Siegel came in for four days to finish it up. The whole story is there to read in Seigel's book. It's all there. Widmark and everything. Don Siegel was very special. I miss him greatly. I learned how to deal with studio management, producers, difficult egocentric actors and actresses, film editors and writers. I learned economy for "El Capitan." He was a generous man full of love and service. His autobiography is outstanding, and I know it to be true!

H.F.   And the alias "Alan Smithee"?

B.T.   Nobody knows how that alias came about correctly yet. It came about when the picture was finished and Don and I were sitting in the projection room, a little cutting room, looking at the picture. Don Siegel said, "I'm not going to put my name on this picture, these people are full of crap." He asked me how I felt about it and I said I thought he was right. It was my picture except for the four sequences he did. Don said, "I'll tell you what 'Tot', let's go to the DGA and have them hash it out for us."

So we went down there and they brought out every name guy on the council. Everyone had something to say. The guy who was there quietly in the background reminded us that is was past eleven o'clock, and that, "The guys who this means the most to are Siegel and Totten, and in respect for each other, they are not going to have their names in this and no one is going to force them to do it."

So I suggested that we have a "nom de plume." Let's come up with a name that is no name. A name that can't be found in the U.S. census. A name that doesn't exist. So we wrote down the name "Allan Smithee." Now the picture was "Directed by Allen Smithee."

Then, of course, the most important thing is that we were adamant that all the residual money that would be paid over the years be split in half and a separate check be sent to each one of us. So even though "Mr. Allen Smithee" did this big piece of western art work, it's too damn bad that he isn't going to get paid for it. I suggest if anyone wants to know the complete story they read Don Siegel's book. As I said, it's all there.

H.F. Let's talk about *The Red Pony*, Bob. It garnered an Emmy nomination and won "The George Foster Peabody Broadcasting Award."

B.T. That's an interesting story, because they were already going to make it even before I became involved. It was to be an NBC special sponsored exclusively by AT&T. They had spent up all their preliminary development money on trying to get a script which would satisfy everybody. They had six finished scripts, all by different big name writers, and none of them were worth a darn. And they couldn't get a cast that was worth anything because the scripts were so bad and they couldn't get NBC Programming Network approval. In addition, the AT&T people didn't like anything either.

My involvement came as kind of a fluke. The people who were working on *The Red Pony* were up in Sonora and were running out of patience. So they eventually took a hike as their contract allowed. Now they had no director, no art director, and no script. Well, I was having a meeting with some of the guys from the Omnibus Group. One of the guys turned to me and said, "Aren't you a big Steinbeck fan?" I answered, "You bet your bottom dollar." or something like that. He says, "Have you read *The Red Pony*?" "Does a one-legged duck swim in a circle? Hell, yes!" I answered back.

Well they needed a script and they needed one fast. I told them I could do all they asked if they had the money to pay for it. At first they said they didn't have it. Then all of a sudden they found the necessary money, if you can believe that. I said, "Fine!" So I worked seven days and seven nights and wrote a script from the Steinbeck novella. Right off the bat, Hank Fonda said he wanted to do it. Then the minute Fonda said he wanted to do it, Maureen (O'Hara) called and said why wasn't she asked too. We assembled a wonderful cast. In addition to Hank Fonda and Maureen, our stellar cast included Jack Elam, Ben Johnson, Richard Jaeckel, Julian Rivero, Rance Howard, Lieux Dressler, Warren Douglas, and Clint Howard in the lead role of Jody.

H.F. You were particularly fond of Henry Fonda, weren't you?

B.T. I miss him. Oh my, how I miss him. He taught me about being specific with performance. He used to like my way, with the entire story telling in mind — all of the time! He worked hard at overcoming his speech difficulties and trusted me to help him with his scenes. He taught me a lot about bravery. He produced *Twelve Angry Men* for Mr. Lumet. We were working on a World War II epic seventeen years ago, that has remained unfinished. Now there is a lot of talk and planning about finishing this film. We shot for three weeks and were making a fine film. It's certainly worth finishing. Fonda had a super sense of humor. Rance Howard and I were asked to visit him just before he passed away. We did.

H.F.   Anything new on the horizon today, Bob?

B.T.   Well, right now I'm into the last phase which a guy goes into: being completely and totally independent, and packaging my own stuff. But that's not as singular as it sounds. I've had to learn the hard way that I need a lot of help doing that. I have some nice people whom I work with and they are very helpful. It's every day with diligence, just as if I was working for the old Colonel, making sure I'm not tardy or that I don't drop the ball. It involves things that I never dreamed about, like world-marketing and broadcasting. Here I am doing all the managing. It's been too long since I could just get up in the morning and make a western picture show.

H.F.   What kind of western would you like to do now?

B.T.   I have one right now that's the best material ever on Belle Starr. Some might say that Belle Starr has been used to death. But, they better check out Wyatt Earp before they start getting critical. Every time you turn around, somebody is making a new version of Wyatt Earp.

Sure, the character of Belle Starr has been used. But it has never been used right. Those who want to talk about these liberated women of today, they ought to look at the liberated women way back then. There are two or three gals very interested in playing it, and they are as big a name as you'll ever find in the picture business today. I'm very excited about that.

I've also had a burning desire, and it's getting to the point that it's driving me nuts, to do something about Ulysses Grant. I never heard him talked about properly. They seem to want to make him out as some bombastic buffoon, but he was far from that. The documents bear this out well. I want to do his life story very badly. If a guy would really take time to read his history carefully, and really pay attention to his history, you have more there to dramatize into moviework than you can shake a stick at.

H.F.   Just a few more questions, Bob. First of all, how did you get the rights to *The Sacketts*?

B.T.   Well, a guy named Doug Netter went to L'Amour and got the rights to both books we used. Then he hired Jim Burns to do the script by blending the two books. I can't take credit for any of those things. That had already been accomplished by the time they came to me and asked me to direct it.

H.F.   Your greatest achievement in the industry?

B.T.   I liked *The Red Pony*, because I had the most creative control over the entire project. I was really a strong influence. The reason I can gloat that my script won so many awards is that I did no more than to take Steinbeck's work, and make sure that I wasn't going to deviate from it except in one way. I would take the weak father character and the strong hired-hand character and blend them together into one guy. Because then I got a story of survival which I could tell.

H.F.   Finally, Bob, the future of the western film as you see it today?

B.T.   Well, it's going to be pretty tough to make them like they did. If you went out and tried to make a *Shane* today like George Stevens did, or films like *The Gunfighter*, or *The Searchers*, it would be tough to get it done the way those guys back then got things done. First of all, you are not going to have the autonomy or the privacy to do it. You see the sales marketing of today works on "one up" and second guessing each other. That's how they are making western picture shows today. All these "experts" which they have suddenly become, standing there and looking at the video assets. You really don't have a director anymore, and that's too had.

H.F.   Thanks for this wonderful interview, Bob. I really learned a lot.

21

Virginia Vale

The B western was a low budget movie and some studios would shoot them in days. Our studio usually had a seven- or eight-day shooting because George O'Brien always demanded an amount of quality.

Virginia Vale was a rarity in the picture business. She came to Paramount Pictures in 1937, started out in bit parts and advanced to playing second leads. She played in *The Big Broadcast of 1938*, the film which introduced Bob Hope's signature song, "Thanks for the Memories." Other early films were *Her Jungle Love* with Ray Milland and Dorothy Lamour, and *Cocoanut Grove* with Harriet Hilliard and Fred MacMurray.

After winning a "Gateway to Hollywood" contest, she was given a contract at RKO, the studio which changed her name from Dorothy Howe to Virginia Vale. At RKO she played in George O'Brien's last series of six westerns.

Unlike others, Virginia Vale did not want to hang on after her Hollywood welcome seemed over. In 1942 she made a clean break and never really looked back. Only recently has she been "rediscovered" and film festivals and collectors have started taking a renewed interest in her career.

I met Virginia Vale at the Knoxville Western Film Caravan in 1993 and have spoken with her many times since. In the following interview she talks about her early career at Paramount Pictures, but mainly the B westerns which gained her fame, and about her work with George O'Brien, whom she respected enormously.

H.F. Virginia, could you say something about your childhood, and any show business aspirations you might have had?

V.V. Certainly! I was born in Dallas, Texas, and I guess I was just born to show business. When I was just a little bitty tyke, if someone needed a song or a dance or a little pantomime, I was there to do it.

H.F. Were your mother and father involved in show business?

V.V. No, they weren't. My family was not theatrical in any sense of the word. I was in the Dallas Little Theater working in a play and the director asked me if I would like to audition for a talent scout from Paramount who was coming to town. I said, "Of course." So I did a little one-person scene for him and he asked me if I would send some pictures to Hollywood. I did and came out for a test. The test was successful and I was signed at Paramount. I was there for a year and a half, and that's how it all began.

H.F.   When was this?

V.V.   This was 1937. A long time ago. As I said, I stayed at Paramount for a year and had some bit parts as everyone who starts out does. Then I had some second leads in a couple of pictures.

H.F.   What pictures were these?

V.V.   Oh, I was in *The Big Broadcast of 1938* with Bob Hope. I played one of Bob Hope's three wives. It wasn't a big part but I was in five or six scenes. I had a lovely wardrobe, and the marvelous song, "Thanks for the Memories" came from the film. The song won the Oscar that year.

In fact, after the picture was over there was a radio show and they asked me if I would come in and sing Shirley Ross's part in the song. So I was on the air with Bob Hope the first time "Thanks for the Memories" was aired. I'd almost forgotten that until someone reminded me. It was funny because I asked them how they wanted it done, and they said I should do it just like it was done in the movie. Well, in some portions of the song in the movie there was no singing, just music. They said, "No, you can't do that on the radio, you have to sing it straight through." Anyhow, it was lots of fun.

H.F.   Any recollections of Bob Hope?

V.V.   Not really. Because I only had one short scene with him when he was thrown in jail for not paying alimony to all of us wives.

H.F.   You mentioned some other second leads.

V.V.   After *Big Broadcast* I did the second lead in *Her Jungle Love* with Ray Milland and Dorothy Lamour. That was fun. It was my first experience on location. We went down to Laguna to shoot the scene where we find them marooned in the jungle. The other big part I had at Paramount was the second lead in *Cocoanut Grove* with Harriet Hilliard and Fred MacMurray.

H.F.   Why did you leave Paramount?

V.V.   Like I mentioned, I stayed with Paramount for a year and a half, and after that old option was dropped, my agent called me one day and asked me if I would be interested in entering the Jesse Lasky "Gateway to Hollywood" contest. It was for singing and acting. I said, "Sure!" So I did it and won.

Virginia Vale

Rhonda Fleming was an entrant in this thirteen week contest, and Kirby Grant was the male winner. Gail Storm was the winner of the following series. That's how I got the name Virginia Vale. The Award was a contract at RKO, the name Virginia Vale, and a feature role in the film, *Three Sons*.

H.F. So Virginia Vale is not your real name.

V.V. No, it's Dorothy Howe. That's the name I worked under at Paramount.

H.F. Then you gravitated into the B westerns, is that correct?

V.V. I did some featured parts at RKO, and was loaned out to Producers Releasing Corporation for the lead in three pictures. Then I did George O'Brien's last series of six at RKO. I don't know if it was because they didn't have any plans for me or if they thought we worked together well, which we did. I did a number of short subjects with Ray Whitley who was a singing cowboy. I did bit parts and small parts at RKO. I was there two years. Again, the option was dropped.

H.F. How did that option work?

V.V. Usually it is six months, six months, and then for a year at time. I don't know why mine was dropped. I guess it was just my destiny. The last year I was in the business I only worked three weeks. That was 1941-42. My mother and I talked it over and I felt it was obvious that I was never going to be another Joan Crawford or Betty Grable or Myrna Loy, so I freshened up my shorthand and typing I had learned in high school and went to work as a stenographer. So that's how I got out of the business. But I certainly loved it.

H.F.   How did it feel coming to Hollywood as a young girl?

V.V.   Well, when it's been your ambition to do something in the theater or in the movies or perform in any sense of the word, then any step upward is exciting. And we also had wanted to come to California for years, so everything just fell in place when we came out.

H.F.   You are remembered mainly for your westerns. Did you know much about horsemanship when you came to Hollywood?

V.V.   Not too much. When I was a kid, about ten years old I guess, I spent four or five days on a ranch in Texas. We rounded up sheep, and I guess I did not have enough sense to be afraid. But other than that, I had never ridden until 1937-38 when I first came out here. But I did know how to ride.

H.F.   Can you say something about the B westerns and what distinguished them from the major western films?

V.V.   Most of them were by a studio. Each studio would have its main star. Republic had John Wayne, Roy Rogers and Gene Autry. RKO had George O'Brien as its big western star. The B western was a low budget movie and some studios would shoot them in four days. Our studio usually had a seven or eight day shooting schedule, because George always demanded an amount of quality.

Believe me, I am not denigrating the others, but I think George always demanded a bit more. B westerns were made to fill in for major motion picture at the Saturday matinee, or the double feature. They were all full-length films. As I mentioned, I made six with George O'Brien, and it was fun.

That was the end of George O'Brien with RKO. I don't know whether it was time to end the contract, or whether his patriotism got the better of him. Because that is when World War II came along and he was an officer in the Naval Reserve. And so in 1942 he went into the Navy and Tim Holt took over as their western star.

H.F.   Anything in particular you recall about George O'Brien?

V.V.   Well, I don't have anything very exciting to say about George except that he was a real gentleman. I haven't really worked with anybody in the business that wasn't a gentleman. Maybe I give off the air that I expect people to be gentlemen. But he was also a gentle man. As far as I knew him he was very soft-spoken, very well-mannered, a very caring man. And he was a *good actor*. It's a shame that once he started in westerns, he ceased to be in big productions, because he was a good actor. Later on, after he came back from the Navy, he was in bigger productions but only in feature parts. Of course, he was older and younger cowboys had taken over. That's understandable and that is the business. I wish he had had more opportunity to show his real acting ability.

H.F.   You mentioned that Tim Holt replaced George O'Brien at RKO. Did you do any work with Tim Holt?

V.V.   Only one movie, *Robbers of the Range*. Tim was an excellent actor.

H.F.   So you just decided to leave the business in 1942!

V.V.   Yes, I did. I left in forty-two. I decided to quit the business since the business more or less quit me. I decided to make a clean cut, and hardly ever thought about it after that. I closed the door completely and it wasn't opened again until someone heard that I was still alive and around. He wrote me and asked me if I would do an interview with him. I said, "Sure, let's do it on paper." So he wrote a bunch of questions down and I answered them and sent it back. Since then I have been invited to film festivals which I think are wonderful. They are fun, and meeting the fans, you don't dream that they are still out there. New fans too!

H.F.   You go back a long way in the movie business, Virginia. Could you give us a bit of a synopsis as you knew it?

V.V.   As far as I am concerned, I was pretty naive about the whole thing. I wish I had been more aggressive. But I was told at the beginning to let my agent do all the contracts, and all the searching for parts, so I never said a word. I just sat back and did what I was told. Had I been more aggressive and hounded the producer's offices and head of the studio or the casting department as to their plans for me, I might have stayed in the business and been another Joan Crawford. Who knows?

H.F.   Any directors who were particularly helpful?

V.V.   Oh, I haven't even thought of directors' names for nearly forty years at least. But Dave Howard did the last three of the George O'Brien's. The other one I can think of is Ed Kill who took over when Dave died.

H.F.   Were you nervous in front of the camera when you started out?

V.V.   No, nothing bothered me. I loved it, I loved to be on stage. I don't know if that is conceit or what it is. But I loved to be on stage. It's such a thrill. It really makes you feel as if you accomplished something.

H.F.   You were very young when you came to Hollywood. Did success at an early age spoil you at all?

V.V. I don't think so. But you always want to move higher so I never really felt I was a true success. I never really attained the goal that I wanted to attain.

H.F. Was it a big letdown when you realized that you couldn't?

V.V. No, I guess that I'm just too practical a person. But you love the business. You love the attention, you love the slipping into somebody else's life when you play a part, even a small part. You miss it. Sure you miss it, but having a regular pay check coming in is pretty nice.

H.F. Do you have a family?

V.V. No, I don't have any family. I'm the last of my family. I never married. I almost did a couple of times, but I just chose not to. I've been in love, but I never married. I guess I never found the right person, and I'm pretty independent myself. No brothers, and no sisters. I have one cousin in Arkansas.

H.F. When you come to film festivals like Knoxville, you are surprised that people remember you!

V.V. Yes, but it has to be the older ones who remember you on the big screen. But it's wonderful to see younger people under forty or even under fifty who are interested. And they are interested because of cable TV, it's done the whole thing. Otherwise the B western would have died out completely.

H.F. Anything you are particularly involved with today?

V.V. Oh yes! I am very involved in figure skating. I'm a judge and in other ways, I'm serving the figure skating sport.

H.F. Some of the standard questions, Virginia. When you see the industry today, how do you feel about it?

V.V. Well, the products I find rather disturbing. I don't like violence and hear of millions of people who don't like violence but you still get it. I'm not a writer, and maybe I shouldn't say a word, but there seems to be very little script. There really isn't a beginning, a middle and an end. I'm not really crazy about all that sex either. I'm old enough to realize that so much is not necessary. Another thing is they use the camera so much and there are no words going on. There is a shot of the face which lasts for ten seconds, and there is no dialogue. To me personally, a lot of what is out there today is not very palatable. But it is to a lot of people so they will continue to make money.

H.F. Any ambitions to get back in the business?

V.V. I've gotten calls from people asking why I don't get into commercials or other avenues of the industry. But I don't need that struggle at my age.

Not any more. But no matter how long you've been out of the business, or no matter how clean you cut it, you never give up loving to perform.

H.F. You've been a real trouper. Any sustaining philosophy?

V.V. That's a little deep for me to answer. I guess I deal in clichés like "live and let live." There are things I accept today but I don't necessarily condone them. When I was a kid, my dad left home when I was eight years old and my mom and I had a real tough time. I think it's through her that I developed my practical side and my independence so that I can look after myself. And nobody ever gave me a penny. Everything I have ever gotten has been through my own work or whatever talent I have.

H.F. Are you fully retired now?

V.V. I retired from Lockheed in January 1977 after thirty-four years. I decided that as soon as I could handle things the way I want to do, I was just going to quit and play. I have a few reasons for getting up: I do Meals on Wheels three days a week; I'm very involved in figure skating, so I have to judge test competitions; and I try to ride at least once a month. Of course, I have to look after my little home and all those kinds of things. And it's wonderful.

H.F. All those years at Lockheed, Virginia, did people know about your career in movies?

V.V. Some of them did. I never went around saying I was in the movies, because that was in the past.

H.F. Thanks so much, Virginia!

V.V. Oh, this has been just great. Thanks for the opportunity.

22

Virgil Vogel

Great directors are usually those with a lot of balls. I had no formal training as a director. But directing is like any command position. You should know every position beneath you, and all major parts of picture making.

Prolific Virgil W. Vogel has been a director, writer and producer in Hollywood for over fifty years. Born in Peoria, Illinois he came West right out of high school. An Air Ace during World War II, he flew twenty-four missions over Japan, winning numerous medals and citations including the Distinguished Flying Cross.

Vogel learned the picture business from the ground up, beginning as a mail boy in the editing room, and graduating to being a cutter and finally a film editor at Universal in 1940. From there he went to the optical department where he learned the art of creating special effects.

He got his directing break in 1955 with the science fiction film, *The Mole People*. Several pictures followed including *The Land Unknown*, a man-encounters-dinosaurs epic conceived long before *Jurassic Park*. Then in 1980 he directed *Beulah Land*, a polished TV production and a generational look at the life of a southern family, which carries the viewer through the Civil War and its aftermath.

But it was in television, where Virgil Vogel began working in 1957, that we see his true and lasting imprint — an imprint and legacy that has been equaled by few. To date, he has directed well over four hundred hours of programming, including series episodes, numerous pilots and TV movies, and several mini-series.

Vogel has directed almost every type of show, yet more than half his efforts over the years have been westerns, a genre he understands as completely as anyone. Included in his list of credits are ninety episodes of *Wagon Train*, forty-five episodes of *Big Valley*, and twelve hours of the twenty-five hour mini-series *Centennial*. He directed seventeen episodes of the recent *The Young Riders* series, and in 1991 the National Cowboy Hall of Fame honored him with their "Wrangler Award as Best Director of a Western TV Show." In 1993 he was named "Wild West Director of the Year," at the Tuolumne County Wild West Film Fest.

In the following interview Virgil Vogel talks about his more than fifty years in the film and TV business. He talks about the stars, their talents and their limitations. His special friendship with the great Barbara Stanwyck for whom his admiration knows no limits. He talks about his many series: Ward Bond and Robert Horton in *Wagon Train*, Lee Majors in *The Big Valley*, Lorne Greene and Pernell Roberts in the early years of *Bonanza*. He is candid about his views, precise in his comments about directing, and calls each separate issue the way he sees it.

H.F. Virgil, it's a long way from Peoria, Illinois, to Hollywood, California. What prompted you to make that long trek?

V.V. Well, I came West right out of high school. I arrived in California the day my uncle, Lee Garms, was fired as cameraman for *Gone with the Wind*. He was one of the most-noted cameramen out here. So I was just lucky to be at the right place at the right time. I was very young.

H.F. But was there a particular reason to head West?

V.V. Adventure! Sheer adventure. But I had some problems too. I had been in the automobile business in high school. Yet, I was a musician and was promised a job in San Francisco. I was looking for a job in a Big Band, but I couldn't make the Union in San Francisco, so I came to Los Angeles to see my uncle before I went home.

My uncle said he was going to make a picture in about six months, and if I wanted to stick around he would give me some kind of job. I was working on his picture when war was declared. The Germans invaded Poland in September 1939. He got me a job on his picture as a mail boy. I had a couple of friends there. One was Billy Asher. Later, he directed a lot of the *I Love Lucy* shows. Then he did *Bewitched*. He was producer and director of the show and married its star Elizabeth Montgomery. He and I became very good friends. We worked together at Republic. My first real experience was in film editing. We were run around guys in the editing room.

H.F. No experience before that at all?

V.V. Like I said, just as a mail boy. I would clean pictures but it was always in the editing room.

H.F. Then the war came along. How did it affect your career?

V.V. When the war came along it was grabbing all the young men. The studios were keeping everybody they could. They needed someone badly in the optical department, so I spent about a year in there. We'd call it the effect department, montages and that. It was a great background. Then my own number started coming close, so I joined the reserves in the Army Air Corps. I had about six or eight months training, and Universal let me go back on pictures as an assistant cutter. I did a picture with Charles Boyer and Barbara Stanwyck and it was a great experience.

H.F. How much active duty did you spend in the Air Corps?

V.V. I spent three years and I did a lot of combat. I was a pilot and an instructor. First on the B17s, then on the B29s. That was a big airplane back then. I flew twenty-four missions over Japan. I won the Distinguished Flying Cross, Air Medals and a Unit Citation.

H.F. And after the war?

V.V. Universal took me back as an assistant cutter. I worked there and met Bob Parish who became a good friend of mine. He was working in the Optical Department like I had. Billy Asher was there at Universal too. Well, Bob Parish got a job cutting for the film *A Double Life* which won a Best Actor Oscar for Ronald Colman in 1947. It was a lovely job. I worked about nine months on it and got to know George Cukor very well. After that I did the same kind of job in *Mr. Peabody and the Mermaid* with William Powell and Ann Blyth. After that Universal made me a full-fledged film editor. I worked in that capacity for about three and a half years. Later, I did *A Touch of Evil* with Orson Welles.

After I cut about twenty-four pictures, Universal made me head of the department. Then they put me on the staff. There were about thirteen men who ran the studio. I sort of became the official editor of the studio, with all the assistants working under me.

H.F. That must have been a great source of satisfaction?

V.V. No, not really. I really didn't like the executive work. So I told Ed Muhl, the studio head, that I really had to do something else or I was going to leave. He was very upset. I might also add that he was the most underrated man in Hollywood ever. He was a great executive, but he didn't have a chance. Everyone just knew him as Ed, and he couldn't get any respect. I told him that I had to do something else. I didn't like the fact that I lost my identity as a person. He said he would see what he could do, and asked me what I would like. I told him I'd like to be a director. He said that if this is what I want, he would do what he could. About six months later he gave me a picture called *The Mole People*. Then I did *Ma and Pa Kettle*.

H.F. Then you had no formal training as a director?

V.V. That's right! This was a new direction for me. Directing is like any command position. You should know every position beneath you. This was good training. Remember, by now I learned editing, a major part of picture making. So many people today edit who don't know how or have the background. I had spent fifteen years in editing by now. I also spent a couple of years in the optical department, so there is no optical effect around that I don't know how to do. I had already seen the day of the "special effect" as you call it. It's not hard for me to understand.

Before Universal went broke, I asked them if I could do something called *Sword of Ali Baba*. I wanted to take the old Arabian Nights pictures Universal made, take the stunts out of them, and write a story about it. I hired a fine writer and was ready to go when the studio went broke.

H.F.   Universal was a major studio. What happened?

V.V.   Well, Universal Studios did not believe in television, so they started lagging behind the others. The other studios were at least putting their toes in the water.

H.F.   And what happened after you left Universal?

V.V.   I went to Europe and did a picture called *Terror in the Midnight Sun* in Sweden. The only recognizable name was Bob Burton. He was a good solid actor. The rest of the cast was Swedish. Half of them didn't speak English. I was very young and every challenge was fun. The cold weather got me. Sixty degrees below zero way above the Arctic Circle where we were shooting. It was the northernmost tip of Sweden, where Sweden, Norway and Russia meet.

H.F.   Was this the late 1950s?

V.V.   Yes, the end of 1957 I believe. I came back home after the filming and a friend of mine who I directed *Ma and Pa Kettle* for was now with CBS. He called for me and wanted me to come over and produce *Wagon Train*. I didn't want to work as a producer. I wanted to work as a director. So he said I could do both.

H.F.   Did you have a particular leaning toward westerns or the West in general at the time?

V.V.   Let's just say I had a special feel to work in the picture business. I was not a horseman. Anything around pictures is what I loved, and it was great working on them. He gave me an eight-year contract and I started out almost in complete charge of the show. I came up with most of the stories which we did, and I wrote some. We would turn out a screenplay nearly every week.

H.F.   You had some very good scripts!

V.V.   Yes they were. They were really great. But we stole from so many stories. There wasn't a movie made that we didn't steal at least something [laughing]. We even did *Great Expectations* and gave Charles Dickens screen credit. We were blatant and brazen in those days. We were doing so many shows. This went on eight years.

H.F.   Were you with the show the whole time?
V.V.   Yes! But Robert Horton left after five years and that changed things.

H.F.   How about Ward Bond? A fine actor with a powerful presence on the screen!
V.V.   Well, Ward Bond was Ward Bond. The same way he was on the screen. He wasn't very different. Tough, blustery, a little bit of a braggadocio. Not heavy though. Like most people, if you called them on it they will shape up, no matter how much power they have.

H.F.   Did the two of you get along?
V.V.   Well, this is an open secret. The first two years were all right. The third year, I was called up to the office. They said that Ward didn't want me on the show this year. I asked, "Why?" They said he didn't like the way I treated the crew. I was too nice to them. He'd like to see more discipline.

H.F.   How did you handle that? Bond was a big star at the time.
V.V.   I asked them how they liked my pictures. They said my pictures were the best. Then I asked them about the schedule costs. They said my costs had been the lowest. So I explained that if I was making cheaper pictures and better pictures, are you going to fire me because I treat another person well? They said I made good sense. This was the third year as I said. The same thing happened the fourth year and the fifth year.

H.F.   Was this well-known?
V.V.   As I said, it was kind of an open secret. I knew how he felt about me, and he knew how I felt about him. Of course, his politics were pretty right wing. In fact, they were way out. Yet, He still made pretty good friends with the crew. They were union men, but they liked him and he liked them.

H.F.   He was quite close to John Ford. He was one of that inner circle in Ford's Stock Company.
V.V.   Oh yes! John Ford was also a good friend of mine. He would come to the set of *Wagon Train* and give me the big wink. He would argue Bond to death. Ward would jump off his chair, give him his fan, give him his light. And most of the time, Ford would ignore him. John Ford would have made a great actor.

Well, about six months before Bond died, the edit production guy came up to me and said, "Well, kid, you finally made it." I asked him what he meant. He said that Bond was in his office last night and said he didn't want any starring roles unless I directed them. That he finally said I was the best director in town. Six months later he died. I think that killed him.

H.F.   And the show was never quite the same!

V.V.   Of course, Horton left and the show really went down. To give you an example, Horton would get six thousand fan letters a week, and Bond would get six. Nobody else would get any letters. But Horton left the show on his own free will. He wanted to do other things. I thought it was wrong and I told him so at the time. He didn't want himself locked into a contract. That contract would have made him one of the richest men around. Then the show closed. I was tired of Universal by this time so I left. The first thing I did was work for Aaron Spelling. He loved my work and started giving me shows. Then I went to *Bonanza* and did seven *Bonanzas*. I won the Director of the Year Award in 1965 for *Bonanza*.

H.F.   What do you recall of Lorne Greene?

V.V.   Lorne Greene was a sweetheart of a guy, a very nice guy. But his was not my style of acting. He was too slow. Too pedantic. I tried to put some life into him, but he was very set in his ways. He had been a very, very successful radio announcer in Canada. I admired his ability, but thought he could do much better. He'd argue how much better could he do. He was very successful. You can't argue with success, but I did try.

H.F.   Were you there when Pernell Roberts gave up the show?

V.V.   Yes! Pernell hated the show. I was sympathetic to anyone who doesn't like what he is doing. Other directors wanted to work with him. He said, "Virg, here I am thirty-five years old and I'm walking around calling someone 'Pa'!" The other guys got themselves their first big raise when they went on strike, but he refused to join them. They made big money and he just wanted out. Anyway they let him out.

H.F.   After *Bonanza*!

V.V.   I did some more work with Aaron Spelling. Then I did *Mission: Impossible* with Peter Graves. Eventually, I wound up on *The Big Valley*. Somebody in the *Bonanza* group took a dislike to me and I never worked for them again.

H.F.   I've heard you say how you thought the world of Barbara Stanwyck. She had a remarkable capacity as an actress to show both a hard and a soft side to her.

V.V.   I'll say this. Barbara Stanwyck was a very soft, wonderful, and well-refined lady. She was very small. Her first husband abused her quite a bit. She finally divorced him and married Robert Taylor. I had given Barbara a starring role every year I was with *Wagon Train*, sometimes two, and the last year I gave her three starring roles. I really loved that lady. I still had a commitment with *Bonanza* but dropped it to continue with *Big Valley*. I stayed with *Big Valley* four years and directed every other episode. Of course, Barbara was the star.

And I had a wonderful cast. Barbara played Victoria Barkley, a strong-willed widow, who headed the Barkley clan of cattle ranchers. Then there was Richard Long and Peter Breck as her two sons. Linda Evans was the gorgeous sister, and Lee Majors played Heath, the rebellious half-brother.

H.F. I always enjoyed Lee Majors work. He had an interesting quality.

V.V. We had him on *Big Valley* when he just came off the North Hollywood playground. He was a star athlete. He played college football somewhere in the south. I think it was Alabama. He was very nice and very fresh. He had a good career. In fact, he just did something last year. Lee has worked all that he has wanted to work. The whole group in *Big Valley* was a great group.

H.F. You said earlier that you were pretty easy going with your casts? Would you like to comment on that?

V.V. Everybody has his own style. You learn a lot through trial and error. That's the best way. For me it was best because it got things done. But I'm smart enough to try different things with different people.

H.F. Anyone in particular whom you found difficult to direct?

V.V. I'll tell you a little story. Once I was doing a little thing called *Here Comes the Brides*. The star of the show didn't get along with my assistant. The man was a crackerjack of an assistant. A real good one. I had a second assistant, Chris Morton, who is still a good friend today.

Now this was twenty years ago and we were working on the Columbia back lot. The star of the show had a habit of always being in his dressing room and never on the stage. So when you needed him you had to call. He was making deals with his brokers and his investments. Well, we were running the scene with one of the girls, and my assistant wanted somebody to read the lines from behind the screen for the show's star. I reminded him that the star wasn't going to like this at all. But my assistant wanted to roll immediately because of a tight schedule.

He yelled, "Roll the cameras!" We started the scene. The star saw the red light and suddenly burst in "What the hell are you guys doing!" he yelled. I said that we were shooting the scene, and he starts a raving argument with my assistant. They are screaming at each other. Finally, the star storms off the stage. I stayed around to calm my assistant, but they never threw a punch.

Then my assistant goes to the phone and calls the unit manager. He told him about the fight. He said to the unit manager, "You are going to back me, aren't you?" The unit manager thought for a moment and said, "I don't know. Can you act?" So that afternoon I had a new assistant.

H.F.   Those directors who impressed you the most?

V.V.   Of course, John Ford has always been my idol. George Cukor was wonderful. And George Stevens was just great. Former cameraman. Great directors are usually those with a lot of balls. How Stevens handled people, I don't know. But I liked his style when he made pictures. *Shane* was a true screen classic. One of the very best. I don't think anyone but George Stevens could have made it the success it was.

H.F.   Anything on the horizon now, Virgil?

V.V.   I have a movie I am preparing, and I hope to shoot it in February in Texas.

H.F.   Thanks so much, Virgil!

V.V.   Thanks, too. It's been good talking with you.

23

Clint Walker

Those fellows who ran the old studios had a commitment to making good movies. There are no more Jack Warners, Louis B. Mayers or Darryl Zanucks. It's an end of an era, and now you have a bunch of guys who wouldn't even know who Clint Walker is.

Big Clint Walker (six feet, six inches tall) almost single-handedly put Warner Brothers on the TV map. His popular TV series *Cheyenne* ranks with *Gunsmoke*, *Rawhide* and *Maverick* as one of the very best in the western genre. Clint Walker's credits, however, go far beyond the hit series he initiated. He soon became a well-sought out and popular leading man starring in such fine films as *Baker's Hawk*, with Burl Ives and Diane Baker; *The Bounty Man* with Richard Basehart and Margot Kidder, *Send Me No Flowers* with Doris Day and Rock Hudson, and *Yellowstone Kelly*. He was one of the infamous twelve in *The Dirty Dozen* with Lee Marvin and gave perhaps his best and most lasting performance in *The Night of the Grizzly*, a fine and no-frills family story.

Yet never during his youth in Alton, Illinois, where he was born in 1927, did Walker ever aspire or think about acting as a career. These endeavors gave him an awareness of the "real world" and a strong sense of professionalism he has never lost.

At age nine he was working odd jobs in a carnival. In high school he worked in a steel foundry. He would caddie in the summer and shovel snow in the winter. Occasionally he'd get a chance to go to the movies.

When he was eighteen, he joined the Merchant Marines and went to Catalina for Maritime training. It was his first taste of the Golden State. With the end of the War, he put his size and strength to use working construction. When his aspirations of becoming a carpenter dwindled, he began working in law enforcement, moonlighting as a bouncer. It was while working security at the Sands Hotel in Las Vegas that he decided to heed the advice of many people who told him he would do just fine in the movies.

With the help of veteran character actor Henry Wilcoxon, he made his

Clint Walker

screen debut in Cecil B. DeMille's grand 1956 epic, *The Ten Commandments*. From here it was a short leap forward to a Warner Brothers contract and the role of Cheyenne Bodie. The series put Warner Brothers and Clint Walker on the big time TV map. Suddenly Clint Walker was a star.

In the following interview, one of the first he has given in many years, Clint Walker talks about his films, his hit TV series, and the many people who have come and gone along the way. He recently lost his wife after many years of a happy marriage. As for the future, he hides nothing. Integrity is of the essence, his convictions and feelings are firm and strong, and he'd like to do some more pictures, some good westerns in particular. Let's hope he does!

H.F. Clint, would you tell us something about your upbringing in Alton, Illinois?

C.W. Sure! I was actually born in Hartford, Illinois, a little Mississippi River town, and raised in nearby Alton. That particular area is where Lewis and Clark crossed the Mississippi on their little trip. We also have a dam there and the Lewis and Clark Bridge. A lot of folks don't know that Alton was also the home of the tallest man in the world. He was eight feet something. His name was Robert Wadlow. As a youngster I would work the river boats, going down the Mississippi and Illinois rivers, pushing barges to Chicago and all the way down to New Orleans.

H.F. But you had no acting aspirations at all during that time?

C.W. No, not really! Those of us who portrayed cowboys, I imagine, had heroes of our own when we were kids. I liked Hopalong Cassidy and Buck Jones. Yet, I always liked going to the movies. The problem was I just didn't have enough time to see too many. There were some Gene Autry's and Roy Rogers'. There were the Hopalong Cassidy's and Wild Bill Elliott's. I recall that Bill Elliott had two guns he wore backwards. When he'd draw, he'd usually cross draw, and when he'd cross draw, they'd come out front ways.

Then, as I said, there was Buck Jones, and later on Randolph Scott. And Gary Cooper whom I met a number of times. Cooper would always kid me about my hats. He'd say that I should get a bigger hat, and of course, I was trying to wear one where the crown wasn't too high. I figured I was tall enough. It was funny meeting some of my heroes later on.

Another thing I recall is falling in love with Shirley Temple when I was about nine or ten. I was going to take my scooter, pack a few clothes and some food, and scooter all the way down to California.

H.F. So you started working at a very young age, and in a sense never stopped?

C.W. I started working when I was nine years old. I'd go to the carnivals and circuses and get various jobs. Jobs like carrying water, setting up milk bottles, or bringing back the baseballs. I'd get jobs in the grocery stores cleaning up. As I got older I'd shovel snow in the winter, mow lawns and caddie at the local golf course in the summer. Lots of people are surprised when I tell them I didn't play football in high school, with my size and strength. But I couldn't. I was always working. I would get out of school at three o'clock, and at four o'clock I would go to work in a steel foundry for an eight-hour shift.

H.F. After high school, what then?

C.W. I didn't quite finish high school. I wound up working for a big paper mill, and then went to work for a glass company loading box cars and glassware. When I was pushing eighteen, I had to worry about going into the service. As I indicated I worked the river boats some of the summers, pushing down as far as New Orleans, so I joined the Merchant Marines. Between ships I also worked a lot of odd jobs. When the War ended in 1945, I began selling vacuum cleaners door-to-door. Then I sold insurance door-to-door. I even tried selling cars. I didn't have any problem with the new ones, but I couldn't sell used cars because there was always something wrong with them, and I couldn't lie about it.

H.F. How did you find your way to California?

C.W. When I joined the Merchant Marines, I went to Catalina for Maritime training. That's how I became acquainted with California. First, I got into construction work. I went to Texas to work as a carpenter, then tried working again as a carpenter in California for a big company. But things didn't work out.

I started to figure on what was the best thing I had to offer. I decided on my size. So I got into the law enforcement game. I worked for an outfit called Newton Detective Agency for awhile. I worked eight hours on the waterfront making sure the long shore men didn't take too many things. Then I'd go to work in a night club for six hours as a bouncer. This was in Long Beach. Then I figured I could make more money in Las Vegas, so I went out there and worked security at the Sands Hotel for a year and a half.

While I was working in Las Vegas there were a lot of picture people who would approach me and say that I should try the movies. At first I thought that was a pretty silly way to make a living. Then I started thinking things over, "What does law enforcement offer me, maybe a hole between my eyes." So I decided to go give it a whirl and eventually I got lucky.

H.F. How did this happen?

C.W. A man named Henry Wilcoxon, a fine actor, helped me a lot. He appeared in many great films like the 1939 version of *The Last of the Mohicans*, *Mrs. Miniver*, and *Cleopatra* with Claudette Colbert, which was directed, of course, by Cecil B. DeMille. He played Marc Antony. Henry Wilcoxon was a very nice man. You couldn't meet a nicer human being.

At the time DeMille was making *The Ten Commandments*, and Henry Wilcoxon in turn had me meet DeMille briefly. DeMille decided he liked me and put me in the film. Wilcoxon had made me take a couple of screen tests, but oddly enough he made sure they were westerns, because he thought I would do very well in westerns — which, of course, I did. That eventually led to a contract with Warner Brothers and the *Cheyenne* series.

H.F. Then you were in *The Ten Commandments*.

C.W. Oh yes! I was the Sardinian Captain of the Guard. I'd sit by the throne all the time. I was wearing a helmet, a cape, and a big sword in my hands. I actually had some lines at one point in the picture, but DeMille came to me and said, "Clint, I'm not only going to have to take your lines away, I'm going to have to take you out of the scene. I hope you know that standing there in that helmet and all, my leading men look like a bunch of stumps around a tree." Anyway, DeMille was very nice to me and said he would make it up later to me. And he would have except as luck would have it, Warner Brothers saw my screen test, put me under contract, and I wound up making *Cheyenne*. But I still was in quite a few of the scenes. I just didn't have any lines. I just stand there looking mean.

H.F. So *Ten Commandments* was your screen debut?

C.W. That was the first part I had in a picture. Before that I had one day's work in *The Bowery Boys Go to Africa*. I played Tarzan. The Bowery Boys were about to take Jane back to civilization and I discouraged them from doing it.

H.F. What do you recall about DeMille?

C.W. DeMille was an extremely demanding man. But he was also demanding on himself. He wouldn't ask anyone to do something he would not do himself. When we made *The Ten Commandments* in Egypt, they were shooting on top of a temple. He climbed a ladder all the way to the top of it. In doing so it created a hole in his heart, and that's what eventually killed him. But he finished the picture. He was that kind of guy.

H.F. What about Charlton Heston?

C.W. I've always had very great respect for Chuck Heston. He's not only a very fine actor, he is a very good human being. I also liked Yul Brynner very much. For me this was a heck of an opportunity. All of a sudden, here I was up there with the biggies. Heck, it was like a kid let loose in a toy store. I was enthralled by the whole thing.

H.F. A real thrill I bet! An epic like that.

C.W. Oh it was. Especially for me being my first picture. Of course DeMille never did anything on a small scale. And almost anything he did would hold people's interest because of the way he did it. He was a stickler for legitimate detail. He'd want things as legitimate and as realistic as he could get them.

H.F. How did he create the parting of the Red Sea? What great special effects!

C.W. I didn't see them do that scene. By that time I think I was at Warner Brothers. But it was quite a project. So many people were involved and it wasn't a scene you could do over and over again. Of course, they had at least three cameras shooting it from different angles. No doubt you heard the joke, "Ready when you are, C.B." which has to do with that specific scene.

H.F. I'd like to hear it!

C.W. There was a joke. After building all the sets and rehearsing all day, after getting all the actors and cameras in place, they finally decided to rehearse it. In rehearsal everybody knew what they were supposed to do. So after the first scene was shot, DeMille says to the cameraman, "Well, how did it go?" The cameraman says, "I'm terribly sorry, Mr. DeMille, there was a hair on the lens." So DeMille hollers to the second cameraman, and that cameraman yells, "Mr. DeMille, one of the horses knocked the camera over halfway through the scene." Finally DeMille hollers at the third cameraman, and the guy yells back, "Ready when you are, C.B.!" It's kind of a classic joke which I am sure almost everybody has heard, but it's still funny.

H.F.   *Cheyenne* really put Warner Brothers on the map as far as TV westerns were concerned.

C.W.   Well evidently it kind of pulled them out of a tight spot. They weren't doing too well financially, so they started off with three shows. They figured mine would be over very shortly, yet mine was the only one that lasted.

H.F.   Then Warners actually put you under contract when you were making *The Ten Commandments*.

C.W.   What happened was that Hal Wallis put me under contract for six months, but didn't do anything with me. Then Warners saw the screen test and went to Hal Wallis and bought my contract.

H.F.   Had you much training in dialogue and delivering lines?

C.W.   I didn't study much. I studied at Paramount, but not a great deal. Even less at Universal. They wouldn't put me under contract or pay me a salary. They just let me come to some of their acting classes for a short time.

H.F.   How valuable are acting classes? I have heard pro and con.

C.W.   It depends on who your coach is and how you apply yourself, I guess. There are certain things you have to learn about acting. You have to learn to hit your mark. You have to learn not to get in the way of the other guy's light, because the camera has to see him over your shoulder. You have to know never to look at the floor and still know where your marks are. It becomes second nature eventually.

H.F.   Did you have a dialogue coach?

C.W.   Yes, I had one for a while. I think they had one at the studio because they were accustomed to making motion pictures. But as TV became more popular they began to do away with a lot of that. They became TV-oriented, and TV became a medium where you did a whole lot more with a whole lot less, and you did it faster.

H.F.   You became a big star very quickly as *Cheyenne*. Did you know a lot about horsemanship and gun work?

C.W.   The riding was something I hadn't done too much of, but they said, "Don't worry, you will either be a good rider by the end of the first year or a dead one." A couple of times I wondered which one it was going to be. We were at a place with huge sandstone formations, and we had to ride through a very narrow passageway in the rocks. When we went through there, the old horse would try to dump me against the rocks. I would bring my leg up alongside his neck to avoid being dumped, and got my canteen smashed flat. I got through it, but once I had a bad back and was very sore that day. I had to do a fast ride around the corner. I couldn't lean enough and the horse went one way, and I went the other.

H.F.   You alternated with *Sugarfoot,* didn't you?

C.W.   Well *Sugarfoot* didn't come along until later. I began having problems with Warner Brothers. They were letting other people do films and I wasn't doing many, so I walked out for a while. When I came back they arranged for me to do less *Cheyennes* and do more feature pictures. They brought in Ty Hardin as *Bronco* and Will Hutchins as *Sugarfoot.* They put all three under the *Cheyenne* banner.

H.F.   So you wanted more feature films from Warner Brothers, and the series was tying you up?

C.W.   That's right! They weren't letting me make films. They kept me too busy doing the *Cheyennes.*

H.F.   How did becoming a big star in the industry hit you?

C.W.   It's a funny thing. I was so busy working that I didn't give it much thought. I was traveling a lot and doing promotion. That is when I came to realize how many people knew me, and I didn't know them from Adam. That TV box has a tremendous capacity to reach people.

H.F.   You said something earlier about meeting Gary Cooper and what a thrill that was for you.

C.W.   Cooper and I would wind up at some of the same functions and be sitting at nearby tables. In between everything we would get up for a drink of water and get to talking. Cooper was a big man, about six foot, three inches or six foot, four inches. I thought he was a good actor and enjoyed the work he did. I seldom ever missed a Gary Cooper picture if I could manage to see it.

H.F.   What about *High Noon* and Cooper's Oscar winning performance?

C.W.   I thought it was good. I thought it was believable. Oddly enough that picture was put on the shelf. It was so badly shot and difficult to put together that they put it on the shelf for a while. Then some cutter got hold of it who was evidently pretty clever, and put it together well enough that it became a classic. What a lot of people don't realize is that in one of the shots, where he is having a showdown with the bad guys facing them on the street, you are so engrossed with what is going on, that you don't notice that a Greyhound bus goes through and over the top of Cooper's head.

H.F. I've seen the movie many times, it's one of my very favorites but I never noticed that.

C.W. Well, watch for it. Then, son of a gun! There it is. They never took it out because they couldn't get Cooper back. He was involved with other things.

H.F. Did you ever try to pattern yourself after a particular star or stars?

C.W. Like any other kid who liked the movies, I guess I did to a certain degree. Sometimes if I wasn't sure about doing something, I'd say to myself, "What would Gary Cooper do? Or what would Roy Rogers or Hopalong Cassidy do in that case?"

H.F. Who is taller, you or Jim Arness?

C.W. Jim's an inch taller. I know him but not real well. I've been up to his house and met his boys. They are nice people. You don't hear much about him anymore. I don't think he wants publicity. All I can say is I liked his acting. I think he did a fantastic job with *Gunsmoke*, an excellent job.

H.F. How about John Wayne?

C.W. I worked with John just a couple of times, very briefly and not on a regular show. One time was when we both showed up at the Hollywood Bowl for some affair. Then a few months before he died, all of us who had been in westerns did something with John. He was doing most of the talking. My wife knew him quite well. I liked his work a lot. He came off as a man's man. When he was in a western, you believed him. He looked the part and played the part, and he did a heck of a job. John, of course, was very conservative. He was a fine patriot who was not afraid to speak his mind. I respected him for that.

H.F. You are best remembered as Cheyenne Bodie. But you made some very good films as well. A good one was *Baker's Hawk* with Burl Ives. It was a great family film.

C.W. You're right. It was a nice little film, and what a nice guy Burl Ives is. He reminds me somewhat of Vincent Price. I worked with Vincent in another western. In *Baker's Hawk*, I played a good no nonsense family man who kind of pinch hit for the sheriff in cleaning up the town.

H.F. How about *The Dirty Dozen*? A great cast, and an exciting film.

C.W. Well, *The Dirty Dozen* was like a vacation. Boy, after doing television for all those years, doing all those scenes — rush, rush, rush — what a pleasure. It took us six months to make that picture. Heck, at times I was off two weeks at a crack. I was able to get around London and visit those fantastic museums.

H.F. Of course, the picture starred Lee Marvin. But there were other big names, and soon to be big names. Guys like Ernest Borgnine, Charles Bronson, Donald Sutherland, and football great, Jim Brown.

C.W. Yes, a great cast. I was one of the Dirty Dozen, a character named Posey. Originally, I was to have a much bigger part in it as an Indian, and even do a rain dance and so on. But the guy directing the picture was Bob Aldrich. He was a heck of a football fan and Jim Brown kind of wound up getting some of my time there. Aldrich was a tremendous fan of his.

H.F. How was Lee Marvin to work with?

C.W. I did a fight scene with Lee in *The Dirty Dozen*. It turned out to be a very good scene. Of course, I was an admirer of Lee. He just had natural acting ability. He was a natural talent. I think he could have done it sleep walking.

H.F. How about Jim Brown back then? A great athlete who later became quite controversial.

C.W. Jim and I used to run in Hyde Park when we had a chance and were not working. He used to say to me, "Don't run easy, just float, man!" Of course Jim was probably one of the finest physical specimens you'd ever hope to see, which is why he was such a great football player. It's unfortunate that he let that racial prejudice interfere with his acting career, because I think he could have had a tremendous career. Especially when there were so many people trying to help him. Who knows! Maybe he is older and wiser now.

H.F. Richard Jaeckel was in that also. He started young in the business and did so much good work. He is often overlooked.

C.W. I'm glad you mentioned him. Richard played one of the M.P.'s. He's probably as nice a person as you ever hope to meet. He's got bad arthritis now and is taking treatments. Richard was a child star and has been in the business forever. And I'll tell you one thing. You'll never find a more professional actor, No sir! He was a no-nonsense actor. When he came, he was on time and was prepared. And the only job he ever did was a good one. He was a good actor.

H.F. How did you like working in England?

C.W. Funny. When I first got to England, I felt very much at home there. I recall walking outside the Royal Palace. It was a warm day and I didn't wear a coat. They had all those Palace Guards standing there with those big fluffy hats. They stand like statues and are not supposed to say a thing or to move.

I'm about to walk by them when I hear a voice. "Hey Clint, won't you give me your 'bloomin' autograph?" As I turned around, there was one of those soldiers talking out of the side of his mouth. At first, I couldn't believe that he had recognized me. But he had. There he was standing there, and he was not about to let me get away. He really appreciated the autograph.

H.F. Let's talk about *The Night of the Grizzly*. What a wonderful movie!

C.W. It was my favorite of all the shows I've ever done. It was a clean movie and a family type. We had so many good people in it. Martha Hyer played my wife. We had Ron Ely, Jack Elam, and Sammy Jackson. It was written by Warren Douglas, one of the sleeping giants of all the Hollywood writers. It turned out to be a beautiful movie. I've seen the thing so many times on TV now that it's a little embarrassing. But people still like to see it. Everyone did such a great job.

H.F. You're a big guy, Clint! When you do these fight scenes, how close do you come to the actual punch?

C.W. On occasion, anybody who does any amount of this is going to get hit, or you are going to hit somebody. But you try not to. Usually when somebody gets hit, it is because somebody misses their mark, or the timing is wrong. Ron Ely, the guy who played Tarzan, actually missed his mark and stepped in too close to me, and I actually cut him. I felt badly about it. On the same show, I cut my foot with the ax but I had to go through with the scene, because in this business you have to move on. You can watch the scene and you will never know that anything happened.

H.F. Do you consider *The Night of the Grizzly* your best acting job?

C.W. I don't know about my best acting, although it was my favorite picture. I did a thing called *Cry of the Wolfe*, where I got very good reviews. They panned some of the other people in the picture, but my reviews were good. I played a heavy in that one.

H.F. You were in *None But the Brave*, which was directed by Frank Sinatra!

C.W. You are right. It was a war picture, and it was Sinatra's first attempt at directing. Sinatra is kind of an enigma. If he's your friend, he's your good friend. He was very nice to people. I think Sinatra just got bored. He was a far more talented man than I ever realized. He had us all over to his home one night for a spaghetti dinner. He entertained us for three hours just telling jokes and funny stories. And he was very good at it, too. If you really watch Frank, he is a very good actor. I felt honored to work with him. We made the picture in Hawaii on the island of Koni. Those Japanese could not speak English and we really had a heck of a time.

H.F. You also did *Send Me No Flowers* with Doris Day and Rock Hudson. This was a different type of picture for you.

C.W. I played the wealthy Texas oil man who had gone to school with Doris. Doris had a cold at the time. She had a fever blister and wasn't feeling the greatest. I had to pick her up, swing her around, and kiss her all at the same time. Unfortunately, I cut her lip. She was a very nice lady. She had that certain quality about her, and I always enjoyed her singing.

H.F. The film industry today, Clint?

C.W. Well I'm not happy about it. There is far too much garbage. There is a lot of stuff done in bad taste, and I don't see the necessity for it at all. We didn't have to do it in our time, and they don't have to do it now.

H.F. Then why is it done?

C.W. Supposedly they say that the R-rating makes money. But they are still making good movies without having to resort to that. I like things like *Lonesome Dove* and *The Sacketts*. I like anything that Ben Johnson does. Ben turned out to be a very good actor, who is also a very likable human being. He was just a working stiff, a wrangler, before he got into acting. Fortunately, he never went through the stage of believing his own publicity.

H.F. Some of your favorite westerns?

C.W. *Shane* was a classic, and you can't find a better bad guy than Jack Palance. Another actor I always liked so much was Joel McCrea. A certain director whose name escapes me, once said that if you give me three scenes that I'll always remember in a picture, that picture will be a success.

I also like all the John Ford westerns. He made beautiful use of the country which was very appropriate. I like Ward Bond a lot. He worked very well with John Wayne in those days.

H.F. Any favorite directors you worked with?

C.W. I can't say that I can name just one or two, because there were so many who were equally good. Gordon Douglas with whom I made three pictures at Warner Brothers was very good. You can't put the people who did TV in the same category, however, because they just didn't get the chance to do the same thing as those who did feature films. The budget, the money, and even the actors at the time, were on a smaller scale. Howard Hawks was a very fine director, and I would have liked to work with him. He, too, was a man's man, and made manly pictures. I like the dirt, the sweat, and the realism.

H.F. Any regrets professionally?

C.W. I think you always have regrets. You can always think of a scene you could have done a little better, or perhaps something you might have tried differently. You know, when I quit the *Cheyenne* series, I should have been more financially-wise. I would have done what Jim Arness did with *Gunsmoke*. They would have given me the show at the time. They would have given me just about anything I wanted. When my eight-year contract ran out, Jack Warner invited me to dine in his personal dining room for the first time.

H.F.   What was that like?

C.W.   I dined with him and we talked. When we talked, he'd always offer me a cigar, but I'd decline. We had a few arguments and disagreements, but at the same time I had great respect for him. He ran Warner Brothers in a way that produced some very fine pictures.

Those fellows who ran the studios had a commitment to making good films. Well, there are no more Jack Warners, Louis B. Mayers, and Darryl Zanucks. It's an end of an era, and now you have guys who don't know who Clint Walker and lots of others are. And many don't even know much about the business of making pictures. The studios are owned by shoe companies and oil companies. What they are only interested in are the bucks, and unfortunately, many times they are not all that creative.

H.F.   Then on the whole the film business has been good to you?

C.W.   It's been an education. If I had it to do all over again, I'd do some things differently. I plan to go back. I lost my wife, and I'm going to try to get back in shape and make some more pictures. I'd love to do some good westerns. I'd love to work with Ben Johnson. I've never worked with him. When you work with people like that, you actually do a better job yourself because you are motivated by them.

H.F.   I've heard from so many people that in terms of sheer decency, those who were involved in making westerns, the crews, the actors, the wranglers, etc., were among the best people in the industry.

C.W.   That's true! This is true. You don't find many pretentious people. Again, take Ben Johnson. I mentioned how I would love to work with him. Ben's a fine actor and put him a western and he's right at home. He was a real cowboy and did so well on film. Likewise, I was a deputy sheriff, and got paid lots more money to do it on film. The bullets weren't real and I got to win. There's still a lot of good people out there in the industry, but I don't like the cheap stuff and all that bad language.

H.F.   You have lots of company out there!

C.W.   It isn't necessary. It's in bad taste and it sets a very bad example for our young people. I think there is an element out there that actually does it for that purpose. And that is unfortunate. Well, a lot of things are less than they should be today. I don't know whether people are going to wake up or not.

H.F. Do you think there will be a revival of the western film?

C.W. It's a funny thing about westerns. For a while nobody would do a western. Now they are doing them again, at least more than before. Also I think more and more people are yearning to get out of the big cities, have a garden, and maybe go hunting or fishing. It's the type of lifestyle that would be favorable to a renewed interest in the West.

H.F. I want to thank you, Clint!

C.W. Listen, you are entirely welcome. It's been a pleasure talking with you.

24

Marie Windsor

Today I think the westerns are so overproduced that they are losing touch with the simple westerns we enjoyed so much.

Marie Windsor has been dubbed the Queen of the "Bs" by *The New York Times*. And on November 6, 1994, the Roxie Cinema in San Francisco saluted the woman who has also been called "Hollywood's most underrated actress." One month earlier she had been honored by the Screen Actors Guild Society at the Academy of Motion Picture Arts and Sciences building in Beverly Hills.

Introduced by Charlton Heston when she was honored by the Screen Actors Guild Society, two of her most highly-acclaimed pictures were featured, *The Narrow Margin* (1952, RKO), and *The Killing* (1956, United Artists) — one of the first films directed by Stanley Kubrick, and for which she won the *Look Magazine* Award for Best Supporting Actress. In 1983 Marie Windsor was awarded a star on the Hollywood Walk of Fame, recognizing a career spanning seventy-six feature films, one hundred thirty television shows and dozens of stage productions.

Of her seventy-six pictures, twenty-two were westerns; and over her forty-year career some of her distinguished leading men included John Wayne, George Raft, John Garfield, Sterling Hayden, David Niven, Marlon Brando, James Garner and Abbott & Costello. While off-screen she is regarded as one of the most considerate, charming, and helpful film personalities, volunteering much of her time on behalf of her fellow performers, on-screen she has played (in the words of film historian Ephram Katz) "aggressive, domineering, downright nasty, and vicious types." Her roles as tough independent women led to stronger females parts in years to come. "Marie Windsor is the best of the female heavies," cited Ian Cameron in *Movie Magazine*.

Among her western films are *The Fighting Kentuckian* with John Wayne, *Hellfire* with Bill Elliott and Forrest Tucker, *Dakota Lil* with George Montgomery and Rod Cameron, *Little Big Horn* with Lloyd Bridges and John Ireland, *The Tall Texan* with Lloyd Bridges and Lee J. Cobb, *Day of the Bad Man* with Fred MacMurray, *Support Your Local Gunfighter* with James Garner and

Marie Windsor

Cahill— U.S. Marshal with John Wayne.

    Her numerous TV credits include *Tales of Wells Fargo, Cheyenne, Lawman, Gunsmoke, Wyatt Earp, Rawhide, Maverick,* and *Bonanza.* One of her proudest accomplishments is her founding role in the development of the Screen Actors Guild Society, which celebrated its twentieth anniversary in 1994.

    Marie Windsor has been married to Jack Hupp, a Beverly Hills realtor and former all–American basketball player, for more than forty years. She is also an accomplished woman in fields other than acting. In the past she has designed her own clothes, has been an outstanding western rider, an expert skeet shooter (she has won eleven trophies), and a fine artist who has sold more than a hundred paintings of her own. Marie Windsor recently retired from the Screen Actors Guild Board after twenty-five years of service. Upon her retirement from the Guild, she was made Honorary Chairperson Emeritus of the Film Society.

H.F.   Marie, you were born and grew up in Utah. Can you say a bit about those years?

M.W.   Certainly. I was born in the little town of Marysvale, a little town of two hundred-fifty to three hundred in the southern part of Utah, about two hundred miles south of Salt Lake City. It was mainly a farming and a little bit of a mining community. When I was about nine, someone gave me my first horse. I learned to ride bareback because we didn't have enough money for a saddle I recall it was a little tiny horse called "Silver Queen."

H.F.   Did you get bit with the acting bug at an early age?

M.W.   Yes, Yes, Yes! My grandmother, whom I called "Gunga" would take me to the movies every week. She was the town's postmistress and loved to take me to every movie that came our way. Gunga would always read the subtitles to me, and that developed a love affair with movies that never left me. I had a crush on Clara Bow and wanted to be like her. I would stage shows on our porch when I was eight.

H.F.   Were your parents in show business?

M.W.   No, they never were. No one in our family had ever been in show business, in fact. But my parents went along with this dream of mine. My mother drove me about thirty miles away on the dirt roads to take dancing lessons. Later I got involved in our little school plays. We had only one school and it covered grades K to twelve.

I ended up graduating high school in only three years. I think the principal saw that between my parents and my grandmother, they couldn't afford to send me to college. So they gave me some subjects to study on the side and eased me through high school quickly. But I'm not sure this was a great idea because I missed out on a lot of the English which I should have received.

H.F.   But you did go to college?

M.W.   I went to Brigham Young University for two years and studied art and drama. I won two contests there. In 1939, I was "Miss Covered Wagon Days" which was something like a Miss Utah contest which we didn't have in those days. I was also "Miss D. & R.G. Railroad." Then my grandmother and my mother found an expensive school of acting. They thought it was in New York. They were wrong; it was in Hollywood. So I went to Hollywood and enrolled in the Maria Ouspenskaya School of Drama. I moved into the famed Hollywood Studio Club. However, after a while my parents just couldn't afford to continue supporting me at the Studio Club.

H.F.   But you didn't give up!

M.W.   Well, I had already completed six months of the nine-month course and the tuition had been paid in full. So I saw an ad in the newspaper for a cigarette girl at the Mocombo Club, which back than was the movies leading nightclub. I just hated the job, and one night while I was helping a man on with his coat, he saw the tears in my eyes. He said to me, "You're not happy with this job, I guess." I told him "No!" He asked me if that was because I wanted to be an actress. I told him, "Yes," that I was going to school and working at night. Well, that man who found me sobbing over my cigarettes, was Arthur Hornblow, the producer. He told me that a friend of his was LeRoy Prinz, the dance director, and they were casting for a little picture they were going to do at the Hal Roach Studios.

The picture was called *All-American Co-Ed* and they were casting at Paramount. Mr. Hornblow introduced me to LeRoy Prinz and I got the job. It was a two-week job at sixty-six dollars a week. So that is how I got my Guild card and began my acting career. This was 1941.

H.F. So you got hooked on films the same year as the country went to war?

M.W. Oh I was "hooked on films," as you say, long before I got my guild card. But I was pretty starry-eyed and thrilled because I got a job in pictures. *All-American Co-Ed* was about a bunch of high school kids and was made at the Hal Roach Studios. It starred Frances Langford and Jon Hall. Johnny Downs, Noah Berry Jr., and Harry Langdon were also in it. The theme was that someone came to the school to put on a musical, and we were all vegetables. LeRoy Prinz's wife was a "tomato." Someone was the celery girl. I was the "carrot girl." Anyhow it got me my Guild card.

H.F. Was there a lot of work for you now?

M.W. Really only a lot of bit parts basically. I did a Kay Kyser movie called *Playmates* that same year. Then I did something called *Call Out the Marines* the next year. So I thought things might be better in New York. I went on an interview and got myself cast in a road show called "Henry Duffy's Merry-Go-Rounders." We opened in Detroit, played Buffalo, and closed in Washington, D.C. My main purpose was to get closer to New York to do radio, which I did. I played a heavy on a program called *Romance on Honeymoon Hill* for about a year. I did several Jergens' commercials with Walter Winchell. I must have done two hundred radio shows during the three years in New York.

H.F. You also did some live theater!

M.W. The big break happened when I was called to replace Karen Stevens on Broadway in Gertrude Neissen's *Follow the Girls*. I was a heavy once again and the play was a big hit. I was in it for about six months when someone from MGM saw me and arranged for me to test at Metro. That's how I got my stock contract there.

H.F.   And how many films did you do at Metro?

M.W.   I was under contract for two years. During that time I was kind of buried in pictures where I usually had just a few lines. But there was also an advantage. I was given lessons daily in singing, dancing, and acting by the most qualified coaches in town. I also married Ted Steel, an orchestra leader whom I had known from the soap opera days, but that only lasted eight months. It was when I left the studio and started to free-lance that my career really began to build.

I had a scene with Margaret O'Brien in a film called *Unfinished Dance* in 1947, which also starred Danny Thomas and Cyd Charisse. I did the *Romance of Rosy Ridge* with Van Johnson and Janet Leigh. Then I did *Song of the Thin Man* with William Powell and Myrna Loy.

H.F.   What do you recall about William Powell?

M.W.   He was a charming, darling man. Everybody adored him. He was really a sophisticated, charming man, very witty, and sharp. Myrna Loy was also a very lovely lady. I would see her at friends homes, but I never became buddy, buddy with her.

H.F.   *Force of Evil* with John Garfield in 1948 really helped to establish you as one of those beautiful, blunt and rotten-to-the-core women, that you did so well on screen. What was it like working with John Garfield who was so charismatic?

M.W.   I played a gangster's wife who fooled around with John in *Force of Evil*. And you're right. It did begin that new and lasting phase in my screen life as the second woman or the heavy. I'd take roles that the bigger stars turned down. You see, I wasn't afraid to dirty my hands with tough, unsympathetic roles.

As for John Garfield, he was shorter than me. He was very gracious about standing on a box so when we met each other it didn't look like I was taller than he was. He was rather introverted on the set, but he did have lots of charisma.

H.F.   You did a wonderful western in 1949 called *Hellfire* with Bill Elliott!

M.W.   That was terrific. It really was. It was one of my favorite movies. Everybody liked Bill Elliott as far as I know. He fought very hard to get me in the movie. He had seen a movie and a screen test I had made, and he was determined to have me in the lead, despite the fact that Herbert Yates wanted someone else. It was done by Republic Studios and was an off-beat western which really carried quite a punch. A lot of good western people in that like Paul Fix, Forrest Tucker and Denver Pyle.

H.F.   Because of your western orientation, did the studios put you into more westerns than other films?

M.W. No, not necessarily. I appeared in about seventy-five movies and did twenty-two westerns. Then, of course, I did a lot of television westerns, several things at Warner Brothers, but again, they were not the bulk of my TV work.

H.F. But did you get a special joy doing the westerns?

M.W. Yes, *I loved them*. I loved the people that make westerns. They are down to earth, you feel comfortable with them. I was really honored when I was given "The Woman of Western Fame Award" at The Sonora Film Festival in 1993.

H.F. You worked with John Wayne. What do you remember about him?

M.W. I made three films with John Wayne. The first was a western called *The Fighting Kentuckian* for Republic Pictures in 1949. John Wayne produced the picture, and Duke and Oliver Hardy work together which makes this film very different. They play a couple of frontiersmen. He changed over the years naturally, because the last one I did with him in 1973, *Cahill— U.S. Marshal*, he was sick and not up to his usual self. I played his ex-wife in that. But he was still fun and charming. He was always very nice to me. In the early days at Republic, he was sure full of the devil. He and the guys were always playing jokes on each other and there was a lot of laughter. But through it all he was always very professional, and the crew was always crazy about him.

I did one non-western with John in 1953. It was called *Trouble Along the Way* and was directed by Michael Curtiz at Warners. It was a nice sentimental picture with John as a disillusioned and divorced ex-football coach who tries to come back by coaching a rag tag team at a Catholic college. Donna Reed and Chuck Connors were in that, too.

H.F. Any favorite movies you appeared in, Marie?

M.W. I have three. I have already mentioned *Hellfire* with Bill Elliott. Then, of course, there was *The Killing* in 1956, which was what really put Stanley Kubrick on the map as a director, and for which I won the *Look Magazine* for Best Supporting Actress that year. Stanley was only twenty-six years old at the time, and sent a telegram from England when I was recently honored by the Film Actor's Guild Society. I was the femme fatale who set up poor Elisha Cook, Jr. One of the best lines was when Sterling Hayden said to me, "I know you like a book, you little tramp. You'd sell out your own mother for a piece of fudge."

H.F. You mentioned three films!

M.W. The third, of course, was *The Narrow Margin*, which I did for RKO in 1952, and was produced by Stanley Rubin and directed by Richard Fleischer. In fact, Stanley Kubrick saw me in that picture and made a mental note which later led to my casting in *The Killing*. It was a real thriller. I played a gangster's widow with a heart of gravel. When Charles McGraw tells me, "You make me sick to my stomach." I snap back, "Yeah, well use your own sink." It would define the film persona which I carried through much of my films.

H.F. Yet with all your film work, your beauty, and your talent, you never really became a front rank star!

M.W. Well part of me feels a disappointment that I never became a really big star. I think a lot of things happened to hamper my career. At five feet nine inches, I was too tall for most leading men. And I never had that so-called classic face. With film noire waning, I never really got a chance to find an audience outside the B-Movie action film. But when I first started hearing people calling me "The Queen of the Bs," I thought it was kind of a compliment. I guess it's better to be the queen of something rather than the queen of nothing. Some critics have called me "the best of the female heavies."

H.F. Other disappointments?

M.W. Well, I'd have to say that I always had dreams of buying my parents a house in California and doing so much for them. But I never made much money in my life. It was always month-to-month making car payments, paying the rent.

H.F. You have appeared both on stage and on the screen. Any preference? You have won, too, a couple of awards for your stage work.

M.W. Yes, I have. I have received an award from the *L.A. Weekly*, a Los Angeles Critics Award for *The Shadow Box*, and the College Award from the Burt Reynolds' Jupiter Theater for my work in a play called *The Bar Off Melrose*. As to having a preference between stage and screen, the answer is "No." They are both fascinating. They both require a lot of different things from you emotionally, because you are dealing with different people. There are advantages to both. You love the reaction of a large audience on stage. On the other hand, it's such a pleasure to know that something you put on film is there forever and ever.

H.F. Any film stars whose work you particularly admired?

M.W. Well, as I got older, I loved the Joan Crawford parts particularly. Then I always wanted to play things like *Mrs. Miniver*.

H.F. How about the directors?

M.W. King Vidor was one of my favorites. Then Stanley Kubrick to be sure.

H.F. The industry today, Marie?

M.W. I feel it is a lot harder for people to get started today. There are too many actors and there are too few parts. The actors nowadays, I think, have a far greater basic background of studying drama and acting than most people did in my day. The kids are really working hard to perfect themselves. In the early days, a lot of the success people had was because they had screen personalities. Sometimes it didn't necessarily have to do with their talent.

H.F.   How about the movies coming out today?

M.W.   I disapprove of about ninety percent of them, I don't like all that blood and thunder. They don't know how to tell a story subtly and leave the imagination to the viewer. I think these movies go well because the world is absolutely in a stage of self-destruct. But I do love things like *Howards End* and almost everything Tony Hopkins has done.

H.F.   When you see the westerns of your era, and the westerns of today, what do you think?

M.W.   Today I think the westerns are so overproduced that they are losing touch with the simple westerns that we enjoyed so much. *Shane* is one western which I still love. The acting is great. It was well cast. The photography was marvelous. Of course Ben Johnson was in it, and it's hard to forget Ben in anything. Ben Johnson is "Mr. Nice Guy" for sure. But primarily it was a good story. John Ford, remember, always chose good stories and directed them wonderfully.

H.F.   You have received your share of honors lately. It must really be nice being remembered so well for your work.

M.W.   It's mind boggling. For an actress who hasn't made a picture since 1981—and never became a genuine above-the-name title star—there's consolation in belated recognition. I feel like I'm in a dream and I don't want to wake up.

H.F.   Thanks Marie!

Index

Numbers in **boldface** refer to pages with photographs.

237